The Princeton Review

Word Smart
Junior

Build a Straight A Vocabulary

by C.L. Brantley

Random House, Inc., New York

D0196821

Copyright © 2002 by The Princeton Review, Inc.
Illustrations copyright © 1995 by Jeff Moores.

All rights reserved under International and Pan-American
Copyright Conventions. Published in the United States by
Random House, Inc., New York, and simultaneously in Canada
by Random House of Canada Limited, Toronto.

ISBN: 0-375-76257-4
Second Edition
Manufactured in the United States of America.
10 9 8 7 6 5 4

ACKNOWLEDGMENTS

I would like gratefully to acknowledge the help of Julie Shaffer, Whitney Shaffer, Shannon Graham, and the curriculum developers and teachers who offered their advice and input throughout the writing of this book. I would also like to thank my true, good friends for standing by me through thick and thin. They know who they are.

CONTENTS

Introduction

You have probably been learning vocabulary words in school for a long time now, right? Your teachers make you copy down the words, then you go home and look them up in a dictionary and write down the definition. Maybe you even have to write a sample sentence. Do you ever stop to think about why you are being taught vocabulary?

Not if you're like most people, you don't. You just do your homework as quickly as possible, and probably forget the words and their meanings by the time you hand in your assignment. Well, we want to change all that.

Don't worry, we're not going to tell you to ask for extra assignments, or make a bunch of flashcards, or read a hundred words out of the dictionary every night. Not that it would hurt you to do those things, but it wouldn't do much good either. That's because when you are just starting to build an adult vocabulary, a vocabulary that will help you succeed in high school and college and beyond, the best way for you to learn new words is by *reading or hearing them in context*.

HERE'S HOW THIS BOOK WORKS

Word Smart Junior is designed to help you learn as enjoyably as possible by reading important vocabulary words in context. There are eight stories included here that follow the adventures of Bridget, a street-smart kid from New York, Babette, a mysterious French girl, Barnaby, a boy genius with a wild head of hair, and Beauregard, a huge black tomcat with a crazy past.

Around six hundred and fifty words are covered in this book. Whenever one of them appears for the first time, it will be in boldface (**like this**). If you come across a word you don't know, see if you can figure out its meaning in context. Don't interrupt your reading by looking up every unfamiliar word unless you really have to. Just try to enjoy the story from start to finish, then go back and look up the words you don't know.

USING THE GLOSSARY AND DOING THE QUIZZES

If you do have to look up a word right away, there is a glossary at the back of the book which defines all the bolded words and uses them in sample sentences. Take a look in the glossary whenever you get confused.

At the end of each chapter are some quizzes you can do to make sure you understood the words you just read. The answers are in the back of the book (don't peek ahead of time!). If you miss some of the questions, look up the words you didn't understand in the glossary. Also, make sure you go over our special pronunciation guide at the beginning of each glossary entry, so you'll know how to say the words properly on your test drive.

Okay, that's about all you need to know. Start reading, start learning, and prepare to impress the pants off everyone you know with your new, improved vocabulary!

Chapter 1

The Fateful Meeting

Allow me to introduce myself. My name is Beauregard, a gentleman cat from a long line of South Carolina aristocrats. My **ancestors,** from my father way on back to my great-great-great-great-great-great-grandfather Lucius, have resided in the homes of the finest families of the South. We are known as much for our perfect manners and grace, as we are for our size (I, myself, stand nearly four and a half feet tall when I walk on my rear **limbs**). Our good breeding is also obvious from our beautifully kept, glossy coats. Mine is completely black, and I spend a good deal of time each morning grooming and smoothing it to perfection (one never knows whom one might meet).

That afternoon, I was as happy and **content** as can be, taking a well-earned nap on the softest, sunniest patch of grass in the Bois de Boulogne, a large and beautiful park in Paris. As for what I was doing in France, well, I am forced to admit that I was a bit wild in my youth, and my family thought it best that I take a long trip until some of the scandals died down. Yes, it's true, I've always been one to go out until all hours, eating catnip and singing loudly with my tomcat friends, and chasing young lady cats around. Those were the days! I remember one beautiful cat named Felinia. She and I used to . . . well, that's a story for another time. Let's just say my folks thought it best that I do my **gallivanting** on foreign soil.

But I **digress.** As I said, I was taking my afternoon **siesta,** which ordinarily I wouldn't have interrupted for anyone or anything. But I knew that little girl was in trouble from the minute I laid eyes on her. She was trying to act calm and **nonchalant,** just smacking on her bubble gum and strolling through the Bois as though she didn't give a hoot about anything in the world, but she wasn't fooling anyone but herself. She wasn't from Paris, you could tell that from the New York Yankees cap she wore backwards on her braided head. I couldn't see anyone that looked like her parents around, so I just put two and two together and figured she was lost.

Well, this little girl was so full of **anxiety** you could practically see the worry coming out her ears, so, today, I decided to make an exception, and interrupt my siesta. She had plopped herself down on a bench and was sort of kicking her feet around in the dirt. I was just about to go up to her to see if I could do anything to help, when Babette came along and the two struck up a conversation. I was somewhat curious, as cats can be, and a little worried, so I decided to stick around to make sure they were all right. Of course, I hadn't the slightest suspicion that later that day I would be involved in a plot to overthrow the Elephant Empire . . .

✑   ✑   ✑   ✑   ✑

"You're an American," said Babette, matter-of-factly.

Bridget jumped a little. She wasn't expecting to hear someone talk to her in English, and she definitely wasn't expecting to run into someone like Babette—black hair, black clothes, black sunglasses that **concealed** most of her face. In fact, the bright red lipstick she wore was the only thing that added any color to her outfit. Bridget usually thought lipstick and all that "girlie" stuff was silly—she was a tomboy, herself—but this girl didn't seem silly at all. Actually, she was very grown-up and **sophisticated.**

"Yep, I'm American," replied Bridget, trying to look casual. "So what?"

"What are you doing here?" asked Babette.

"I'm just sitting on a bench minding my own business. You got a problem with that?" growled Bridget. She didn't mean to seem **gruff** or unfriendly, but for some reason she didn't want this strange, older girl to know she was afraid.

"I have no problem," said the French girl. "I am simply curious. Where is your family?"

Bridget heaved a sigh and stared down into the dirt. "I lost them," she mumbled.

"Oh, I see. You are an orphan. You lost them in an accident?"

"No, not in an accident. In the Louvre. Accidentally in the Louvre. I mean, we went to that stupid art museum, and I lost them. I mean, they lost me. Or we lost each other. Anyway, they're not here," said Bridget. She bit her lower lip. She knew she was babbling a bunch of nonsense, and she didn't want to blow her cool.

"Ah," said Babette, her eyebrows appearing above her sunglasses.

"Who is this girl?" thought Bridget. "What's all this 'ah' stuff?" She had had about enough of this conversation.

"Hey, just who are you and what do you want?" demanded Bridget. "Can't you see I'm busy **loafing**? Talking with you is messing up my plans to sit around doing nothing all day."

"Why don't I help you find them?" Babette replied. She had an odd way of not responding to what people said.

Bridget was **baffled.** She just couldn't figure this out. Why would this girl, who wasn't even an **acquaintance** of hers, much less a friend, want to help her? Besides, Bridget didn't like owing people favors. She especially didn't want to be **beholden** to some mysterious French girl she'd only just met. On the other hand, she probably knew Paris well, and Bridget had to admit that finding her parents wasn't a bad idea.

While Bridget was puzzling over this **quandary,** Babette repeated her offer, "Come, let us go find your family."

"Back off, Frenchie," snapped Bridget. "Who says I need your help?"

"My name is Babette, and you are obviously in need of assistance. We can go search for your family now, if you will get up and come with me." She didn't seem to mind Bridget's **hostile** tone of voice. In fact, she seemed completely **oblivious** to it.

Bridget could tell there was no way to change Babette's mind. She was obviously **adamant,** and **circumstances** being as they were, it seemed the best thing she could do was to take her up on the offer. But Bridget, being a New Yorker and naturally **reluctant** to trust people, still wondered if Babette had some **ulterior** motive for wanting to help her. Was she a space alien disguised as a human looking for someone to do weird experiments on? Was she one of those people who kidnaps children and sells them to the gypsies? Bridget decided to ask her straight out.

"Why do you want to help me?"

"Frankly, I am quite bored and have nothing better to do," sighed Babette.

Bridget grinned. Now *that* was an answer she could believe. This Babette might be as cool as she looked after all. She got up and offered her hand to Babette.

"My name's Bridget," she said. "Let's get going."

Babette shook her hand and they started walking away.

"How did you know I was American, anyway?" asked Bridget, as they rounded a curve in the path and headed for the street.

"You are, well, **conspicuous.** You stick out, you see? Your hat, your blue jeans—these are very American clothes. Your hat is very nice, especially. Very **chic.** All the most stylish Parisians want to wear these hats."

"Thanks. You're pretty chic yourself," said Bridget. "I'll tell you what. If you find my parents, you can have the hat. Deal?"

"Deal," said Babette. It seemed like she was smiling, but it was hard to tell what was going on behind those dark sunglasses.

The two new friends walked out onto the busy sidewalk to begin their mission. And if they had paused to look over their shoulders, they would have seen that they were not alone. A gigantic, elegant black cat was following right behind them.

Bridget and Babette had been walking along in silence for a while when suddenly, Babette came to an **abrupt** stop in front of what looked like an apartment building. In fact, it was such a run-down, ugly apartment building, it might have been safe to call it a **tenement.**

"We must go in here," she said.

"Well . . . um, okay, I guess," said Bridget, **hesitantly.** She didn't like the look of the place at all. "What is this building, anyway?"

"It is a **dormitory** for all the science students at the university," Babette replied as she opened the door. "It is where all the young geniuses live—when they are not in their laboratories, that is. We are here to see my friend Barnaby. He is American, like you. It is my belief he may be able to help us find your parents."

"Great," chirped Bridget, as they walked into the building, followed by Beauregard the cat. "Let's find him."

"I must warn you, Barnaby has his **quirks.** Just odd little habits, of course, but some people are put off by them," Babette calmly explained as they walked up the stairs.

"What kind of quirks?" asked Bridget, who was becoming more nervous and **uneasy** about this whole thing with each step they took.

"Nothing to worry about, really. His most noticeable **idiosyncrasy** is his hair. He has hair unlike any other person's—it is his trademark. He is also the most brilliant person I know. He entered the university when he was only ten years old. A 'boy wonder,' I believe they called him. But he is still so young, and he is excitable. Ah," she said, stopping in front of a plain wooden door. "Here is his room. Knock, please."

Bridget gave the door a couple of **tentative** taps with her right hand. She was almost grateful there was no response.

"He's not in. Let's go," she said.

Babette smiled and started beating the door with both her fists. "Don't be so **timid** about it. Barnaby! Barnaby!" she yelled. "Open this door at once!"

Just then the door jerked open and a strange looking boy poked his head out. His hair was bushy, long, and pale, and stuck a couple of feet off his head in every direction like a crazy lion's mane. Beneath that wild mop, his face was that of any ordinary boy. To call him **unkempt** would be putting it mildly. It looked like birds had nested in his hair, and his lab coat looked as though it had never been anywhere near a washing machine. The "boy wonder" seemed **bewildered** at first, as if two girls and a giant cat had never paid him a visit before, but after a few seconds, he smiled widely and flung the door open.

"Hey, Babette!" he cried, **beckoning** her into the room with a wave of his hand. "Come in here, quick. You have to see my latest experiment."

The place was filled with bubbling test tubes, strangely colored liquids, a bunch of dead insects, and a huge **array** of vegetable plants— everything from alfalfa to yams.

"As you can see from all my little green friends here, my experiment is **botanical** in nature. Yes, Babette, I have long been tortured by the **plight** of plants, the innocent vegetable in particular," he **lamented**. "Oh, how the poor plants suffer! They have such beauty but, unfortunately, no legs or arms, so they can't fight off these cruel and **despicable** bugs!" He smashed his hand down on a pile of dead mealy bugs. "Until now, there was no choice but to spray these lovely vegetables with poisons so **toxic** they polluted the soil and **contaminated** the waters. But no more! My invention will do away with these poisons. They simply won't be needed anymore—they will be completely **obsolete**! At last we will . . . hey," he paused suddenly, "who let that cat in here?"

All eyes turned to the cat who was, it appeared, sleeping in the doorway.

"I have seen this cat before," said Babette. "He chases pigeons in the Bois de Boulogne and makes **amorous** advances toward every female cat he sees. Oh, he is so ridiculous, yet so harmless."

They all giggled, and the cat seemed to grumble in his sleep.

"Yes, well, er, as I was saying, at last we will defeat the creeping killers," Barnaby muttered.

"Man, something smells **foul** in here," said Bridget, wrinkling up her face. "What stinks?"

"Aha! You see? It works!" cried Barnaby, clapping his hands.

Bridget looked puzzled. "Are you nuts or something?"

"Not at all, not at all. Allow me to explain. What you smell are gym socks. Dirty gym socks that have been worn for an entire semester without a wash and left in a locker. You don't like the smell, eh?" asked Barnaby, smiling. He paused for a moment. "Well, let me tell you something. Bugs hate the smell. But it goes beyond a simple **aversion** to the smell of gym socks. They **detest** the smell so much they can't bear to come near it. It also **inhibits** the growth of some plant fungi, but it doesn't stop it altogether. Those socks even killed these mealy bugs," he said, wiping his hand off on his lab coat. "Yes, the day of the bug is over. No longer will these pests destroy crops and cause **famines**."

"Preventing starvation is a wonderful cause. But surely, Barnaby, there are not enough disgusting gym socks in the world to keep insects off all the crops," offered Babette.

"An **astute** observation. You're as sharp as ever. No, unfortunately, there aren't enough socks to go around. So I've been trying to capture the **essence** of the disgusting gym sock, the thing that makes it tick. Is it the odor of foot? The sweat? The toenail grime? Once I discover this, I can use a variety of ingredients to create a **synthetic** spray that has the same effect as the real thing. It will be very **potent.** Oh, yes. No one will doubt its power. But it will not be poison."

Bridget rolled her eyes. Barnaby seemed a little full of himself, and **pompous** people always really **irked** her. "Look, my name's Bridget and Babette here thinks you can help me find my parents."

"So you've lost your parents, huh? I know exactly how you feel. Yes, you have my **sympathy.** I once lost my parents for an entire year. Or, rather, it seems I forgot to call them for an entire year while I was studying tropical bird songs in the Amazon rain forest. So you could say they lost me, I suppose. It's upsetting either way. Yes." Barnaby scratched his head. Bridget wasn't sure, but it looked as though he had pulled a wristwatch out of his bushy hair. Or maybe he already had the wristwatch. "Time to check the solution!" he cried.

The young scientist scurried over to a large beaker full of bubbling, smoking, grayish liquid and carefully calculated the temperature, all the while mumbling to himself. Then he filled an eyedropper full of bubbling blue liquid from another beaker and added it to the gray muck. Next, he **agitated** the unholy mixture by picking up the beaker and giving it a shaking so **vigorous** it made him break out in a sweat.

"Ladies," he announced, "you are about to witness scientific history!" With that he began a countdown. "Ten, nine, eight, seven, six . . ."

Barnaby never reached the end of his countdown. Around "four" a terrible rumbling began. Then an explosion. Then, a horrible, horrible smell.

"Quick! We must **vacate** the building at once! Out! Out!" shrieked Barnaby.

The girls and the cat were all too happy to **comply.** They ran out the door and down to the street. There they stopped to catch their breath (which they had been holding for a couple of minutes).

"Oh, what a stupid **blunder!**" gasped Barnaby. "How could I have made such a mistake?"

"There, there," said Babette, not very convincingly.

"It was my **ego** that made me do it. My foolish pride! I thought I was smarter than the great Vogelstellenstein, a scientist **renowned** the world over for his brilliantly simple discoveries! How I **envy** his genius! It was he who suggested cigar smoke as an insect repellent. Naturally, since cigar smoke is a **carcinogen,** I thought it was best not to encourage farmers to smoke in their fields, **lest** they develop lung cancer. How was I to know gym socks could be worse than cigars?" Barnaby seemed near tears.

"Look, don't sweat it. Um, I mean, quit worrying about it," said Bridget.

"Yes, I suppose you're right," he said, changing moods abruptly. "After all, I'm only an **amateur** when it comes to botany. My true profession is physics. Still, I do enjoy **dabbling** in the other sciences. But this little accident doesn't **bode** well for me. It's the third explosion I've caused this week, and the university said they'd have me sent home if I continued to destroy their property. I guess my announcement of my great discovery was **premature.** I must do many more tests to **verify** the results so that I can be absolutely certain they are correct. In the meantime, I should probably go try to straighten up."

"Nonsense," snapped Babette. "We have a more important matter to take care of. Let the university sort through all the broken glass and **debris.** We must find Bridget's parents."

"I apologize. Of course. Where do we begin?" asked Barnaby.

"I thought you were supposed to know that," said Bridget. She stared down at her sneakers sadly. This whole thing was beginning to seem hopeless.

"Come, Bridget, there is no need for such **dejection**," said Babette. "Barnaby is always full of good ideas."

"Naturally!" agreed Barnaby. "Now, let's see. If you want to cover a lot of ground, the best way is in the air! What we need is some kind of hot-air balloon. I could design one by tomorrow morning."

Bridget perked up at this idea. "A hot-air balloon, huh? Why didn't you say so? Let me show you two a little trick I picked up back home."

With that, Bridget began chewing her gum, her jaws and cheeks pumping furiously. Then she slowly blew a large pink bubble, bigger than a beach ball, toward the sky. And, to Babette and Barnaby's (and Beauregard's) amazement, she began to lift off the ground!

"Oh, my, you Americans are incredible!" cried Babette.

"How **convenient**," remarked Barnaby. "A hot-air balloon you can carry in your mouth!"

With a loud *smack,* Bridget sucked her gum back into her mouth and plopped back down in from of them. "How about it, guys? I can't look down very well while I do that. But if you hold onto me, you can look for me."

"Sounds fascinating," said Barnaby.

Babette agreed. So Bridget took a deep breath and began to create a blimp made of bubble gum. As she rose into the air, her two friends grabbed on—Barnaby on the right leg, Babette on the left—and they began their ascent.

But just as they became airborne, Barnaby let out a squeal.

"Aaaiieee! That cat just jumped on my leg!"

"So we have a **feline** stowaway, eh?" said Babette. "Careful, then, Barnaby. The last thing we need is to drop a hundred-pound cat on some innocent Parisian."

Soon, the four of them were floating above the rooftops of the city, eagerly searching for the misplaced parents. Unfortunately, they didn't notice the angry black clouds forming overhead.

You can see what I mean about those kids needing help, now, can't you? That Barnaby, for instance. He certainly knows how to put words together, but being **articulate** doesn't necessarily mean you have common sense. And Babette—well, she's obviously just out for a bit of excitement. She's not **naive,** that's for sure, but even the most worldly-wise girl needs looking after now and again. Bridget? She seemed tough enough, all right, but I figured she just might have gotten a little big for her britches, if you'll pardon the expression.

And as for me, well, a **trauma** like that frightening gym-sock explosion should have been enough to **deter** me from any further involvement with that bunch of crazy kids. The decision to jump on Barnaby's leg was pretty **spontaneous.** I just saw them floating away, and the next thing I knew, I was floating away with them. It wasn't long after takeoff that I realized we might be in trouble. The sun was setting and the air was unusually **sultry** for a fall day, sticky and hotter than the Fourth of July. A **gust** of wind blew some damp air into my face, which I was grateful for at first. But then another gust came, and I realized it had started to rain—big, fat, heavy raindrops. Then, all at once, everything let loose. The air became so **turbulent** it felt as though we were riding a roller coaster. The rain came down in buckets. I was reminded of the **monsoons** of southern Asia, those winds that brought such heavy rain. How well I remember the lazy evenings I used to spend in Bangkok, waiting out the storms with a beautiful, exotic . . . but I **digress.** Back to the subject.

The winds swirled around us faster and faster, until they built up such **velocity** I feared we would be thrown far off course. But there was nothing I could do except hold on tight (and hope Barnaby held on tight) and wait for the storm to die down. When it finally did, I almost wished we were still high in the air being whipped by wind and water. We had landed safely in a grassy field, but our relief quickly gave way to fear. We were immediately surrounded and taken prisoner—the helpless **captives** of the jackal army.

✍ QUIZ #1 ✍
Relationships

Decide what relationship the following pairs of words have to each other. If they have similar meanings, write "S" next to the pair of words. If they have opposite meanings, write "O" next to the words.

1. anxiety :: uneasiness
2. hesitant :: reluctant
3. chic :: unkempt
4. carousing :: gallivanting
5. sophisticated :: naive
6. suspicion :: trust
7. quirk :: idiosyncrasy
8. premature :: tardy
9. amateur :: dabbler
10. despicable :: foul
11. acquaintance :: close friend

✍ QUIZ #2 ✑
Relationships

Decide what relationship the following pairs of words have to each other. If they have similar meanings, write "S" next to the pair of words. If they have opposite meanings, write "O" next to the words.

1. gruff :: hostile
2. conspicuous :: concealed
3. tentative :: timid
4. oblivious :: astute
5. inhibits :: assists
6. bewildered :: baffled
7. potent :: weak
8. toxic :: contaminated
9. abrupt :: sudden
10. comply :: disobey
11. tenement :: mansion

✍ QUIZ #3 ✍
Fill in the Blank

For each sentence below, choose the word that best completes the sentence.

1. Mark was the happiest guy at the party when the girl he had been staring at all evening finally noticed him and _____ him to come over to her.

   a. babbled **b.** loafed

   c. beckoned **d.** agitated

2. When the little girl dropped her ice-cream cone in the dirt, the ice cream man felt _____ for her and gave her another one for free.

   a. sympathy **b.** envy

   c. dejection **d.** aversion

3. Sally hadn't planned on traveling to the beach for the weekend, but the weather was so beautiful that she made the _____ decision to hop into her car and head for the shore.

   a. amorous **b.** vigorous

   c. pompous **d.** spontaneous

4. The invention of compact disc players made turntables and vinyl records practically _____.

   a. obsolete **b.** renowned

   c. synthetic **d.** articulate

5. Barry got a reputation for being the coolest kid in school because he always acted _____, no matter what was happening to him or around him.

   a. content **b.** nonchalant

   c. adamant **d.** turbulent

6. "I agree, much stricter punishments are needed to _____ cheating in the classrooms," said the prinicipal, "but spanking the students is against the law."

   a. irk **b.** vacate **c.** deter **d.** verify

7. Until the recent article in *National Geographic*, people didn't know about the _____ of the blue-tongued skinks, the little lizards who are hunted down and killed by the hundreds every day so their skins can be used for belts and wallets.

   a. essence **b.** ego **c.** gentility **d.** plight

✍ QUIZ #4 ✍
Matching

Match each word on the right with a word on the left that has a similar meaning.

1. siesta	a. speed
2. ancestors	b. indebted
3. convenient	c. nap
4. blunder	d. foretell
5. beholden	e. warm
6. sultry	f. handy
7. ulterior	g. starvation
8. array	h. sleeping quarters
9. velocity	i. plant-related
10. detest	j. forefathers
11. botanical	k. hate
12. bode	l. collection
13. dormitory	m. mistake
14. famine	n. other

✍ QUIZ #5 ✍
Matching

Match each word on the right with a word on the left that has a similar meaning.

1.	carcinogenic	a.	difficulty
2.	lest	b.	situation
3.	exception	c.	seasonal wind
4.	limbs	d.	for fear that
5.	circumstance	e.	trash
6.	quandary	f.	cancer-causing
7.	digress	g.	stray
8.	captives	h.	prisoners
9.	gust	i.	special case
10.	feline	j.	upsetting experience
11.	monsoon	k.	legs and arms
12.	trauma	l.	blast
13.	debris	m.	catlike

Chapter 2
The End of the Elephant Empire

It was no ordinary army of jackals that had taken us prisoner. These soliders wore metal armor and helmets that made them a most frightening pack of dogs. That is, I think Barnaby, Babette, and Bridget were frightened. I, of course, am a cat. And cats, as everyone knows, feel a certain, shall we say, **animosity** toward most creatures of the **canine** persuasion. I felt nothing but **contempt** for these puny pups. One on one, I could have handled any of them easily. But since we were greatly outnumbered, and our wrists and ankles were tied up, I decided to keep myself in check. Besides, I had a feeling we wouldn't be prisoners for long.

"I never learned about any place like this in geography class," said Bridget, shaking her head. "Boy, when things go wrong . . ."

"Something tells me we're not in France anymore," agreed Barnaby.

"I could ask them where we are, if you like," offered Babette.

"Yeah, if you spoke Dog you could," snorted Bridget.

"They're jackals, actually, and I did pick up a working knowledge of their language while I was on safari last year. Their poetry is excellent, although somewhat primitive."

Bridget tried to think of a clever **retort,** but all she could say was, "Yeah, right. And I hear they're all portrait painters in their spare time. 'Dogs Playing Pool' by Fido is one of my favorite pieces."

Barnaby snickered.

"There's no need to be **sarcastic,**" replied Babette calmly, turning away from her companions. Then she made some odd growling noises, followed by a short bark and a couple of whimpers, apparently in the direction of the guard behind her. She got no response.

"They don't seem to understand you," Barnaby commented.

Babette ignored him, and repeated her "question" to the guard.

"Save it, sister," barked the dog suddenly, in English. "Your accent is hurting my ears. And pick up your smart aleck friend there. Kind of **awkward,** isn't she? She's tripped over her own feet."

Bridget had, indeed, fallen over from the sheer shock of hearing the dog speak. Babette helped her up, but she remained stunned, and just stood there, **gaping** at the jackal.

"Close your mouth, kiddo," said the jackal. "And let me give you a word of advice. You're in the animal kingdom now. This is our **domain.** And as long as you're on our turf, you would do well to be a little more respectful and a little less **impudent.** For example, I didn't like the way you knocked our artistic abilities just now. You shouldn't **disparage** things you know nothing about, and from what's come out of your mouth so far, that's a lot. Do I make myself clear?"

Bridget continued to stare.

"Do you **comprehend** what I have just told you? Quit giving me that **bovine** stare. You look as dumb as a cow," he snarled.

"Yes. I'm very sorry," stuttered Bridget.

"That's better. Now look, we have nothing against you humans personally. But too bad you have that cat with you. We absolutely **loathe** cats, sneaky little devils, mostly spies. And you should have known better than to land in the middle of a troop movement."

"But we didn't mean to come here!" blurted Barnaby. "We just ran into **adverse** weather conditions above Paris, and . . . ."

"Oh yeah? Then how do you explain the cat?" yipped the jackal. "But as I was saying, we really have nothing against you; even the cat might not be so bad. We've hired cats as spies now and then ourselves. But you have to understand, the situation here is tense. Until a few days ago, the jackal army was united in the revolution. We were working to overthrow the Elephant Empire and hold free, democratic elections open to every animal that **inhabits** this region, from antelopes to zebras. But General Horace got greedy. He decided to turn the revolution into some kind of holy war. 'All creatures must come under submission to the word of Dog,' he said. Well, that's the last thing we needed, to get rid of one **authoritarian** government only to replace it with an even crazier dictatorship."

The jackal shook his head in disgust.

"Well, our Colonel Cano spoke up against the idea right away. But as it turned out, Horace wasn't prepared to accept any form of **dissent** or disagreement, and he planned to have Cano executed. So, that same night, Cano and all of us broke off to form our own **faction.** We're hoping other animal armies will help us carry out the revolution and keep Horace out of power."

"And where are you taking us?" asked Babette.

"We're taking you back to camp. Colonel Cano will want to meet you," he replied.

"Thanks for the information," said Bridget, who had somehow regained the ability to speak. "By the way, my name is Bridget, and this is Babette and Barnaby."

"I am Lieutenant Lassiterius. Folks call me Lassie for short."

Bridget thought it best not to make a joke.

When they reached camp, they saw many soldiers gathered around, as if waiting for something to happen. At first they were quiet and patient, but after five minutes or so, they started barking and stomping their feet, **clamoring** for whatever it was they were waiting for. Finally, a big, important-looking jackal with grayish fur appeared at the front of the room, and with one sharp bark, he silenced the **boisterous** crowd. From the way he looked, so noble and powerful, so full of **dignity,** Barnaby, Bridget, and Babette correctly assumed it was Cano.

He began speaking in Jackal, and you didn't have to understand the words to know that Cano was a gifted **orator** who knew how to hold an audience. He barked, growled, leaped around, and yipped his way to such a stirring climax that all the jackals, including Lassie, began to howl with excitement.

"I'd follow him anywhere," sighed Lassie. Then, suddenly, he let out a bark in the colonel's direction.

Cano's ears pricked up as he noticed Lassie. He came right over.

"It's **unanimous**!" cried Cano. "We voted, and every single jackal has agreed to fight til the end to keep Horace out of power."

"I told you not to doubt our loyalty, sir," said Lassie. "That was some speech you just gave."

"Well, to tell the truth, I hadn't planned on giving a speech. It was just one of those **impromptu**, spur-of-the-moment things, you know? I **ad-libbed** the whole thing."

"Well, it was pretty amazing for a speech you made up as you went along. You were speaking from the heart, and we're with you. We'll teach that wacko a lesson," the lieutenant replied.

"I believe *fanatic* is more accurate than *wacko*, Lassie. He's not crazy, he's just, well, let's just say he's dangerously full of enthusiasm and **zeal**."

"Anyway, look what we found on patrol today, Colonel," said Lassie, jerking his head toward the prisoners.

"I see, I see," said the jackal. "A few humans and . . . hey! Beauregard, you old son of a gun, what are you doing here?"

Cano had trotted over to the cat and seemed very glad to see him.

"You know him?" asked Lassie and Barnaby. They were both **astonished,** but for different reasons.

"Know him?" laughed the colonel, "Why, back in the old days, Beau and I used to run the undercover division of . . ."

Just then the cat growled softly in Cano's ear.

"Yes, well, um, whoops! Heh, heh. What was I saying?" the colonel continued clumsily. "I, uh, must be mistaken. I've never seen this sorry old cat before. Take them all to my tent for questioning."

Babette, Barnaby, and Bridget exchanged perplexed looks. The situation was getting weirder and weirder.

On their arrival at the tent, Cano ordered that they be untied and Lassie began to loosen the ropes.

"Thanks, man, those things were beginning to **chafe** my wrists," said Bridget. "Hey!" she shouted to the colonel. "You got anything to eat?"

"Remember the talk we had about respect, Bridget?" snarled Lassie. "It would **behoove** you to behave with a little more **deference** toward the colonel. After all, he *is* in control of your fate right now."

"Oh, come now," laughed Cano. "These people are welcome here. In fact, they should be treated as foreign **dignitaries,** honored and important visitors from the human world. Bridget is hungry; we should have a feast for her! Lassie, go out and tell everyone that tonight we'll be having a party to celebrate the arrival of new friends and to **revel** in the certain defeat of Horace and the end of the Empire!"

The travelers began to wonder if Cano was always so full of **optimism,** but as soon as Lassie left to make arrangements for the feast, he let out a heavy sigh.

"I don't know how much the lieutenant has told you, but we are facing serious odds. The situation actually looks pretty **bleak,**" he said.

"I can see that," said Babette. "You plan a **coup d'état** against the Empire, and a **feud** develops within your ranks. A very difficult situation, indeed. Can you not find support outside the jackal army?"

"I have considered the possibility," replied the colonel, "but we animals have never had strong alliances. The jackals are the only group that has an army to speak of. Until recently, we were the royal guards of the Elephant Emperor himself."

Cano shook his head and continued, "The ostriches, for example, could be a great help. They seem to favor democracy, and their speed and size make them valuable friends. But, unfortunately, they are known for their **apathy.**

They're happy to bury their heads in the sand and not bother with anything.

"The pandas, strong and fierce as they look, are all **pacifists**. That's right—they don't believe in war for any reason. It's against their religion. On the other hand, the warthogs, nasty-looking creatures, are definitely **belligerent** enough to join us. They like fighting. Waging war is how they get their jollies. But when they don't have a war to fight, they tend to kill each other. No, it's best to steer clear of them. Still, there is some hope. We have **solicited** the aid and advice of the Reptile Republic. It looks as though they are willing to help us. We got word that King Cobra is sending an **ambassador** to our camp tonight—a high-ranking lizard, I believe—to see if there is anything they can do. The reptiles have much to teach us. They have lived outside the Empire for many years now. Frankly, I think the elephants are a little afraid of them," Cano chuckled.

"Tell us more about this Horace character," demanded Bridget. "He sounds much worse than the Emperor."

"You're right there," agreed the colonel. "Horace is the worst kind of **tyrant** imaginable. He expects more than obedience from his animals—he wants them to be absolutely **servile,** slavishly satisfying his every whim. It's been like that for years, and the elephants have always backed him up. He even issued an order that all soldiers must fall to their knees and bow before him, **revere** him as if he were some kind of god! That was the last straw for me. I refuse to **kowtow** to anyone, not even the Emperor, and especially not Horace! I went through basic training with him, for goodness' sake!"

"You said it, Colonel," said Bridget.

Cano took a deep breath. "Horace actually does think of himself as some kind of god—the **omnipotent** kind, at that. You know, all-powerful, all-seeing. But really he's just totally **paranoid.** He was always imagining that there were secret plots and **conspiracies** against him."

"If he's such a rotten guy, why did you go along with him on this whole coup d'état thing?" asked Bridget.

"That's a good question," replied Cano, "and I can only respond with the tired old **cliché,** 'desperate times require desperate measures.' I knew Horace was a kook, but I thought that continuing to live under the harsh rule of the elephants was worse. It wasn't until after we declared our freedom that I found out how truly evil he was. He's an absolute **bigot.**"

"A bigot?" gasped Barnaby.

"I honestly don't know how I didn't figure it out before. I guess before we broke away from the elephants, he kept his **prejudices** to himself. Now he is much more **overt** about his hatred of all other creatures, even ones he's never even met. He feels jackals are the only worthy animals. It's extremely disturbing. To think, not so terribly long ago he was my friend, and now he is my most dangerous **foe.**"

Cano sighed again, and stared off into the distance as if **contemplating** all the events that had led him up to this moment. Soon, he was completely lost in thought.

"Um, maybe we should go wash up **prior** to eating," offered Barnaby, wanting to leave the colonel alone with his thoughts.

"Yes, how rude of me," said Cano, snapping out of it. "You'll find a guest tent outside to the right. Everything you need is there. We'll come get you when the feast is ready."

"Cool. See you later, Cano," said Bridget.

"Thank you, Colonel," said Babette.

And with that, they left the tent. But the cat stayed behind.

I should explain about Colonel Cano and myself. It's true, we were comrades-in-arms back when I was working undercover for the Elede agency of

disparate experiences—traveling with the circus, selling encyclopedias, organizing labor unions, and yes, even spying for the Empire. You see, at the time, humans were guilty of **atrocious** acts of violence against elephants. Hunters would kill them by the hundreds, rip their tusks out for ivory, and leave their bodies to rot. Animals all around the world decided to fight against this senseless cruelty.

Cano and I got together at a meeting of the United Animal Nations and came up with a completely new, offbeat, altogether **radical** idea. We would take our story to the **media**—newspapers, television, radio, the works. We took pictures of the horrors ourselves—elephants lying tuskless in the jungles. Then we went off into the human world and tried to blend in as pets, waiting for the opportunity to put our plan into action.

Of course, it was easy for me. I was used to **cohabiting** with humans, and besides, pet cats usually get to act as mean and persnickety as they want, and no one thinks twice about it. Cano had more of a problem. He was a jackal, and a soldier, and he didn't have much **tolerance** for the whole stick-fetching, tail-wagging routine dogs are expected to put on. But he put up with it somehow.

Finally, I managed to slip a videotape of the elephant hunts to a major television channel. One of the station managers saw it and things just sort of took off from there. There was a huge public outcry. Many countries got together and imposed **sanctions** against other countries that supported the ivory trade—that is, they refused to do business with them or help them in any way. Some even called for **embargos,** refusing to import any ivory at all. Cano and I were mighty pleased with our **audacity.** It sure took a lot of guts and daring to do what we did.

After that, we went our separate ways. I didn't see Cano again—until now. I had no idea the elephants had come back so strongly—too strongly, it seems. I sure didn't like seeing my old friend so upset. After the kids left, we had a talk and **reminisced** about old times. I told him not to blow my cover, that I was watching over these kids, but I didn't want them to know it. And I told him I'd help him in any way I could. Well, he took me at my word. We spent the next hour working out a plan to take care of Horace and the Emperor once and for all.

✎ ✎ ✎ ✎ ✎

"Boy, I'm so hungry," said Bridget, who was resting comfortably on some cushions in the guest tent. "I hope dinner's ready soon. I plan to **gorge** myself until I can't eat another bite."

"I wouldn't go planning an eating **binge** so soon," warned Barnaby. "After all, we have no idea what jackals eat. And whatever it is, it's likely to be raw."

"Yikes, I hadn't thought of that," said Bridget, springing upright. "What are we going to do? Are we going to starve, or what?"

"Hmmm," replied Barnaby, scratching his

bushy head. "We'll just have to put our minds to it and see what we can come up with. Well, what do you know?"

"What?" asked Bridget.

"Look what I found! These must have gotten lodged in my hair that time I blew up the vending machine in the library!"

Sure enough, Barnaby had somehow managed to pull four candy bars, a bag of potato chips, and some bright orange crackers out of his hair. Ordinarily, Bridget would have been surprised at such an event, but with everything that had happened in the past couple of days, she hardly batted an eyelash.

"Wow! Can I have some?" she asked.

"Sure. Help yourself."

As Bridget began to **devour** the candy bars greedily, Babette spoke from the other side of the tent.

"That is an amazing head of hair you have, Barnaby," she said.

"It suits me, I think," he agreed. "You sure have been awfully quiet and **pensive.** What have you been thinking about?"

"I have been thinking about these poor jackals. You see, the French people know what it is to live under the rule of emperors and dictators. It is something you Americans, thankfully, have not had to bear," she said, munching thoughtfully on a potato chip.

"What's your point?" asked Bridget, her mouth full of candy.

"My point is, I feel **sympathy** for them. I think we should help them."

Barnaby and Bridget sat quietly for a few seconds, and were about to reply when Lassie came in through the tent flap.

"Thanks, but no thanks," he said. "I hope you don't think I was **eavesdropping,** but I couldn't help hearing what you said about helping us. We don't need anything from you. Colonel Cano has it all figured out."

"I was only . . . ," started Babette.

"I know, I know. Look, I didn't come to argue. I came to tell you the feast is on. Come on out!"

Babette, Bridget, and Barnaby emerged from the tent to find the camp lit up like a carnival. Torches glowed all around. Seven female jackals were doing the dance of the seven wails—they **gyrated** until they were too dizzy to stand up, then let out seven heartbreakingly **plaintive** howls. And Cano, in his finest cape, sat at the head of a long, low table, a gigantic, wrinkled-up old lizard on one side and a gigantic cat on the other.

"My friends!" he called when the three humans appeared. "Come join us!"

The three travelers joined their host, and introductions were made.

"This is Ambassador Sangfroid, a respected and **venerable** statesman from the Reptile Republic," said Cano. "He has traveled all the way from the Château Guécot to be with us tonight."

"Actually, it's not really a château. More like a large dungeon than a small castle. But I suppose it will have to serve as the reptile **embassy** for the time being, until the jackals can come up with more suitable office space," said the lizard.

Babette and Bridget squirmed uncomfortably at his rudeness. Barnaby was too busy examining the food to notice what was going on.

"Of course," said Cano, good-naturedly. "Please, help yourself to some food."

"You must be mad, Colonel," replied the lizard with complete **disdain.** "I can't stand to smell this boot camp slop, much less eat it."

"Hey!" cried Bridget. "The colonel doesn't have to sit here and have his food **scoffed** at by some stuck-up, **haughty** Gila monster!"

"Foolish child, I am an iguana."

"A pretty **obese** iguana, if you ask me," snapped Bridget. "Maybe it's best if you don't eat anything. Looks like you could afford to skip a few meals."

"Well, I never!" huffed the ambassador, who got up to leave.

"Actually, I think Ambassador Sangfroid looks very strong and distinguished at his current size," said Babette, trying to **appease** the offended lizard.

It seemed to work, because he sat back down and **resumed** the conversation he had been having with Colonel Cano before the three humans arrived. He completely ignored Bridget. Bridget, in turn, ignored him. She turned toward the female jackals and **feigned** great interest in their weird dance steps.

"As I was saying, Colonel, the Reptile Republic is completely **autonomous**—totally independent. We are free to make alliances as we choose. But of course we must choose wisely."

"Surely you can't think that siding with Horace is wise. And your reptiles hate the Emperor as much as we do," argued Cano.

"That's true, but at least the Emperor keeps order. If and when you topple his government, what happens then? We reptiles don't want to live next to a country in a state of **anarchy.** Without an organized system of government, you'll have **chaos** on your hands—complete disorder. Bedlam!" cried the lizard.

"Surely, Sangfroid, you don't think we went into this without a plan," Cano replied. "We have a well-thought-out **agenda.** We have already sent a letter to the Emperor asking him to **abdicate** the throne and set up free and democratic elections. He refused to **relinquish** control, as we thought he would, so we wrote a declaration stating that all animals should have equal say in the government and that we refused to recognize the Emperor as our ruler. Naturally, he **denounced** us as traitors and immediately began releasing false reports about us to the media. Of course, these reports were nothing but **propaganda** designed to frighten the other animals into thinking we were dangerous. But, as you surely understand, we have no choice but to fight for our rights!"

"Please forgive my **skepticism,** Colonel, but so many revolutions fail that I think we have a right to be doubtful," said the lizard. "That is why we are prepared to offer you limited support. We can give you a unit of light lizards trained in electronic **sabotage** to damage the elephant computer networks and telephone lines. These lizards have the natural ability to **camouflage** themselves. Their skins change color to match their surroundings, so they are rarely detected."

"I am grateful for your help, Ambassador," said Cano.

Just then, some awful racket—yowling and crashing—started on the edge of the camp.

"What on earth is that?" yelled the colonel.

"Lassie, can you see what's going on?"

"It seems to be some sort of brawl, sir," replied the lieutenant. "Probably a fight over one of those wail dancers. I'll go check it out."

It was a brawl. And soon the brawl turned into a **skirmish.** Then the skirmish turned into a **melee.** And before Cano's men realized what was happening, they were under full-scale attack by the forces of General Horace and his jackals!

"To arms, to arms!" ordered Cano. "Fight for your lives!"

"Much as I'd like to help, I'm afraid I have to be going," said Sangfroid sheepishly. "The **gout** in my leg has been acting up, swelling something awful, so I wouldn't be much good anyway. Ta ta!"

With that, the ambassador scurried off as quickly as a fat lizard with gout can scurry.

"Don't worry, Colonel," yelled Bridget over the battle noise. "We'll help you!"

In fact, Babette and Barnaby were busy doing just that. Babette, it appeared, had a few more tricks up her sleeve than speaking fluent Jackal. She was running around, karate-chopping dogs like some some kind of crazed ninja. And Barnaby kept pulling stink bombs, firecrackers, and other explosives out of his hair and hurling them at the enemy. Bridget pulled out her bubble gum and began stretching it into a huge lasso, with which she captured several of Horace's soldiers and yanked them to the ground.

But the enemy jackals were **relentless.** They fought on and on, refusing to give up. But Cano's soldiers wouldn't **yield** either, and finally, after several hours of battle, they got the upper hand. Beauregard even managed to capture General Horace himself.

Then they heard the footsteps. Heavy, loud footsteps.

"Oh, no, the elephants are coming in from the north!" cried Cano, more with exhaustion than fear. "Judging from the sound of their footsteps, they're about a mile from camp! That means they'll be here in **approximately** ten minutes."

"At least **stealth** isn't one of their advantages," Bridget commented. "You can't exactly sneak up on someone with footsteps as loud as that."

"That's no help right now, Bridget," said

Babette. "We have just **subdued** Horace's soldiers, and already we are under attack again. Cano's jackals are tired, many are wounded. We are at our most **vulnerable.** We can no longer defend ourselves!"

Bridget was shocked to see how upset Babette was getting. She had been so cool until now.

"Hey, don't give up yet! We've still got ten minutes!"

"Nine," said Cano.

"Okay, nine," said Bridget. "Anything could happen. There was a **similar** situation in New York during the '86 World Series. It looked like the Mets were going to lose for sure, but the Red Sox's first baseman totally choked, made an error, and we were saved."

"What *is* she talking about?" groaned Cano.

"Well, maybe that's not the greatest example," said Bridget. "All I'm saying is, it ain't over 'til it's over."

"So what do you suggest we do, oh, perky one?" asked Barnaby, his eyebrows raised into high, confronting arches.

"Well, first of all I think we should get a bunch of green paint, a can of root beer, a few bushels of cotton, and some dry toast. Then . . ."

But Bridget didn't get a chance to finish outlining her plan. From the east came the sound of two-footed galloping and what seemed like the throaty quacking of enormous ducks. From the west, came a rumbling sea of black and white.

And from the south, a really revolting snorting noise and a **repulsive** piggish odor.

Bridget, Barnaby, and Babette looked around wildly, fearing for their lives, but Cano leaped with excitement.

"It's the ostriches! And the warthogs! And even the pacifist pandas!" he cried. "We're saved!"

The allied armies arrived at the camp, gathered around Cano, and pledged their support to him just as the elephants began to arrive. A huge wall of gray legs, like granite columns, thundered into view, stopped, then broke into neat formation to make way for the chief, the father of their clan, the **patriarch** of the pachyderms—the Elephant Emperor himself.

The two forces, a hodgepodge of birds, dogs, hogs, and bears on one side and the giant elephants on the other, faced each other uncomfortably. Finally, the emperor spoke.

"Cano," he boomed. "Are you the one responsible for stirring this whole thing up? Did you instigate this rebellion?"

"Yes, but as you can see, I'm not the only one who's tired of your rigid, **dogmatic** rule," yelled Cano.

"I've had about enough of all this," replied the emperor. "All of you, go on home. Cano, if you and your soldiers turn yourselves in, you will not be harshly punished. I am prepared to be **lenient**."

"You just don't get it, do you?" said the colonel. "This isn't a childish prank. We don't want an emperor anymore. We want democracy! We want democracy!"

The crowd behind Cano began cheering and chanting in their assorted languages.

"Hmmph," said the elephant, frowning. "I have my doubts about this whole thing, but just because I am **dubious** doesn't mean you are wrong."

"You mean, you will step down?" asked Cano, both shocked and hopeful.

"Well, I should warn you, a dictatorship such as ours has certain advantages over democracy," said the elephant. "For one thing, we have no **bureaucracy**—no confusing lines of authority, no piles of paperwork, no useless officials to bog things down. What I say goes, and that's that. It's very efficient."

"But it's not fair!" argued the colonel. "We must have a say in our own government!"

The crowd mumbled agreement. The emperor stood for a moment in deep thought. Not a sound was heard throughout the camp. Several minutes passed before he spoke again.

"Okay, then, you shall have your elections. I certainly don't want a bunch of ungrateful, unhappy subjects. We might as well get the ball rolling immediately. Cano, I guess you and your army are in charge. The country will have to be under **martial law** until an election can be arranged," he said.

The animals, realizing that they had won without fighting a single battle, cheered with joy. The emperor, recognizing that it was useless to stand in the way of democracy, let out a sigh of **resignation.** Then some serious partying began.

Babette pointed out to Barnaby, Bridget, and Beauregard that touring a country immediately after a revolution, however bloodless, is usually not wise. Everything is in a state of **upheaval** and confusion, and it's impossible to find a hotel room. It was agreed that they should take this opportunity to thank their hosts and be on their way.

They began walking back to the clearing they had landed in. But as soon as they reached the open field, a blinding flash of rainbow-colored light and a great whooshing of air engulfed them, and they promptly disappeared from the face of the planet.

✍ QUIZ #6 ✍
Relationships

Decide what relationship the following pairs of words have to each other. If they have similar meanings, write "S" next to the pair of words. If they have opposite meanings, write "O" next to the words.

1. abdicate :: relinquish
2. animosity :: contempt
3. deference :: impudence
4. foe :: comrade
5. gorge :: devour
6. anarchy :: chaos
7. melee :: skirmish
8. lenient :: authoritarian
9. tolerance :: bigotry
10. impromptu :: ad-libbed
11. zeal :: apathy
12. reminisce :: forget

✍ QUIZ #7 ✍
Relationships

Decide what relationship the following pairs of words have to each other. If they have similar meanings, write "S" next to the pair of words. If they have opposite meanings, write "O" next to the words.

1. pacifists :: belligerent
2. dissenting :: unanimous
3. radical :: traditional
4. servile :: haughty
5. disdain :: scoff
6. dogmatic :: flexible
7. disparage :: praise
8. paranoid :: trusting
9. autonomous :: independent
10. pensive :: boisterous
11. feigning :: pretending

✍ QUIZ #8 ✍
Fill in the Blank

For each sentence below, choose the word that best completes the sentence.

1. It was obvious that Lance felt
   _____ toward the girls'
   softball team because even before he saw
   them, he had made up his mind that they
   were lousy players.

   a. audacity **b.** reverence
   c. prejudice **d.** dignity

2. The kids called Marlon "dog-face" because
   his pointed teeth, shaggy hair, and his habit
   of hanging his tongue out of his mouth gave
   him a sort of _____ look.

   a. canine **b.** bovine
   c. plaintive **d.** awkward

3. Cassie was being _____ when she
   said, "I can't wait to go have my wisdom
   teeth pulled. It will be more fun than
   Disneyland!"

   a. sarcastic **b.** adverse **c.** fanatic **d.** overt

4. During the student council elections, my opponent handed out tons of pamphlets filled with lies and twisted stories about me and my plans as student council president, but most students knew it was just a bunch of _____, and I won the election anyway.

   a. agenda **b.** embargo
   c. propaganda **d.** media

5. The military overthrew the government in a bloody _____.

   a. resignation **b.** coup d'état
   c. feud **d.** upheaval

6. During the holiday, Margie _____ donations of canned goods from her neighbors for her school food drive.

   a. solicited **b.** comprehended
   c. contemplated **d.** denounced

7. Sheldon was not usually a troublemaker, but when the lunchroom served gruel for the fourth day in a row, he _____ a riot in the cafeteria, and led a crowd of students to the secret supply of chocolate pudding the cook had been keeping for herself.

   a. sabotaged **b.** clamored
   c. gaped **d.** instigated

8. Genghis Khan was a powerful
_____ who ruled with an iron
fist and crushed anyone who tried to disobey
or disagree with him.

   a. ambassador b. orator
   c. tyrant d. patriarch

9. Mr. Spalding, our social sciences teacher, is a
_____ old man who has taught
at our school for forty years and is respected
and liked by the whole town.

   a. vulnerable b. omnipotent
   c. disparate d. venerable

10. Ambassador Black hosted a big party at the
American _____ in Tokyo.

   a. domain b. embassy
   c. camouflage d. bureaucracy

11. Jacob was _____ in his
efforts to get Samantha to date him—he
asked her out five times before she finally
gave in.

   a. repulsive b. dubious
   c. atrocious d. relentless

12. Mindy sent me a Valentine's Day card that
said "Roses are red, violets are blue, sugar is
sweet, and so are you," which I thought was
pretty _____, but it was
nice of her anyway.

   a. similar b. clichéd c. obese d. bleak

✍ QUIZ #9 ✍
Matching

Match each word on the right with a word on the left that has a similar meaning.

1. retort
2. astonish
3. loathe
4. inhabit
5. faction
6. camouflage
7. chafe
8. behoove
9. dignitary
10. revel
11. kowtow
12. prior
13. conspiracy
14. cohabit

a. delight
b. hate
c. rub
d. live with
e. bow
f. reply
g. hide
h. surprise
i. secret plot
j. important person
k. live in
l. benefit
m. group
n. before

Matching

Match each word on the right with a word on the left that has a similar meaning.

1. sanction
2. binge
3. eavesdrop
4. gyrate
5. appease
6. resume
7. skeptic
8. yield
9. approximately
10. stealth
11. subdue
12. martial law
13. resignation

a. overhear
b. doubter
c. conquer
d. revolve
e. punishment
f. military rule
g. spree
h. give in
i. acceptance
j. calm
k. begin again
l. sneakiness
m. about

Chapter 3
Space Hippies Freak Out

Barnaby, Babette, Bridget, and Beauregard lay
flat on their backs, staring up at a large
mirrored ball that was spinning and casting
multicolored light all around them. The smell
of incense hung heavy in the air. They were all
feeling a little **disoriented**. After all, not thirty
seconds ago they had been standing in a
grassy field. Now they had no idea where they
were or what was going on.

"Is this hell?" whispered Bridget, to no one in particular.

"I think it's a disco," responded Babette.

Suddenly a voice thundered all around them.

"Aw, man, Janice! You've gone and done it again. I keep telling you that isn't a disco ball—it's a highly sensitive teleportation device!"

The four friends sat up and stared at each other in wonder. This was all very unusual.

"You cats just hang loose for a sec," continued the voice. "I'll be right there."

"Cats?" questioned Barnaby. "But there's only one cat."

"That's just an old hippie expression," said Bridget. "It just means 'guys.' Do you think ...?"

But Bridget's question was answered before she asked it. Through the door walked a hippie so hippie-ish he was practically a **caricature** of himself—long hair, a scraggly **goatee** on his chin, granny glasses, and a flowing Indian robe.

"Peace," he said, making a V-shaped sign with two fingers of his right hand.

Now, you'll have to admit, this was an extraordinary turn of events. I think I ought to give you some background information to help clear things up. As you may have guessed, we were all feeling a bit **fatigued** after our battle with the jackal fanatics. But even though we were worn out, we were all still eager to get back to Paris and commence our search for Bridget's parents. The last thing we needed was to have our plans thwarted yet again. Only this time, it was a spaceship, not bad weather, that threw a wrench in things.

That's right, we were "beamed up" against our will, right off the ground and onto a spaceship. And not just any spaceship, either. We suddenly found ourselves aboard the **infamous** pirate ship, the *Far Out*, captained by the **notorious** space hippie, Wobbly Philstein. At one time, everyone in America knew his name, and they knew about the pranks he and his followers pulled on politicians they didn't like. The worst was when he somehow managed to dye the Speaker of the House bright red from head to toe as some sort of protest against the Speaker's plans to cut spending on education and public television. The FBI was never exactly sure who the **culprit** was in this crime, but Wobbly kind of gave himself away when he got on television and asked the Speaker whether he was "better red than dead or better dead than well read." That statement alone made him a prime suspect. Later, the FBI even discovered he had a tattoo of Big Bird on his arm, and that he was a known watcher of "Masterpiece Theater."

So the FBI named Wobbly the number one most wanted man in America, and a manhunt **ensued** the likes of which the country had never seen. Police officers, Secret Service agents, even regular citizens were searching every barn, barrel, and basement for the hippie. But he was too **crafty** for them, and managed to **elude** his pursuers for months.

The rumor cropped up that Wobbly was planning to **defect** to the Netherlands, a country known as a **refuge** for misunderstood **bohemians,** a place where hippies, artists, musicians, and other uninsured free spirits with kooky or **eccentric** habits could feel safe. Later, however, it was revealed that Wobbly had been in Mexico all along, building a spaceship out of old tour buses. Destination: Far Out. Yes, he and his followers blasted off, and the authorities were forced to give up their hunt. Outer space, unfortunately, does not fall under the FBI's **jurisdiction.**

Gradually, the frenzy over Wobbly **ebbed,** and things returned to normal. Many even suspected his spaceship fell apart during takeoff, and that Wobbly and his buddies were now probably **deceased.** But they were obviously wrong, because there he was, standing in front of us, very much alive.

✎ ✎ ✎ ✎ ✎

"I am Captain Wobbly Philstein," announced the hippie. "You can call me Captain Wobbly if you want, but plain Wobbly is cool, too, if you don't dig the military thing."

"I'm Bridget, and this is Babette and Barnaby," Bridget replied. "And this cat apparently is a spy named Beauregard, but he doesn't talk to humans."

Barnaby and Babette giggled.

"You aren't from the government, are you?" Wobbly asked suspiciously.

"No," said Bridget.

"Well, then everything's groovy! Welcome aboard the *Far Out*. Come on and meet the rest of the crew."

The kids followed Wobbly down a long hall that looked like the inside of a bus. Only a few candles were glowing, so the light was dim. There seemed to be someone in there playing the sitar, but the air was so **dense** with incense it was impossible to be sure. It was very peaceful.

Then they passed into another room, which also looked like the inside of a bus. Only this room, unlike the **previous** room, was in a state of **pandemonium.** All sorts of music were being played **simultaneously,** resulting in a terrible jumble of noises. Men, women, and children were swirling and dancing around the room, banging tambourines and finger cymbals in a kind of spiritual frenzy. And one guy was actually swinging by his heels from a chandelier, his face completely covered with hair and beads. Babette barely had time to admire the orange velour **upholstery** on the beanbag chairs before a group of spinning girls whisked her into their dance.

"Is this some kind of religious **cult**?" shouted Bridget over the racket. "If so, I'm telling you right now, I will *not* let you shave my head."

"No, we're not a cult," Wobbly yelled back. Then he shouted over to a woman with long blond hair who had her back to them, "Hey, Janice, cool it, will you? We've got company, remember?"

Janice turned around. She was very beautiful. She had a daisy painted on her cheek, and her face looked calm and **serene,** especially her peaceful blue eyes. She smiled at the visitors, then stood up on her seat and held her hands out in some sort of gesture to the crowd. She looked like a queen. In fact, it was clear she was the **matriarch** of the merry band of hippies, because they all quieted down when they noticed what she was doing, then stood as if awaiting orders.

"Hey, everybody, looks like we have some more Deadheads aboard," she announced.

"What do you mean?" asked Barnaby, rather alarmed. "We are not dead, and neither are our heads."

"Naw, man," said a hippie in dark sunglasses standing next to him, "the Dead was a band. As in the Grateful Dead, you dig?"

"Yeah, we dig," said Bridget. "We don't exactly live in a pop culture vacuum on Earth, ya know."

"I can dig that," Wobbly said. "Before you guys go back to Earth, you should come to a sit-in with us. We're **en route** to Alpha C right now so we can protest a new outer space curfew. The governing body wants us all in our spaceships by nine o'clock every night. That's so square!"

"It sounds like a good cause," said Bridget, "but we really have to get back. I've misplaced my parents."

"Count yourself lucky. I had to blast off into space in order to misplace mine," replied Wobbly.

Bridget looked down sadly at the brown shag carpet.

"Hey, I'm sorry, man," said Wobbly, seeing that his joke had not been appreciated. "I didn't mean to be **flippant** about something that's got you so low. But you see, it's like this—I can't beam you back down right now. The teleporter is stuck in 'up,' and I can't fix it myself."

"Can't you land us somewhere on Earth? We could pick a hidden spot so no one would be able to sneak up and arrest you," Bridget offered.

"No can do, sister. The *Far Out* probably wouldn't survive a **descent** through the Earth's atmosphere. And if the descent didn't get us, going back up probably would. We could try to position ourselves over one of the holes in the **ozone layer,** but that would only help a little. There are plenty of other layers of gas ready to burn this bus up."

"You mean I'm stuck here? I'm going to live out my life as some sort of space **vagrant**—no home, no family, no money?" wailed Bridget. Her lower lip began to tremble and her eyes welled up with tears.

"Hey, don't knock it, man. The wandering life of a **nomad** is full of adventure. There's nothing like the freedom of pulling up stakes and moving on whenever you feel like it," raved Wobbly. "Of course, being a **pauper** isn't all that much fun. Which reminds me . . . you kids don't have any money, do you? I'll **reimburse** you as soon as we get to Alpha C."

At that point Bridget lost it. She sat down and began sobbing loudly.

"Hey, man, what's all this **lamenting** about?" asked Wobbly kindly. "I said I'd pay you back."

Janice, who had been talking with Babette and Barnaby over by the ship's controls, made her way over to Bridget.

"Nice work, Wobbly," said Janice. "First, I accidentally beam them up, and now you make them cry."

The captain shrugged helplessly and wandered off.

"Your name's Bridget, right?" asked Janice in a soft, comforting voice.

Bridget nodded. She even stopped crying quite so hard. There was something nice and **maternal** about Janice, and it made her miss her own mother a little less.

"Don't let Wob upset you, honey," she said. "I know he seems cold and **dispassionate,** but he's really not uncaring. We'll get you back home, I promise. We're actually stopping at a space station on the way to the sit-in to do a little shopping and pick up supplies. I'm sure we can fit a trip to the mechanic into our **itinerary.** We'll get that disco ball fixed."

Bridget nodded and managed a small smile.

"There, now, that's better," said Janice. "Say, I know what you need. You need to do a little yoga."

"Um, I don't know . . . ," Bridget hesitated. She was **wary** of strange Indian exercises that didn't involve running, jumping, or sweating.

"It'll help you center yourself. Right now you're all out of balance. Yoga can restore your **equilibrium.**"

Bridget was **vacillating.** On the one hand, Janice was so cool that she wanted to go along with her, but on the other hand, the whole yoga thing seemed dangerous. What if she got into one of those twisted-up positions and couldn't get out?

"Don't sweat it, honey," Janice assured her. "I'm about to teach my daily yoga class now anyway. Unfortunately, life on a remodeled tour bus can be pretty **sedentary,** and we all know that sitting around all the time isn't very healthy. That's why we do yoga. Kind of works the kinks out. Join in if you want, but only if your decision is completely **voluntary.** I'm not forcing you."

The fact that other people were going to join her kind of took the pressure off, so Bridget decided to try it. She **donned** the baggy muslin trousers Janice loaned her, and they were ready to begin.

The first exercise was more like sleeping than stretching. Janice told everyone to "get **horizontal,**" and they all just lay down flat on the floor. After concentrating on breathing for a while, Janice told the class to stay on their backs but lift their legs up into a **vertical** position, straight up in the air, **perpendicular** to the floor.

"Then," she said, "when you're ready, lift your lower back off the floor, supporting it with your hands, and stretch your legs out over your head, so your knees are close to your face and your legs are **parallel** to the carpet. This pose will **stimulate** the flow of blood to the brain."

"I think it's definitely working," groaned Bridget. "My head's about to explode."

"Hmmm," said Janice. "Maybe this is too

hard for a **novice.** Since you're a beginner, I'll start you off with something less **strenuous.** Bring your legs down, and I'll show you how to **meditate.**"

Bridget wriggled out of her pose and sat up. Janice came over and sat down cross-legged in front of her.

"Meditation," explained Janice, "is basically just deep thought. But in yoga, you don't meditate on a particular problem or concrete issue. It's much more **abstract,** you know? You just think, but not about anything solid. Just close your eyes and let your mind relax. Understand?"

Bridget nodded. Janice helped her get into the correct position.

"Now then, as you do this, weird ideas may come into your head. Don't fight them, they're just **subconscious** thoughts, thoughts that you're not aware of all the time because they're hidden away in your mind. One time when I was meditating, I got so caught up I began to **hallucinate.** I opened my eyes and found myself floating in an endless sea of non-dairy whipped topping with chocolate sprinkles falling on my head, and a great maraschino cherry moon shining and **luminous** overhead. It was so cool."

Janice smiled in a vague sort of way. Bridget was a little concerned, although finding herself in a bowl of whipped topping didn't sound all that bad.

"I mean, it wasn't really there. I was just seeing things, dig? Anyway, I don't think that will happen to you," Janice assured her.

Bridget closed her eyes and began her meditation, and Janice went back to the rest of the class. Over by the control panel, Babette, Barnaby, and Wobbly were having a conversation.

"Captain Wobbly, I must say, I **marvel** at your mechanical abilities," said Barnaby. "It's truly amazing that you managed to build such a fine spaceship out of ordinary tour buses."

"Yeah, well, it could have been a fine ship, but the feds were breathing down my neck, you know what I'm saying? I had to hurry," said Wobbly. "For one thing, it's not that easy to **navigate.** The *Mayflower* was probably easier to steer than this baby. But the thing that burns me most is the transmission."

"You mean the gears?" asked Babette, somewhat shocked. "A spaceship with gears? I expected 'hyperdrive' and 'warp factors' and things like that."

"You've got to work with what you have," replied Wobbly. "And for the *Far Out*, that meant a **manual** transmission. I was trying to build an automatic transmission for her back in Mexico, but I ran out of time. So until I get the parts I need, gears are shifted the old-fashioned way—by hand."

"Hmmm, automatic transmission," mused Barnaby, scratching his head and pondering the problem. "You'd need a timing belt, for starters, right?"

Suddenly, something fell out of Barnaby's hair and under the captain's seat.

"Barnaby!" gasped Babette. "Don't tell me you had a timing belt stuck in your hair!"

"Well, not exactly a timing belt," said Wobbly, who had pulled the object out from under his seat. "More like the latest issue of *Women and Men of Science: The Swimsuit Edition.* There are some pretty **risqué** pictures in here."

"I only read it for the articles," said Barnaby, blushing slightly. "I like to keep up on what my colleagues are doing. Give it back!"

Barnaby leaped at the magazine, but the captain held it out of his reach. The two scuffled over the magazine until Wobbly suddenly cried, "Hey, my contact lens!"

"You wear contacts?" asked Barnaby, who lost interest in the magazine for the time being. "But doesn't that make your granny glasses a bit **redundant**? I mean, what do you need glasses for if you wear contacts?"

Wobbly paid no attention to his question. He was busy trying to find his contact lens in the dense brown shag.

"Got it!" he chirped, after a couple of minutes. "Man, that was close. Now, what were we talking about?"

"Your life story," said Babette, seizing the chance to change the subject. "You were going to tell us how you became such a scandalous hippie, and how you met Janice, and how you decided to get married and blast off into space together."

"Well, first of all, Janice is not my **spouse,**" replied the hippie.

"Oh, I am so disappointed," frowned Babette.

"How come?"

"Ah, well, it seemed so romantic," she sighed dreamily. "Two outlaw hippies, chased from Earth, finding love among the stars."

"You'll have to forgive her. She's French," whispered Barnaby.

"Hey, man, don't get me wrong," he told Babette. "I mean, she's not my girlfriend. Our relationship is strictly **platonic,** but I do like her just fine. But we outlaws can't get romantically involved, dig? Wild, **unbridled** affections only get you in trouble."

"Hmmph," huffed Babette, crossing her arms over her chest.

"I can see we aren't connecting on this topic," said Wobbly. "Maybe I should tell you about how we got where we are. Actually, it started back when I was a teenager. My mother, who was a hippie herself, said to me, 'Bob, I want you to be rich.' "

"I thought your name was Wobbly. Why did she call you Bob?" asked Barnaby.

"Well, that happened when I was born. Supposedly, she wanted to name me Bob Weir Philstein, but she got confused. She was way out of it when it came time to fill out the birth certificate, and when they asked her what she wanted the name to be, she just kept saying 'Wob Beir, Wob Beir.' She **transposed** the 'b' and the 'w.' At least, that's the best explanation we could come up with. Anyway, she always called me Bob.

"So, as I was saying, she wanted me to be a very rich and powerful businessman—a **tycoon,** if possible. Let's face it, being a hippie isn't that **lucrative,** and she decided someone better start making some money, or she'd wind up old and homeless. Man, was I sad. I didn't want to leave my friends and I seriously doubted I had the **capacity** to be successful in business. As I set out for New York City, I was afraid. Afraid I'd be laughed at. Afraid I'd be fired. Afraid I'd never be hired at all.

"As it turned out, my fears were completely **unfounded.** New York was a boom town. I was hired right away, and I discovered I had a real **aptitude** for business. It just came naturally. Soon I was a millionaire. Man, I mean, I was rolling in bread . . ."

"'Rolling in bread'?" whispered Barnaby to Babette. "What does that mean?"

"I have no idea," she whispered back. "It's another one of those hippie **idioms.** At least, I don't think he actually rolled around with loaves of bread. We will have to ask Bridget."

"But my wealth had a price," continued Wobbly. "First of all, the stress gave me stomach **ulcers**—open sores in my stomach."

Babette and Barnaby **winced** at the thought of such a horrible thing, almost as if they felt pains in their own stomachs.

"But the worst was that I had given up all the values that were important to me. Yes, for money I was willing to **forsake** every social and political cause I once held sacred. Man, I even worked for a company whose only purpose was to **deplete** our country's natural supply of kale. If they keep it up, there will be no more kale in the United States by the year 2020!"

Barnaby and Babette stared at each other, obviously shaken.

"That was the last straw. I had to do something. The country was going down the tubes, man, and I had to stop it. I became active, dedicated, **militant** in service to the cause. That's when the pranks began.

"I wrapped the White House with recycled toilet paper. I dumped a truckload of compost on the floor of the Senate. And, as you may have heard, I turned the Speaker of the House bright red with vegetable dye. Sure, some people said I was nothing more than a **vandal,** but these were hardly acts of senseless spray painting and destruction of property.

"By the time of the red-dye prank, I already had a following of several dozen. But my life was changed forever when I met Janice."

"Aha!" cried Babette. "I knew it. You are crazy about her. You **dote** on her, admit it!"

"Back off, Babette," said Wobbly. "I'm no love sap. I do owe her a lot, though. Before I met her, I was full of anger. My pranks were getting more and more dangerous. I was even starting to have violent thoughts. Janice chilled me out, helped me become more **moderate.** But by that time, the government already wanted me dead, and I was getting tired of spending all my time **evading** capture, so we beat it down to Mexico, followed by tons of like-minded hippies. It was an **exodus,** man; whole populations picked up and left the country. The government folks probably thought we were doing them a favor. Anyway, the rest you already know. Whoa, man, we're already at the mall! We'd better slow down."

Wobbly jammed his foot onto the clutch and shifted clumsily into first gear. The whole ship **lurched** forward. Bridget, deep in her meditations, fell over sideways. Beauregard, who had been **lulled** into a deep sleep by the incense and sitar music in the other room, came in to see what had so rudely awakened him. He fixed an angry stare on the captain.

"Sorry, man," said Wobbly with a little wave of his hand.

Bridget, suddenly awake, was full of excitement. "I've got it!" she cried.

Janice and a couple of other people from the yoga class came over and helped her up.

"Did you have some kind of vision?" Janice asked.

"The perfect counterplay to the pick-and-roll! Somebody get me some paper—I've got to sketch this out and send it to the New York Knicks!"

"A basketball formation? How **profound.** How deep. What an important insight into the meaning of life," said one of the hippies in a **snide,** mocking tone.

"I'd wipe that self-satisfied **smirk** off my face if I were you, Ralph," **cautioned** Janice. "Should I tell everyone what your great insight was? It was rather **prosaic,** if I remember. Totally dullsville. Boring. Something along the lines of 'Oswald acted alone,' right?"

Ralph grumbled and walked off.

"Let's go see what Wobbly's up to," suggested Janice. "I think we're almost at the mall."

Janice brought up the idea of stopping at the mechanic's shop, getting the disco ball fixed, and returning Barnaby, Babette, Bridget, and Beauregard to Earth before heading to the sit-in. Wobbly didn't take to the idea immediately.

"But, baby," he whined, "we've got a **rendezvous** with Stan the Fruit Man in less than four hours. If we don't meet him when we're supposed to, we won't have any RSGs for the sit-in!"

"RSGs?" asked Bridget.

"Red seedless grapes," said Janice. "Great snack food. **Ideal** for sit-ins. Anyway, look, Wob, that's a pretty **flimsy** excuse for kidnapping. You know you can get some grapes at Alpha C. We have no right to drag these kids to a sit-in that could last all day and night. If they decided to come of their own **volition,** that would be another story. But they obviously want to go back to Earth, and we should help them, so unless you can come up with a stronger reason than your desire for snack food, I suggest we return them to their planet."

Wobbly unhappily agreed, and pulled the *Far Out* into the airlock of a spaceship service station. He honked the horn, and a stooped-over, gray-haired man in greasy coveralls came shuffling out. Wobbly, Janice, and the kids jumped out of the ship.

"Yeah?" asked the man, whose coveralls had the name "Bruce" sewn on the breast pocket.

"Our teleportation device is stuck in 'up.' We need to get these kids back to Earth right away. Do you think you could help us, um, Bruce?" asked Janice as sweetly as possible.

"My name's not Bruce," grumbled the mechanic. But fortunately, he agreed to take a look at the disco ball.

After only a **cursory** examination of the broken ball, he came right back out and announced that all his attempts to fix it were **futile.**

"Well, there you have it," said Wobbly. "Let's be on our way."

"Hold it, Wob. What do you mean, futile? You barely looked at it!" Janice told the man whose name wasn't Bruce.

"I mean useless. Unsuccessful. There's only one thing that could fix it, and that's . . ."

"Duct tape?" asked Barnaby.

All eyes turned toward the boy genius, who stood there holding a roll of shiny gray tape.

Bridget and Babette exchanged knowing smiles.

"Well, I'll be," said the mechanic. "Boy, give me that tape, and I'll have you fixed up in a jiffy."

He was true to his word. Within five minutes, they were waving good-bye and heading toward Earth. Within fifteen minutes, however, the engine had coughed to a stop. Wobbly began banging his head on the steering wheel.

"This is some kind of **omen,** man. A sign, dig? Something's trying to tell us our days of going to sit-ins are over."

"Calm down, Wobbly," said Bridget. "Barnaby here is mainly a physicist, but he's pretty **versatile.** I'll bet he can fix it. He's a genius!"

"Such **optimism.** Such a cheery outlook. Don't you see, it's hopeless?" he moaned.

"Well, I'm not sure I'm such a genius," said Barnaby, trying to sound **humble,** "but since Captain Wobbly seems too upset to fix it himself, I guess I can take a look."

Bridget and Babette followed him to the engine room.

"Hmm," said Barnaby, after examining things for a minute. "It looks like Wobbly's been pretty **lax** about changing the oil in this spaceship. You're supposed to do it every three months. I'd say, judging from all this clogged-up goo, that he hasn't it done it in, well, a really, really long time."

"Never mind that," said Bridget. "Can you fix it?"

"I'm not sure," he replied. "It would take the proper tools and the **finesse** of an expert to chip out the clog without damaging the engine."

"Nonsense," said Babette. "It just needs a good whacking."

"Are you crazy?" asked Barnaby. "You can't simply hit a machine and expect it to work."

"Barnaby, we are in the middle of a **crisis** here," said Bridget through clenched teeth. "If we don't fix this engine, we'll be adrift with a bunch of freaked-out hippies forever. Who knows what could happen? They might start playing Grateful Dead **medleys** on their guitars! Get the picture?"

"I see. The situation is desperate indeed. Whack away, Babette."

Babette examined the engine for a moment to select a good spot. Then she took a few cleansing breaths and, with a loud "hiyah!" karate-kicked the engine, which promptly sputtered back to life.

Barnaby and Bridget were impressed. They began heaping praise on their French friend,

extolling her many and varied talents. Finally, they could return to their planet. They returned to the front of the ship to say goodbye.

When they got there, things were not all peace and love, to say the least. The hippies were in the middle of an ugly argument. Sure, a few of them were quietly chanting or meditating, but the **predominant** feeling in the room was definitely anger. And the anger was directed at Wobbly.

"You **hypocrite**! How can you tell us to do one thing while you do something else?" yelled one woman. "You said we should give up our worldly belongings and stop being dependent on money. You said that's the only way we'd be free. And this whole time you've had a million dollars in high-yield bonds invested on Earth! Admit it—Stan the Fruit Man is your broker!"

"I resent your tone, Sunshine," replied Wobbly. "I am your captain. Show me the proper respect, or I'll have to punish you for **insubordination**."

That didn't sit well with the hippies, and Captain Wobbly suddenly had an uprising on his hands, a **mutiny** on the *Far Out*. Somehow, Janice remained calm throughout the fight. She walked over to where Barnaby, Bridget, Babette, and Beauregard were huddled in the corner.

"Even space hippies lose their cool sometimes," she explained, "but there's no reason you should have to **witness** such **discord** among people who usually live so peacefully together. Come on, let's go to the transporter room. I think we're within beaming range."

The kids and the cat followed Janice to the room they had first appeared in. She hugged them all, scratched Beauregard's head, and gave them **identical** love-bead necklaces.

"Keep these as something to remember us by—**mementos** of your brief **excursion** into space," said Janice.

"We will," said Bridget, who was feeling a little sad at having to leave her new friend.

"Now, then," began Janice, as she approached the teleporter controls, "you all just huddle together in the middle of the floor. I'm not sure how precise this disco ball is, but you'll wind up on Earth somewhere, at least."

The disco ball began spinning, pink and green and yellow and blue flashing everywhere. Soon Barnaby, Beauregard, Babette, and Bridget were enveloped in a warm, melting feeling.

"Have a nice trip!" yelled Bridget, just as she began to disappear.

"Oh, we will," replied Janice. "We will."

✍ QUIZ #11 ✍
Relationships

Decide what relationship the following pairs of words have to each other. If they have similar meanings, write "S" next to the pair of words. If they have opposite meanings, write "O" next to the words.

1. infamous :: notorious
2. elude :: evade
3. vagrant :: nomad
4. horizontal :: vertical
5. perpendicular :: parallel
6. abstract :: concrete
7. tycoon :: pauper
8. platonic :: romantic
9. luminous :: dim
10. cursory :: thorough
11. sedentary :: active
12. dispassionate :: caring
13. lulled :: soothed
14. novice :: beginner
15. futile :: useless

✍ QUIZ #12 ✍
Relationships

Decide what relationship the following pairs of words have to each other. If they have similar meanings, write "S" next to the pair of words. If they have opposite meanings, write "O" next to the words.

1. militant :: moderate
2. volition :: free will
3. bohemian :: eccentric
4. pandemonium :: serenity
5. aptitude :: capacity
6. discord :: harmony
7. wary :: cautious
8. flippant :: respectful
9. simultaneously :: separately
10. jurisdiction :: control
11. ebbed :: decreased
12. ideal :: perfect
13. prosaic :: profound
14. omen :: sign
15. humble :: proud

Fill in the Blank

For each sentence below, choose the word that best completes the sentence.

1. All my careful plans and hopes for a happy outdoor jamboree were _____ by an unexpected snowstorm.

    a. disoriented **b.** fatigued
    c. thwarted **d.** ensued

2. Donating blood is a completely _____ action, strongly encouraged but not required.

    a. extraordinary **b.** crafty
    c. voluntary **d.** itinerary

3. Dad kept _____ on the issue of whether or not to have a swimming pool put in the back yard, but after months of going back and forth, he finally decided to go ahead.

    a. vacillating **b.** hallucinating
    c. stimulating **d.** meditating

4. After college, Andy decided he wanted to be a juggler, but his mother advised him to take a more _____ job so he could make enough money to pay off his loans and get his own apartment.

   a. strenuous b. subconscious

   c. lax d. lucrative

5. The president of Acme, Inc. decided to throw a big office picnic, and told all her employees that their _____ and children were also welcome.

   a. culprits b. cults

   c. matriarchs d. spouses

6. If you must borrow money from friends, be sure to _____ them as soon as you can, or there might be hard feelings.

   a. lurch b. reimburse c. forsake d. lament

7. Mr. Kroft told Timmy he was taking away his issue of *Swimsuits Spectacular* because the pictures were too _____ for a ten-year-old, but we think he just wanted the magazine for himself.

   a. unbridled b. risqué

   c. redundant d. en route

8. After I got off the Whirl-a-Twirl ride at the fair, it took me a while to regain my _____ and walk straight without feeling dizzy.

    a. upholstery b. goatee
    c. equilibrium d. nomad

9. Whenever Penny travels to a new place, she always picks up a little _____ to remind her of her trip.

    a. memento b. medley c. idiom d. ulcer

10. Bruce threatened to _____ to Canada if the American ice hockey teams didn't start performing to his satisfaction.

    a. dote b. commence c. wince d. defect

11. Myra was a(n) _____ for calling her neighbors lazy when she hadn't even left her house or mowed her lawn in over a month.

    a. hypocrite b. witness
    c. vandal d. exodus

✍ QUIZ #14 ✎
Matching

Match each word on the right with a word on the left that has a similar meaning.

1. unfounded
2. refuge
3. deceased
4. dense
5. previous
6. descent
7. maternal
8. don
9. marvel
10. navigate
11. manual
12. transposed
13. deplete

a. shelter
b. unsupported
c. fall
d. wonder
e. dead
f. use up
g. thick
h. hand-operated
i. former
j. reversed
k. steer
l. put on
m. motherly

QUIZ #15
Matching

Match each word on the right with a word on the left that has a similar meaning.

1. snide
2. rendezvous
3. versatile
4. optimism
5. finesse
6. crisis
7. extol
8. predominant
9. insubordination
10. mutiny
11. identical
12. excursion

a. skill
b. main
c. praise
d. flexible
e. mean-spirited
f. trip
g. disobedience
h. same
i. date
j. hopefulness
k. uprising
l. dangerous situation

Chapter 4

Curtains for Caspar

Down we went, splash, right into the Mississippi River. I knew it was the Mississippi because there's just no mistaking that muddy water, so **opaque** it's doubtful sunlight's ever touched its bottom. Needless to say, the situation filled me with **chagrin.** In the first place, as you may know, cats do not enjoy being thrown into water, even nice warm water. But this water was not nice and warm; it was absolutely **frigid.** In addition, after our adventure with the space hippies, my fur had taken on the **subtle** smell of incense. Nothing so **obtrusive** that you'd notice it right away, of course, just a trace of perfume. I kind of liked it, and then here I was having it rinsed off me by brisk brown currents. Yes sir, I was fit to be tied.

It's a good thing Bridget still had her gum, because the waters, which were already flowing quickly, started gaining more and more **momentum.** We soon felt as though we were being blasted by a fire hose. I never thought I'd have occasion to praise a child for **incessant** gum chewing (where I'm from, children are frowned on for chewing gum at all, much less all the time), but Bridget had raised her habit to the level of art. She blew an enormous bubble in the shape of a raft, and managed to pull us all aboard.

It was pretty rough sailing for a while. It kind of felt like we were caught in a washing machine spin cycle, but finally we drifted off the main river onto a more peaceful stream and I was able to check out our **locale.** It was Louisiana swampland. Spanish moss hung thickly from the trees, **obscuring** our view of the sky and sun, so that even at midday it seemed like **dusk.** The water gradually stopped flowing altogether, becoming stale and **stagnant.** There were also plenty of alligators hanging around—every now and then a green, scaly head would **emerge** from the murky water, as if to check us out, then sink back below the surface.

I was glad we hadn't drowned, of course, but the situation made me nervous. When we washed ashore, Bridget, Babette, and Barnaby tumbled out of the raft and flopped down on the ground, **exhausted** by our struggle with the rapids. But I was too edgy to rest. I had a feeling danger lurked behind those trees. And, besides, my fur needed some serious grooming. I took it upon myself to keep watch. Unfortunately, there's only so much one cat can do . . . .

"This is getting ridiculous," said Bridget, sitting up after her rest. "Where are we now?"

"Judging from the plant and animal life, and the amazing size of the cockroaches, I'd say we're in southern Louisiana," replied Barnaby, who was holding up an enormous brown bug by one of its fuzzy hind legs.

"Yuck," Bridget said, wrinkling her face into a **grimace.** "Put that nasty thing down, man."

Barnaby dropped the creature, and it scurried off noisily into the swamp. Babette stretched and sat up, and the three began discussing what they should do next. But their conversation was suddenly cut short by a blood-curdling scream.

"Rrrairrow!"

The kids jumped to their feet and spun around. Not three feet behind them was a **monstrous** man, as big as a bear, as bald as an egg, with four huge arms stretched out to grab them, and Beauregard, hissing, clawing, and yowling up a storm on top of his head.

"Oh, my," gasped Barnaby. "What could explain such a **mutation?** What did his parents feed him when he was little? Or perhaps it's **genetic**—maybe his brothers and sisters all have four arms, too."

"This is no time for note-taking, Barnaby. Run!" screamed Bridget, who had already turned to make a dash for it with Babette.

They didn't get very far, though, because standing right behind them were a short, stocky man in a dark, pinstriped suit and wide-brimmed hat, and a bleached-blonde woman in a short red dress. Ordinarily, that wouldn't be enough to stop two kids fleeing a four-armed monster, but the man happened to have a large gun in his hand—a .44-**caliber,** to be exact. **Circumstances** being what they were, Bridget and Babette stopped running.

By this time, the monster had managed to scoop Barnaby up with one of his arms and had pulled Beauregard off his head with another. He stood, as if awaiting orders, as the boy and the cat struggled uselessly.

"Good boy, **Cannibal,**" said the man with the gun.

"He's a cannibal? Don't tell me you're going to feed us to him! I mean, he eats things other than people, right?" Bridget blurted out nervously.

"Enough already with the questions," barked the man. "If anyone's going to do any **interrogating** around here, it's going to be me. And my first question is, what are you doing out here sniffing around our **loot**?"

"Loot?" asked Babette.

"Don't play dumb with me! You must know we're the dangerous gangsters that looted Mrs. Peychaud's Praline Palace back in New Orleans. We got away with seven crates of pralines. The whole police department must be after us by now. We stashed the loot in our hideout, and you know it. You're after our loot!"

"You like saying 'loot' a lot, don't you?" remarked Bridget.

"'Loot' is real gangster talk, kid. So is 'gun,' if you get my drift. Watch it, or you'll wind up just another nameless **corpse**, floating face down in the Mississippi."

For some reason, Bridget wasn't all that afraid of this guy. He was trying too hard to be **macho**. All that toughness and manliness seemed fake, like an act designed to cover something up. The gun seemed real enough, though, so she decided to keep her mouth shut.

"Ooooh, Verna, these kids are making me really angry! I'd have no **qualms** about shooting them. I figure they got it coming," growled the gangster, waving his gun around.

"Don't kill them yet, Snake," cooed Verna in a high, little-girl voice. "We might be able to use them in our plan, don't you think?"

"Say, baby, that's not a bad idea," said Snake, brightening up. "Not bad at all. You kids better be glad Verna's got such a level head. Cannibal! Grab these two and take them back to the hideout!"

The possibly people-eating monster gathered up Bridget and Babette with his free arms, and started back through the swamp, followed by Snake and then by Verna, who was slowed down because her six-inch high heels kept sinking into the mud.

The hideout turned out to be a one-room shack furnished with a couple of cots and a few chairs. Snake wasted little time pulling four chairs together and tying Babette, Bridget, Barnaby, and Beauregard up with their backs to each other. And, as soon as his captive audience stopped whining, he began to tell them all the details of his evil plan. Gangsters and villains always tell the good guys all the details of their evil plans. It's practically **inevitable.** Unfortunately for the captives, Snake found it necessary to **recount** his entire criminal life story before getting around to the plan at hand.

"I'll tell you kids, I've led a life of crime that would put Al Capone's to shame," he began. "Sometimes I'm even shocked by my own **depravity,** my complete and utter wickedness. It started when I **disregarded** my first traffic signal. The light was red, and I ignored it. I just drove right on through. 'Yeah, baby, yeah,' I said to myself, 'this is living. This is freedom!'"

Barnaby, Bridget, Babette, and Beauregard rolled their eyes, but Snake paid them no mind.

"After I got a taste for crime, I just couldn't stop," he continued. "Next I tried **polygamy.** Of course, you're only allowed to be married to one person at a time. I made it my goal to have a wife in every state! I wanted to be the biggest polygamist this country had ever known! I know what you're thinking. 'Fifty women? Is there no limit to this man's **debauchery**? Has he no shame?' I'll tell you—I lost my sense of shame the day I ran that first red light."

"Did you? I mean, did you manage to trick fifty women into marrying you?" asked Barnaby.

"Well, not exactly. Dames aren't that easy to **dupe.** I'd try to **lure** them in with fancy dinners and jewelry, but most of them got wise to me before I managed to get them to the altar. Many of the women I meet show great **discernment.** If I try to pull a fast one on them, they see right through it every time."

Over in the corner, Verna was smiling to herself.

"But, anyway, the coppers never wised up, and that's the most important thing. Then I tried my hand at **blackmail.** I got some old pictures of Heather Locklear, the actress, dressed in some very embarrassing outfits from the mid-1970s. You should have seen the collars on some of those shirts! And the bell-bottoms! I won't even tell you about her hair. Oh, sure, she begged me not to show them to anyone. 'I was just a kid!' she said. 'I didn't know what I was doing!' But her begging didn't do any good. Sure, I told her, I'd keep the photos to myself—for a price, baby, for a price!"

"Don't tell me she actually paid you off?" said Babette.

"I'm sure she would have, Miss Smarty-Pants, but unfortunately, just as I was about to start barraging her with threatening letters and mysterious phone calls, the whole '70s look came back into fashion. Well, as they say, life is a balance sheet—and sometimes debits outweigh credits."

"Hold it one second, uh, Mr. Snake," snapped Bridget. "Life is a balance sheet? What kind of metaphor is that for a gangster to be using?"

Snake was visibly flustered. Bridget was obviously hitting a sore spot.

"I mean, maybe 'life is a big bank heist' or even 'all the world's a cage', but 'balance sheet'?" she continued, gathering confidence. "That's not gangster talk, that's a comparison only an accountant would make! You're a **fraud**! A phony! I knew there was something weird about you. This whole evil plot thing is a **hoax,** isn't it?"

"Okay, kid, you got me," said Snake. "Yeah, I was an accountant. For twenty long years I sat at the same desk at Ingalls & Marks, **languishing** in a sea of numbers, slowly having the life force sucked out of me. And, since you're so smart, you probably figured out that 'Snake' is just a **pseudonym.** My real name is Caspar, but Verna here **dubbed** me Snake because she said Caspar's a name for friendly folks, and I have **malice** in my heart. That's right, baby, mean and evil intentions.

"Why, you ask? I'll tell you why—because I've spent my life juggling other people's money, making sure they wouldn't go to jail for tax violations, sometimes even touching up the books, if you know what I mean, while I earned a **pittance** of a salary. Rich businesspeople **exploited** my mathematical abilities, and you know what I got in return, after twenty years? A gold-plated pen. Sure, it was the erasable-ink kind, but still, it wasn't nearly enough!"

"Take it easy, honey," cooed Verna, "you're getting sweat stains on your suit!"

"I can't help it," huffed Caspar the Snake. "You kids just will never understand. You can't imagine the **monotony** I had to put up with—doing the same things, saying the same things, eating the same things day in and day out. But I have a news flash for you—you're wrong about the evil plot. I may have failed as a gangster so far, but I'll get my recognition yet. My name will be remembered throughout the entire world!"

"Oh, yeah, you're a regular **menace** to society, aren't you? What a threat you pose," laughed Bridget. "What do you plan to do, loot another candy store?"

Babette and Barnaby chuckled. Surprisingly, even the four-armed monster sniggered to himself in the corner.

"Shut up, Cannibal," said Snake. "What if I told you that I plan to blow up the one thing that keeps the city of New Orleans from being flooded over by the Mississippi River? What if I told you I'm going to destroy the **levee**?"

Babette gasped. "But the city of New Orleans is below sea level! If you blow up the levee, nothing will hold back the waters! The entire city will be destroyed!"

"What reason do you have for doing that? What's your **motive**? The innocent people of New Orleans have done nothing to you," reasoned Barnaby.

"In the first place, don't kid yourself about the people of New Orleans," said Snake. "In the second place, I already told you I want to go down in history as the world's most evil gangster. And you kids are going to help me."

"No way, man, I won't be your **accomplice**! I won't help you commit such a crime!" yelled Bridget, struggling against the ropes that bound her.

"Oh, yes, you will. I'm afraid you don't have a choice," laughed Snake. "See, to blow up the levee, I need to use a whole boatload of dynamite. And a boatload of dynamite is the kind of thing that might **arouse** the suspicion of a watchful river cop. I can't afford to have any coppers nosing around and spoiling things for me now, can I? That's where you come in. I'm going to put you in an even bigger boat full of even more explosives. You'll be a **decoy**, see? The river cops will be so busy questioning you, they won't even notice my **modest** little boat quietly sailing along the edge of the levee. And by the time they figure it out, it'll be too late!"

Snake began to laugh a crazy villain laugh, then he turned abruptly and walked out of the cabin. Verna, who had been standing quietly in a corner, was fidgeting nervously.

"Verna, you can't really be in favor of this. You don't seem like the kind of woman who would **advocate** the senseless destruction of an entire town!" pleaded Bridget.

"That shows what you know!" squeaked Verna in her high voice. "Until I met Caspar, I mean Snake, I was just another substitute teacher. I wanted to make it in show business, but all the movie producers told me I didn't stand a chance because of my voice. Snake gave me the confidence to pursue my dreams. He says as soon as we're rich, he'll buy a studio and make me a big star!"

"Yeah, that'll happen," muttered Bridget.

"Ooooh, you kids think you're so smart!" twittered Verna, stomping her high-heeled foot. "I'm going to help Snake with the boats. Cannibal, keep an eye on them."

And, with that, she turned and stormed out. Finally more or less alone, Bridget, Babette, and Barnaby tried to figure out some way to stop the would-be gangsters.

"Well," said Babette, "the first thing I need to do is get out of these ropes. My legs have fallen asleep."

"Good luck," said Bridget, looking over her shoulder at her own bound wrists. "I've been twisting my hands around, trying to work on these knots. They're tied pretty tight. And the rope is so rough, I think I've given myself a couple of **lacerations.** Maybe if we . . . hey!"

Babette was standing, free of her ropes, in front of her. She was shaking out her legs.

"Mmm, that's better," she said.

"Babette, how did you get out so fast?" asked Barnaby.

"A little trick I picked up in China. Also, I am double-jointed in every joint," she replied.

Cannibal grunted suddenly and began lurching toward Babette.

"Watch out! " cried Bridget. "The monster's behind you!"

"Do not worry. I have a theory about this monster."

"I sure hope it's right, whatever it is," said Bridget, closing her eyes to keep from seeing Babette get eaten.

"You are not a monster at all, are you?" Babette asked, turning to face Cannibal.

The giant four-armed man hesitated for a second or two, then shook his head and let out a sigh.

"Indeed, no, young lady. At least, not on the inside," he said in a high-class British accent.

If they hadn't already been sitting, Bridget and Barnaby would have fallen over from shock.

"It can talk!" observed Barnaby.

"Naturally, dear boy" he replied, as politely as possible. It's hard to be **civil,** after all, when people are referring to you as "it." But Cannibal was obviously a person of good breeding. Looking to Babette, he asked, "If I may inquire, how could you tell I am not the dumb beast Snake and Verna think I am?"

"Actually, it was your breath. While you were carrying me, I caught a whiff of it. It smells like Earl Grey tea. Not a drink I would think people-eating monsters favor too much," said Babette, smiling.

The giant laughed. "No, I suppose not. Allow me to **commend** you on your sharp powers of observation. You are very **perceptive** indeed! I had just finished my tea when you children arrived. I'm afraid we weren't introduced properly. My name is Rupert."

He extended his lower right hand and Babette shook it.

"I am Babette, and these are my friends, Bridget, Barnaby, and Beauregard, our cat companion."

"Let me ask you something, Rupert," snapped Bridget. "Do you really think you're going to get away with destroying New Orleans? A guy like you is pretty hard to miss. The police will **apprehend** you and the rest of your gang before you can say 'crumpet'!"

"Please, you mistake me, Bridget," protested Rupert, gesturing with all four arms. "This is the first I heard of this terrible plot. I had no idea what they were up to."

Bridget looked doubtful.

"Really, you must believe me. It was a mistake," he said sadly. "I am a lonely man—misunderstood, shunned, and **ostracized** even in my hometown. I wandered around the world trying to make friends, but people ran from me in horror. I became a complete **introvert,** shy and unwilling to talk to other people. I have been living the **solitary** life of a **recluse,** all by myself in this hut in the swamp, starved for contact with other human beings. When Snake and Verna arrived, I was overjoyed. I was willing to put on the act they seemed to expect of me, **pantomiming** and grunting like Frankenstein's monster, as long as they would stay and keep me company. I see now that it must end. But what can we do? I am strong, but Snake has a gun."

"Well, I have an idea," said Babette. "First of all, Rupert must sneak out the back. When Snake comes . . ."

Just then, Snake opened the door. He had

changed out of his gangster clothes, and into a fishing outfit, yellow slicker and all. He still had his gun, though, and it was pointed straight at Babette.

"Yeah, sweetheart?" he asked. "I'm all ears. Tell me what you're going to do."

Babette stood frozen to the ground, speechless.

"I thought so," he sneered. "Cannibal, you've been very bad. Tie the girl back up."

Fortunately, he hadn't come into the room in time to hear Rupert speaking. Babette gave her new friend a little nod that told him it was okay to tie her up again. Her plan had been spoiled, and there was no sense in letting Snake find out that Rupert had turned against him.

Once she was secured in her chair, Snake picked up his speech where he had left off.

"It's show time, kids," he announced with a laugh. "The boats are loaded and we're off to dampen New Orleans. I **estimate** our sailing time will be about three hours, so we'd better get a move on if we're going to make it before dark. I'm going to stuff dynamite in every crack, **crevice,** and cranny along that little old levee."

Through the door of the hut came Verna, also dressed in fishing gear.

"What do you think, Snake?" she asked, modeling her new outfit.

"Very convincing," he replied. "Now remember our **aliases**—we are Myra and Blake Turner, two ordinary people out to catch a mess of catfish."

"I thought your alias was Snake," said Bridget.

"That just shows what you know about gangsters," said Snake. "Snake is my pseudonym, but for special crimes, you have to use special aliases, see? Now, Cannibal, pick up these kids and put them in the big boat outside."

Rupert obeyed, lifting all four captives and their chairs off the ground. It was a little difficult to get them through the door all tied together like that, but he managed without bumping them too much. In a matter of minutes, they were sitting on a boat, surrounded by piles of dynamite.

"We're going to tow you kids until we're almost there," explained Snake, "then we'll cut you loose and send you down the river ahead of us. And that's the last you'll hear from us until . . . KA-BOOM!"

Snake laughed, Verna tee-heed, and Rupert frowned. The three of them got into the smaller boat, started the motor, and slowly pulled out into the water.

Several hours later, after they had been cut loose and sent on down the river, Babette finally thought it was safe to untie herself and her friends.

"I only hope Rupert can stop them in time without getting himself shot," she **fretted,** pacing up and down the boat. "We must try to attract the attention of the police and tell them what is happening."

"But how will we convince them that we aren't the ones up to no good?" asked Barnaby. "Why should they believe us, when we are completely surrounded by dynamite?"

"We must make them understand how **grave** the danger is," replied Babette, who was flapping her arms wildly in an effort to attract the attention of a passing patrol boat.

She succeeded in hailing it, but unfortunately, Barnaby was right. No matter how hard they tried to convince the police that the city was in **jeopardy,** the police refused to believe them.

"Please," begged Bridget, "we're wasting time. You have to stop Snake now or you'll have a **catastrophe** on your hands!"

The two river cops who had come aboard looked at each other and smiled.

"Now you must think we're awfully **gullible**," said one officer. "We weren't born yesterday. Here you are with a boatload of dynamite, and you expect us to think someone else in another boat is trying to blow up the levee. That's a real laugh."

Both cops chuckled, which enraged Bridget.

"How can you be so **callous** and insensitive? I'm trying to tell you the entire city is about to be flooded, and you seem completely **indifferent**! Well, if you two won't do something about this, I will!" she cried, running toward the edge of the boat.

Just as she swung her leg over the side and jumped, a huge explosion crashed through the air. When she came to the surface, clumps of grass and dirt were falling from the sky and the air was filled with smoke.

"Babette! Barnaby! Beauregard!" she called, treading water. "Answer me! Are you okay? Answer me!"

She heard coughing and sputtering not far from her. As the smoke cleared a little, she could see Beauregard swimming toward her. He didn't look at all happy. Two dunks in the Mississippi is two dunks too many for most cats.

"Beauregard!" she cried. "Where are the others?"

But her question was answered when a gust of wind cleared the air. At first she was relieved at what she saw: the levee was still there. The city was saved. But lying on the ground, completely motionless, were her friends.

"Oh, no!" she gasped. "Beauregard, quick, we have to get to them!"

They paddled as fast as they could against the current toward the embankment. Bridget gasped as she looked down at the **pallor** of her friends' faces. She was afraid they were dead. She prodded Babette, then Barnaby, with her foot.

"No, Mom, no!" yelled Barnaby, jumping to his feet. "You can't make me take ballet lessons! Get those tights away from me!"

"Barnaby, get ahold of yourself," cried Bridget, shaking her friend by the shoulders. "You must be **delirious** or something. No one is forcing you to wear tights."

"Ow," said Barnaby, rubbing his head.

Babette opened her eyes and sat up carefully. "Barnaby, are you okay?"

"Tights. Tight-fisted fish in a peddle of pickles," he said politely. "I said don't to be glimming my tulip, pilgrim. No, and no again! Time to pay the spleen!" Barnaby shook his fist in the air, then began staggering around as if he were **intoxicated.**

"Well, obviously he's **incoherent**," said Bridget. "He doesn't look seriously hurt, though. You were both knocked **unconscious** by the explosion."

"Explosion!" repeated Babette, pushing herself to her feet. "Quick! We must find Snake and Verna before they escape!"

They didn't have to go far. Not twenty yards away, Snake and Verna were having a knock-down-drag-out fight. Rupert was standing off to one side, watching with great amusement.

"You worm!" screeched Verna, scratching at Snake's eyes. "You're nothing but a big failure! You barely made a dent in this levee. Some explosives artist you are!"

"I told you, you twit, I was only an **apprentice** explosives artist," he growled, pulling her hair. "I still had a year's worth of study with the Master Blaster before I would have been certified. I told you it would be best if I **honed** my skills by trying some minor explosions first, but you wouldn't wait! Oh, no, you just kept on needling me, and bothering me and **harrassing** me until I gave in!"

"How was I to know you'd be so **inept** you couldn't even blow up one little levee?" she squeaked, kicking his shins. "The only thing you have any skill for is adding up numbers!"

"That was a really low blow," yelled Snake.

"Take that back right now!"

"No, no, no!" she squealed, beating her fists into his chest and sobbing. "We're ruined! We're doomed! And it's all your fault!"

Rupert must have finally had enough of this little **spat,** because he decided to **intervene.** He reached one arm over and pulled the upset woman away.

"Now, now, dear, you're getting **hysterical,**" he said, holding her firmly about three feet off the ground. She didn't even notice that the man she called Cannibal was speaking to her, so angry and caught up was she in her **vain** attempts to free herself from his grasp. But Rupert was far stronger, and he had no intention of letting her go.

"Oh, officers!" he called to the two river patrolmen who had just wandered through the smoke. "I believe we have here a pair of criminals for you to arrest."

Sensing that he was about to be taken into custody, Snake began backing away, trying to lose himself in the smoke. But Babette had her eye on him the entire time.

"Not so fast, Caspar," she said, karate-kicking him across the knees. Then, standing over him with one foot at his throat, she began to feel quite pleased with herself. "Hmmm, let's see, what is that gangster phrase I'm looking for. Oh, yes—it's curtains for you,

Caspar baby."

"Don't **gloat** yet, Frenchie," grunted the fallen accountant. "You may think you've won, but there's still going to be a trial, and I have lots of lawyer friends."

"Yeah?" said one of the cops, who had come to handcuff Snake. "Too bad about that. I'm sure plenty of right-minded citizens would like to **lynch** you right now. Unfortunately, it's our job to make sure an angry mob doesn't string you up before you're tried before a fair and **impartial** jury. But you'll face the **gallows** sooner or later, I'm sure of that."

"Yeah, well don't count your money until the check clears," said Caspar as they led him away with Verna.

"Hey, you don't plan on leaving town any time soon, do you?" one of the cops asked Rupert. "It sure would speed things along if you testified against these two."

"I would be happy to **expedite** the proceedings in any way possible," replied the giant.

"Good, then you'd better come down to the station with us. And you kids had better not go anywhere, either," he said as they walked off. "We'll need your testimonies, too."

"Oh, sure," said Babette and Bridget, nodding as convincingly as possible. But as soon as the police were out of sight, all that changed.

"Man, let's get out of here!" said Bridget.

Babette agreed wholeheartedly. After they found Barnaby, who was still wandering around in a daze, and gathered up Beauregard, who was into some serious grooming, they discussed their options—or, more accurately, option.

"The way I see it," said Bridget, "the only way we're going to cover any serious ground and make up for lost time is by traveling by air again. Of course, that's what got us into this mess in the first place. Still, I don't see any way around it. Are you game?"

"Naturally," said Babette. "The situation can't get any worse."

"I almost wish you hadn't said that," replied Bridget with a little laugh.

A few minutes later, they were on their way up again, floating beneath an enormous pink bubble.

✍ QUIZ #16 ✍
Relationships

Decide what relationship the following pairs of words have to each other. If they have similar meanings, write "S" next to the pair of words. If they have opposite meanings, write "O" next to the words.

1. fraud :: hoax
2. pseudonym :: alias
3. subtle :: obtrusive
4. callous :: indifferent
5. malice :: depravity
6. opaque :: clear
7. introvert :: recluse
8. grimace :: smile
9. debauchery :: sinfulness
10. monotony :: variety
11. stagnant :: moving
12. unconscious :: awake

✍ QUIZ #17 ✍
Relationships

Decide what relationship the following pairs of words have to each other. If they have similar meanings, write "S" next to the pair of words. If they have opposite meanings, write "O" next to the words.

1. jeopardy :: safety
2. apprentice :: expert
3. cannibal :: vegetarian
4. obscure :: reveal
5. delirious :: clearheaded
6. menace :: threat
7. incessant :: endless
8. dusk :: dawn
9. lure :: attract
10. hysterical :: calm
11. exhausted :: refreshed
12. ostracized :: rejected

Fill in the Blank

For each sentence below, choose the word that best completes the sentence.

1. Bugsy Blaine, the bank robber, was caught by the police, but his _____, who was waiting in the getaway car, escaped.

   a. decoy **b.** accomplice
   c. corpse **d.** mutation

2. "We are out of fish today," said the waitress at Cap'n Briny's, "so please _____ everything on the menu except the salad and dessert sections."

   a. recount **b.** interrogate
   c. disregard **d.** commend

3. We thought it was amazingly _____ of Barney to shake hands and sit at the same table with Richard, who was his worst enemy.

   a. modest **b.** impartial
   c. macho **d.** civil

4. I was filled with _____ when I found out that my softball team had to forfeit the game because I didn't show up.

   a. chagrin **b.** qualms
   c. blackmail **d.** lacerations

5. A major league umpire must use great
   _____ to tell the difference
   between strikes and balls in important
   baseball games.

   a. loot b. momentum

   c. discernment d. pittance

6. Carol realized she had been _____
   when she discovered the so-called "organic"
   cat litter she paid $20 for was nothing but
   ordinary sand.

   a. duped b. barraged

   c. dubbed d. lynched

7. The baby-sitter saw Mark and Melanie
   beating each other over the head with their
   dinner plates, but he decided not to
   _____, hoping that they could
   work out their differences themselves.

   a. gloat b. emerge c. arouse d. intervene

✍ QUIZ #19 ✍
Matching

Match each word on the right with a word on the left that has a similar meaning.

1. locale		a. inescapable
2. genetic		b. reason
3. inevitable		c. weaken
4. frigid		d. sharp
5. brisk		e. lonely
6. metaphor		f. quick
7. languish		g. approve
8. exploit		h. location
9. levee		i. dike
10. motive		j. capture
11. advocate		k. take advantage
12. perceptive		l. inherited
13. apprehend		m. cold
14. solitary		n. comparison
15. expedite		o. speed up

Matching

Match each word on the right with a word on the left that has a similar meaning.

1. pantomiming   a. guess
2. estimate   b. disaster
3. crevice   c. unskillful
4. grave   d. crack
5. catastrophe   e. confused
6. gullible   f. paleness
7. pallor   g. hanging tree
8. intoxicated   h. gesturing
9. incoherent   i. sharpened
10. honed   j. easily fooled
11. harrass   k. useless
12. inept   l. serious
13. vain   m. drunk
14. gallows   n. bother

Chapter 5

Monks are Weird, but Wizards are Weirder

You're probably wondering what happened to Snake and Verna. Well, it's an interesting story. Both of them were **indicted** on charges ranging from conspiracy to start a flood to attempted **manslaughter,** and both entered **pleas** of "not guilty." Lawyers for the prosecution got a little nervous that Snake might indeed have some kind of trick up his sleeve, so they granted Verna **immunity** from prosecution in exchange for her testimony—a fancy way of saying that they agreed not to send her to jail if she would agree to rat on Snake. And she ratted on him with great **gusto,** calling him all sorts of dirty names and accusing him of practically every unsolved crime in Louisiana—even dragging up some of his underhanded accounting jobs from way, way back. The jury didn't have to spend too much time **deliberating** before deciding on a **verdict** of "guilty on all counts," but no sooner had the judge pounded his **gavel** and said "court is adjourned," than Snake filed an appeal, accusing Verna of **perjury.** Unfortunately, false statements are **inadmissible** as evidence in a trial.

After all the paperwork was completed and the case was retried, the only thing Snake was convicted of was fishing without a license, for which he received the maximum sentence: a very stern **reprimand** from the judge. Imagine, after all that, Snake gets scolded and Verna gets off scot-free. Justice truly is blind.

But I should get back to the matter at hand. After we took off from New Orleans, everything went along smoothly for quite some time. We had great hopes of landing in close **proximity** to Paris— that is, until an albatross collided with Bridget's bubble and poked a big hole in it. After that, I can only assume we crashed because I don't remember anything except waking up in a very strange place . . . .

✎ ✎ ✎ ✎ ✎

Bridget slowly opened one eye, then the other, and looked around without moving her head. She couldn't see much, really, just a high, gray, domed ceiling faintly lit by a light source she couldn't see. She tried to sit up, but an **acute** pain shot through her head and she lay back down on her cot.

"You shouldn't try to move," said a calm,

deep, man's voice. "You've been very ill. You are beginning to recover."

"Who are you?" groaned Bridget. "Where am I? Where are my friends?"

"So many questions," said the voice. "You are safe. Your friends are in another room. They, too, are **convalescing** from the illness."

"You make it sound as if we've been here a while," said Bridget. "Just how long have I been lying here?"

"It is impossible to say. Time is a **labyrinth,** full of twists and turns—and sometimes dead ends. You may have been here forever. Perhaps you have not yet arrived. No one can be certain," replied the voice.

Bridget tried to roll her eyes, but it hurt too much. "Look, that's very interesting, but it's a little too **ambiguous** for me. Just tell me what time it was, or what day it was, when we got here, and what time or day it is now, okay?"

"Child, don't you see? Your **query** is meaningless. Time is a **myth.** It doesn't exist, at least not as you think of it. It is a fairy tale for people with weak minds."

"Hmmm," said Bridget. "You said before that it was a maze. Well, if time is a maze, I can find my way out, right?"

"Ah, and what is beyond the walls of time? That is the question," boomed the voice.

Bridget decided it was high time for some

action. She pushed herself up into a sitting position and sat very still for a few seconds. The room seemed to be spinning around and she felt dizzy. Finally, the whirling stopped and she looked around.

The room was very old, like one of those ancient churches her parents had dragged her to before she lost them. The difference was that this place was much more **austere.** There were no brightly colored glass windows, no flowers, no furniture except her cot, nothing to liven up the **solemn** gray room except the plain white candles which flickered here and there. A small fire burned in a large stone fireplace.

Sitting cross-legged in the firelight was a small man with a flowing gray beard. He seemed unbelievably old, but somehow also young and full of energy. Bridget stared at him in wonder.

"Does your head hurt much?" he asked. "I can give you something to **alleviate** the pain."

"No, I feel fine," said Bridget, getting off the cot and trying to stand up. "Look, I want to go talk to my friends. Where are they?"

"Child, you must sit!" ordered the old man, lifting his hand in a commanding gesture.

Bridget fell back down on the cot, almost as if the man had given her a shove. Something very mysterious was going on here.

"I do not mean to use force," he sighed, "but I cannot **condone** such silly behavior. You have been ill. Your dizzy spells are likely to **recur.** You must **heed** my advice, or you will surely hurt yourself. Have a drink of water. Rest a while. Then you may walk about—but *slowly.*"

"Yeah, sure," said Bridget.

The old man brought her a glass of cool water, and they sat in silence for a long time. It didn't seem as though he was going to say anything, so Bridget decided to strike up a conversation.

"So, this is where you live, huh?" she remarked. "No offense, but it's kind of **ascetic.** The furnishings are a bit **scanty**—no television, no books, no stereo, no chairs. You don't even have a rug. What is this, a prison or something?"

"This is a monastery. I am a monk," the man answered.

"A monk? That means you belong to some kind of religious **sect,** right?" she asked.

"In a way," he replied. "My brothers and I have devoted our lives to the eternal."

"You have brothers?"

"Brothers in the spiritual sense," he explained. "We follow no organized religion, however. Our practices are not what most people would consider **orthodox.** I'll admit, we are unusual. When we first came together, other religious men and women accused us of **heresy.** Of course, nowadays I'm told people use that word to describe any idea or opinion that seems strange, but back then heresy was a serious crime. We were forced to withdraw from society—but not before several of our brothers were taken prisoner by the **clergy** of another religion. Those clergymen, supposedly so **pious** and devoted, tortured our brothers to force them to **repent** their so-called sins. But of course it is impossible to regret something if you don't feel it is wrong. Many of them died horrible deaths."

Bridget squirmed uncomfortably. This conversation was getting gloomy and depressing.

"I am sorry," said the monk. "I have a tendency to get a bit **morbid** when I think about the past. You seem to be feeling better. For a while there you were hanging in that hazy **limbo** between consciousness and sleep. But now I think you are perfectly **lucid**—no more mixed-up talk about dancing jackals and spaceships, right?"

He smiled a kind and **benevolent** smile. He was so well-meaning she didn't have the heart to tell him that the dancing jackals and the spaceship were real. She decided to let him think he had cured her.

"Yeah, whew!" she said. "I'm glad I'm more clearheaded now. It's all thanks to you, um, what's your name?"

"You can call me Brother Gruffy. You are Bridget, I gather. Come, now. I hereby **deem** you healthy enough to walk around. Let us go check on your friends."

Without any visible movement of his legs, Gruffy was standing. Or, rather, he appeared to be floating just above the ground. Bridget couldn't be sure, because his long white robe covered his feet. He just sort of drifted along ahead of her toward a small door at the opposite end of the room.

On the other side of the door was another room that looked exactly the same as the first. Babette and Barnaby lay stretched out on two simple cots, and another old monk, with a long, flowing, gray beard was sitting in front of another fire. She was about to ask Gruffy about Beauregard, when she was toppled over by a hundred pounds of leaping cat.

Beauregard was obviously happy to see her. He was rubbing his head on her chin, his purrs were deafening, and he even gave her face a couple of rough licks.

"Remarkable," said the old monk by the fire. "That cat has been absolutely **listless.** He refused to eat or drink or even move, for that matter. I was beginning to think he was either very lazy or very bored. I guess he just missed you."

"I guess so," agreed Bridget, who had just struggled out from under the affectionate, hairy, hundred pounds. "I'm glad to see he's doing alright. But how are Babette and Barnaby?"

"Ask them yourself," said the monk. He waved his hand, and suddenly, their eyes fluttered open.

Babette leaped up from her cot and assumed a fighting pose, her hands up and ready for combat.

"Relax, Babette," urged Bridget. "You're not in any danger."

"That's a relief," she sighed, letting down

her guard. "Where are we? How did we get here?"

"We found you while we were out gathering herbs," answered one of the old monks. "You were very weak, and had **succumbed** to some sort of fever. The illness was especially **virulent** in you, much more intense and dangerous than what your companions experienced. We brought you here to make sure you recovered safely."

"That is very kind," Babette replied. "May I ask what sort of place this is? What is your name?"

"My name is Brother Owain. This is Brother Gruffy," he said, with a small wave toward the floating monk. "You are in our monastery."

Over on his cot, Barnaby began to moan.

"Oh, oh!" he groaned, "I'm dying. I'm paralyzed. Help! Get a doctor!"

"You are in no danger of dying, my son," said Owain. "You are perfectly healthy."

"You must be mistaken. I have a bandaged foot that is obviously paralyzed. I must see a specialist," insisted Barnaby.

"I'm afraid you had a large splinter caught in your heel. We gave you a mild **anesthetic** so we could remove the splinter without hurting you. The feeling will return to your foot in a few minutes," explained the monk.

"I don't need some mad monk telling me I'm

not dying! I feel my life just slipping away! It's probably your fault, too! You probably poisoned me with some of those herbs you were just talking about!" yelled Barnaby.

"Shut up, Barnaby," snapped Bridget. "Quit being such a **hypochondriac.** You are perfectly healthy. I think you should apologize to Brother Owain. He's shown a lot of **forbearance** by not giving you a punch in the nose for being so rude."

"Nonsense, child," said the monk. "Violence has no place here."

"Yes, well, sorry," said Barnaby, pushing himself into a sitting position and feeling a little embarrassed by his outburst. "We scientists have a history of being at odds with men of religion. I think it's a healthy competition, but I'm sorry if I **affronted** you. Thank you for helping us."

Owain nodded his head slightly, but said nothing.

"Where are we?" Barnaby whispered to his friends. "I've had the most amazing memory **lapse.** Last thing I remember, I was standing in a boat talking to some police officers."

"I can explain all that later," Bridget whispered back. "But I think we should figure out what our situation here is. All I can tell so far is that these monks are really old, kind of spooky, and that they give **vague** answers to the simplest questions. I asked what time it was, and all I got was some kind of mumbo-jumbo about time being a maze."

"I'm sorry if you think we're being unclear," said Owain, which shocked Bridget because she didn't think he could hear her. "We are not used to speaking with people who look at things the way you do. Please ask any questions you like, and we will make an **earnest** attempt to give you **explicit** answers."

Since Bridget and Barnaby were still too surprised at being overheard so easily, Babette decided to ask the first question.

"I hope I may be completely **candid** and honest with you, brothers," said Babette. "Frankly, there is something strange about you both. You seem so very old, yet you do not look it. You have odd, **supernatural** powers, almost like magic. And this place is unlike any monastery I've ever seen. Please tell us how you came here."

"Yeah, what's your story?" asked Bridget.

Both monks chuckled.

"Our story, you ask? Very well, then," said Owain, "I will tell you. Yes, looking at time the way you do, you could say we are very old. Over nine centuries old, in fact."

"Are you **immortal,** then?" asked Babette.

"Oh, no. We are humans just like you, and just like you, we will die eventually. We owe

our **longevity** to the many secrets of nature we
have learned through the years. We are not
susceptible to the same illnesses as most
people. There are special herbs that grow only
here on a little corner of this island. They give
us **immunity** to the diseases of the body, and
our beliefs help us develop other special
powers.

"It all started when Pope Urban II called on
the European noblemen to make a long
expedition to the Holy Land. A 'crusade,' he
called it. Our goal was to reclaim the **hallowed**
city of Jerusalem from the **heathens,** as we
used to call anyone who wasn't Jewish or
Christian.

"The problem we didn't realize at the time
was that Jerusalem was holy to the Muslims,
too, and naturally they didn't want to give it
up to a bunch of Europeans who just showed
up out of nowhere. But we knights were
practically burning up with religious **fervor.**
We were ready to do anything to **vanquish** the
heathens and take back our city (even though,
technically speaking, it never had been our
city)."

"You were knights in the First Crusade,"
Babette observed. "I have always wondered,
how did the pope convince you to go to a
faraway land to fight people who had simply
been minding their own business?"

"It is difficult to understand," Gruffy offered. "But you should know, Owain and I, and many of our brothers, were not always peaceful men. Before the Crusade, we had **lavish** lifestyles devoted to feasting, chasing women, and fighting each other. We gave in to every **base** human desire. Urban II was an **eloquent** and persuasive pope. Not only did he appeal to our love of battle by promising us a war, complete with blood and **gore,** but he said that by fighting for the Holy Land we would be washed clean of all our sins in the process."

"It seemed like a great idea at the time," agreed Owain. "But once we got there, we realized that what was happening was no ordinary war. It was **genocide.** The other crusaders seemed bent on the **eradication** of the entire Muslim population. We liked a fight as much as the next knight, but the slaughter we saw in Jerusalem and Antioch and Ashkalon left even us **aghast.**"

Owain fell silent, as if remembering those long-ago battles.

Gruffy picked up where he left off. "To make matters worse, the people we were fighting were hardly the barbarians we had been told. They had an extremely rich culture, well-developed sciences, medicine, poetry, art, music, and architecture. How **conceited** we

Europeans were, to think our way of life was so superior! Compared to them, *we* were the barbarians.

"Even though the the war was going well, many of us decided to **desert** the army and **renounce** violence for good. We didn't even know each other at the time, but somehow, separately, we all came to the same decision. We just threw down our arms and wandered off into the desert.

"I wandered alone for many days and nights without food or water. Finally, just when I thought I was about to die of thirst, I saw what looked like a palm tree and a pool of water in the distance. And around the pool stood dozens of men in shining white robes.

"I thought at first I was seeing things, that it was just a **mirage.** But as I got closer, I could see that it was an actual **oasis.** Trees and flowers grew there and the breeze rippled the blue waters of the pond and the robes of these strange men. So shocked was I by their appearance that I almost forgot my thirst. I was covered in dirt and blood and sweat, yet these men seemed to glow from within, and their white clothing was spotless and **immaculate.** They seemed not to notice me as I fell to my knees at the edge of the pool and began scooping water to my mouth with my hands. Then I felt a pair of hands shoving me from behind, and I fell soundlessly into the deep blue water."

"It was I who pushed him," said Owain.

"But why?" asked Barnaby. "Were you trying to drown him?"

"No, of course not, don't you see?" replied the monk. "We had all been bathed in those waters. We came there as ugly men, some of us Muslims and some Crusaders, with sick bodies and even sicker hearts. Those waters changed us inside and out. I wanted him to undergo the same **metamorphosis** so he could feel the same overwhelming joy, the same **ecstasy** as we had."

Owain paused again, but by this time, Babette, Barnaby, and Bridget were so **engrossed** in the story they weren't about to let him stop.

"What happened to you all?" they demanded together.

"It is impossible to explain," answered Gruffy.

The children grumbled with disappointment.

"I can tell you bits and pieces. First, I saw a beautiful, mysterious woman who told me things without speaking. I felt burning beams of light that did not hurt me. I held the whole weight of the world in my arms, but I was as light as a snowflake," he said.

"But that's impossible!" said Barnaby. "You can't be heavy and light at the same time. And you can't be burned without pain."

"There are mysteries in the world, my boy, that cannot be broken down and explained by science. Whatever that pool contained is an **enigma** that cannot be logically accounted for, but something that must be experienced and grasped whole.

"Yet in a way, exactly what or who we saw in the water is **irrelevant**. What matters is *how* we were transformed. I was **overwhelmed,** completely overcome, by feelings of happiness and peace. I have no idea how long I remained beneath the surface, but I was returned to the world on a blast of steam and water that shot me many yards into the air, then suddenly disappeared as quickly as it started. A **geyser,** I believe it is called.

"My brothers welcomed me back, and I noticed that I was now one of them—the same glowing skin, the same white robe. So many things had changed within me. I realized that wealth and beauty and fame and many other human achievements are nothing but passing joys, as **ephemeral** as the morning dew that is gone before the day has even begun. We decided to give up the pursuit of glory and devote our lives to helping the needy, healing the sick, and other such acts of **philanthropy.**

But, as I told you before, Bridget, people wouldn't accept us. Other monks told terrible lies about our actions and our characters, the most vicious **slander** you can imagine."

"We were forced to withdraw to the island of Cyprus, where you find yourselves now," continued Owain. "After the Crusade, Cyprus became a **mecca** for misfits. The war changed people, and many did not wish to return to their old lives. Here we were not bothered by the outside world. But now we know it is time to share our knowledge with others, for the Great and Powerful Oz has spoken to us."

Bridget gasped with surprise at the monk's last words.

"Hold it, brother," she said. "What do you mean, 'the Great and Powerful Oz'? Hey, Barnaby, Babette, check this out. I think we're actually stuck in a EuroDisney exhibit. We're closer to Paris than we think!"

"Child, you are making less sense than usual," said Gruffy. "I hope your illness is not returning. But do I understand from what you are saying that you are trying to reach Paris?"

"That's right," said Bridget.

"Well, then, perhaps we should take you to the wizard himself. After all, he descended from the sky. He must have the power to get you home."

"Sure, I've always wanted to meet the

Wizard of Oz," she said.

"Come, then," said the monk. "We're off to see the wizard."

"Oh, boy," Bridget muttered under her breath. "Sometimes life is just like a movie."

The two floating monks led the travelers down a long corridor to a huge metal door. Owain knocked three times, turned and said good-bye, then both monks vanished into thin air.

"Remarkable," said Barnaby.

Slowly the metal door swung open. Beyond it was a large room with a domed ceiling. The air was filled with smoke, an amazing laser light show was going on, and strange pictures were being projected on the walls, probably by a hidden movie projector.

"Cool," said Bridget. "I haven't seen anything like this since the last Pink Floyd tour."

A voice boomed from some speakers in the ceiling. "I am the Great and Powerful Oz!"

"Can it, bub," replied Bridget. "I'm not some thousand-year-old monk. Come out from whatever curtain you're hiding behind."

"Huh?" boomed the voice through the speakers.

"Sir, whoever you are," said Barnaby, "we know the Wizard of Oz is a fictional character. You appear to have these monks fooled. We don't especially care about that, but there is an off chance you can help us get back to Paris."

Suddenly, a man in a magician's suit, complete with black cape, appeared through a hidden door. He wasn't very tall. He had black hair and a pencil-thin black mustache. And he was definitely walking on the ground.

"Are you from the publisher's office?" he asked as he walked forward. "At last, my work will be recognized! I knew you'd like the idea. I think the title should be 'How to Live Forever Without Really Trying,' part adventure story, part cookbook. It's such a **novel** idea, don't you agree? It's the newest idea in **prose** since *In Cold Blood*! Why . . . oh, no. You're only children."

The man sighed, greatly disappointed.

"What are you talking about?" asked Bridget. "Who are you, anyway?"

"Well, you might as well know," he said. "It seems my book will never be published anyway. I am the Amazing Mumpo. At least, that was my stage name back when I was a famous magician. I had five shows a week in Las Vegas—and the occasional television special. You're probably too young to remember."

Barnaby, Bridget, and Babette had to admit he was right.

"My real name is Milton. Milton Fenlich," he continued, offering his hand for shaking. Introductions were made all around.

"I hope I didn't seem too rude just now," said Milton. "It's just that I've been working on this book for years. I've been **tantalized** by visions of my great work, published in hardcover, attractively displayed in shop windows, and eager customers lining up to buy it. But it's a goal that seems forever out of reach.

"You have no idea how difficult writing a book is. You have to set yourself a schedule and have the **discipline** to stick to it. And you must be **diligent** enough to keep at it. Oh, I worked so hard! But my manuscript has been rejected by every publisher I've sent it to! I'm worthless and so is my book!"

"Come on, there is no need to **wallow** around in a puddle of self-pity. Maybe you can fix the book up so they will like it more. Did they say why they rejected it?" asked Babette, feeling sorry for the magician.

"They said my writing was bad. Oh, sure, my sentences may not have the **euphony** of a Shakespearean sonnet, but at least I was getting a point across. Can't they see what a great idea it is? Even if my writing is bad, surely they could hire a **ghostwriter** to do the writing and still credit me as the author. It is my idea, after all."

Milton sighed heavily again. "It's those monks I feel really bad about. You see, I was doing some shows in Greece years ago, and I rented a little airplane to get from island to island. I had just gotten my pilot's license a couple of weeks earlier. Anyway, I ran into some rough weather one night and wound up making an emergency landing here. The monks saw me coming down out of the sky and, well, they thought I was some kind of powerful wizard. Luckily I had all my gear with me, so I went ahead and did my act. It really wowed them. Especially the laser show. After that, they kind of **nominated** me 'head holy man.' I figured it was better to be a head holy man than a cheesy Vegas magician, so I decided to stay." He chuckled to himself.

"And you know what? These monks actually pay **homage** to me. They bow before me, show me respect, and do anything I say. For example, there's no photocopy machine here, so I had them spend hours **transcribing** copy after copy of my manuscript by hand. Monks have great handwriting, you know. Except for that Owain guy. His writing is practically **illegible.** Anyway, I keep telling them that they'll be doing the world a service, and they seem to like that idea very much, but I still can't help feeling a little guilty."

"Hey," said Bridget, who didn't like the idea of the magician taking such advantage of the monks. "This book you wrote—I don't suppose it **discloses** all the secrets these monks have spent centuries learning about?"

"What if it does?" replied Milton defensively. "They say they want to help people. And when the world finds out these guys have kept themselves alive for nine hundred years with their little potions and teas, people will be beating down the door to get to them."

"But don't you see?" said Babette. "The herbs that they use only grow on a small part of this island. People will come here by the thousands, picking their plants and roaming through their halls. These monks are from a time when faith and honor meant something. You will completely destroy their way of life!"

"I don't think they'll squawk too much about it when they start getting some money from the book sales," he replied. "Ten percent of the profits will be **earmarked** for donation to the monastery. That should keep them happy."

"How can you be such a **cynic**?" cried Babette. "Not everyone is selfish and greedy like you!"

"Oh yeah? Well, you're just a kid. Wait until you get a little older. You'll find out I'm right," he said.

Babette looked as if she was about to give the magician a swift kick, but Bridget put her hand on her friend's arm to calm her down.

"Listen, Milton, it looks like we disagree on this subject," she said. "We don't want these monks hurt. They've helped us. But our main problem is that we need to get back to Paris as soon as possible. I don't suppose you could help us with that, could you?"

"I'd love to get rid of you kids, but I'm afraid I dismantled the plane long ago and used the parts to **augment** my film and laser display. It needed beefing up, you know? The Great and Powerful Oz deserves a great and powerful show. No, I'm afraid the only way off this island is by boat, and I don't have one of those either. Anyway, you'd need a compass to keep you pointed in the right direction."

Barnaby began scratching his head. Bridget and Babette looked at each other hopefully. And sure enough, something came tumbling out of his hair. Babette stooped to pick it up.

"Is it a compass?" asked Bridget.

"No, it is a book," she sighed. Barnaby seemed disappointed. "Do not worry, Barnaby. We cannot rely on your hair for everything. At least we have something to read."

Looking down at the cover, however, Babette's face brightened. She gave Bridget a wink, then turned toward Milton.

"Well, we must be on our way," she said. "I hope your writing improves."

"Get lost," muttered the would-be author.

Beauregard, Babette, Bridget, and Barnaby were happy to **oblige**. Once they were back out in the hall, Babette began looking around for the monks.

"Where do you think they are?" she asked. "Owain? Gruffy? Brothers?"

Suddenly, the two monks appeared, floating ahead of her.

"Yes, child?" said Owain. "I hope the wizard has helped you."

"Well, actually, we prefer to solve our own problems. Why don't you three go down to the shore and find us a good place to set sail from," she said to her friends. "I want to say good-bye to the monks."

After thanking the brothers for their help, Bridget, Barnaby, and Beauregard left the dark monastery and walked out into the bright sunlight and down to the shore. Most of the beach was rocky, but they soon found a patch of soft sand where they sat and waited for Babette.

A few minutes later, she came strolling down the beach.

"Are you all ready?" she asked. "Bridget, we'll need another bubble, I suppose. France is west of here, that is all I know."

"Wait a minute, Babette, what did you tell those monks?" asked Barnaby.

"I told them that sometimes the best way to help people is to let them make their own mistakes," she said. "And I told them Milton is no wizard."

"Did they believe you?"

"No. But then I gave them the book—*The Grand Illusion: The History of Motion Pictures from 1918 to the Present*. It should explain Milton's little light show. I do not think he will be head holy man for long."

Everyone was relieved. As Bridget prepared to blow her boat, Babette offered one last detail.

"You know, the cover of the book had such a lovely picture on it. An adorable little dog and a girl with shiny red shoes," she said with a grin.

Bridget and Barnaby laughed heartily.

✍ QUIZ #21 ✍
Relationships

Decide what relationship the following pairs of words have to each other. If they have similar meanings, write "S" next to the pair of words. If they have opposite meanings, write "O" next to the words.

1. ambiguous :: explicit
2. indicted :: accused
3. austere :: solemn
4. lavish :: scanty
5. orthodoxy :: heresy
6. aghast :: shocked
7. eradicate :: vanquish
8. ephemeral :: permanent
9. augment :: increase
10. base :: pious
11. ascetic :: luxurious
12. philanthropy :: genocide
13. prose :: poetry

Relationships

Decide what relationship the following pairs of words have to each other. If they have similar meanings, write "S" next to the pair of words. If they have opposite meanings, write "O" next to the words.

1. condone :: approve
2. susceptible :: immune
3. slander :: praise
4. alleviate :: ease
5. enigma :: mystery
6. benevolent :: virulent
7. hallowed :: holy
8. verdict :: decision
9. gusto :: listlessness
10. affronted :: offended
11. vague :: lucid
12. disclose :: hide

✍ QUIZ #23 ✍
Fill in the Blank

For each sentence below, choose the word that best completes the sentence.

1. Sheila refused to _____ for smashing all of her brother's model airplanes with the heel of her shoe—she said she'd do it again in a heartbeat.

   a. recur **b.** succumb **c.** repent **d.** renounce

2. I used to think the Amazing Melvin had _____ powers, but now I see he just used tricks and mirrors to fool us into thinking he really could do magic.

   a. supernatural **b.** immortal

   c. inadmissible **d.** immaculate

3. John congratulated his sister on her _____, because it was her moving and persuasive speech that finally made their father give them permission to go to the concert by themselves.

   a. perjury **b.** forbearance

   c. longevity **d.** eloquence

4. My embarrassment was _____ when I discovered my skirt had been tucked into the back of my pantyhose since I came out of the bathroom an hour ago.

   a. acute **b.** conceited

   c. earnest **d.** irrelevant

5. Miriam was _____ in Colonel Thompson's stories about big game hunting in Africa, so she didn't even notice that her date had left with another woman.

   a. overwhelmed **b.** disciplined
   c. engrossed **d.** nominated

6. Until I saw one with my own eyes, I always thought the existence of werewolves was just a silly _____.

   a. mirage **b.** myth **c.** geyser **d.** oasis

7. David Livingstone led an important _____ to try to find the source of the Nile River.

   a. sect **b.** clergy **c.** limbo **d.** expedition

8. The aliens finally returned Kevin to earth, but he had a huge _____ in his memory, so he couldn't tell us what he'd been doing for the past twelve years.

   a. lapse **b.** fervor **c.** ecstasy **d.** proximity

9. Mary was such a hardened _____ that she believed that most charities were just scams to cheat people out of their money.

   a. anesthetic **b.** hypochondriac
   c. ghostwriter **d.** cynic

10. After Phyllis caught the flu, the mumps, and the chicken pox one right after another, her parents sent her to her grandmother in Florida so she could _____.
  a. wallow b. deliberate
  c. tantalize d. convalesce

✍ QUIZ #24 ✍
Matching

Match each word on the right with a word on the left that has a similar meaning.

1.	query	a.	gloomy
2.	mecca	b.	question
3.	heed	c.	accidental killing
4.	plea	d.	center
5.	morbid	e.	request
6.	deem	f.	declare
7.	gore	g.	abandon
8.	manslaughter	h.	mallet
9.	gavel	i.	listen to
10.	desert	j.	blood

✍ QUIZ #25 ✍
Matching

Match each word on the right with a word on the left that has a similar meaning.

1. metamorphosis   a. maze
2. labyrinth   b. set aside
3. novel   c. dedicated
4. reprimand   d. transformation
5. diligent   e. respect
6. euphony   f. new
7. heathen   g. pleasant sound
8. homage   h. unreadable
9. transcribe   i. scold
10. illegible   j. nonbeliever
11. earmark   k. copy

Chapter 6
Heir We Go Again

Setting sail from Cyprus on
a bubble boat went
pretty smoothly. It wasn't
the fastest way to travel, but
Bridget's bubble balloon had
proven hazardous to our health
recently, and we decided
we'd better play it safe. The
problem was, we only had
a general idea of which
direction to take. Barnaby
once again showed how
diverse his scientific talents
were by using his knowledge
of astronomy for the purpose
of **nocturnal navigation**—that is,
steering at night. He knew the
names and positions of quite a few of the stars, and
when you know where the stars are, you know
where you are. More or less, anyway. Bridget, for
all her street smarts, and Barnaby, for all his genius,

and Babette, for all her worldly wisdom, didn't know enough about plain old geography to figure exactly which way France was.

So, we wound up stopping to ask directions a lot, and it's a good thing Babette was there. She has an **innate** talent for picking up foreign languages. It truly is something you're born with, I think. I can only speak four or five, myself, no matter how hard I try, but Babette hears a few words, and the next thing you know she's chattering away with ease. Anyway, we stopped off at several of the Greek islands, but Babette kept getting conflicting advice, so once again we were left to our own devices. Nevertheless, we seemed to be making reasonable progress until, as we got out to look for food on a very small, deserted island, we were suddenly swept off our feet and left swinging upside down in a net that was hanging from a tree.

✎ ✎ ✎ ✎ ✎

"This is making me really dizzy," groaned Bridget, who was struggling mightily to get herself free of the net.

Barnaby was taking a more **passive** approach. "Look, Bridget," he said. "It doesn't do any good to struggle. You're just tangling us up more. Just keep still."

But Bridget wasn't the kind of girl who could calmly hang upside down on a strange island.

"Babette," she said. "Does this net feel very strong to you?"

"Actually, no," replied Babette. "The cords seem very **flimsy**. You are thinking I should try to chop through them?"

"Wait a minute!" cried Barnaby. "We're almost twenty feet in the air! If you chop through the net, we'll fall on our heads."

"What we have here is a **dilemma**, Barnaby," said Bridget. "If we just wait here and do nothing, we'll probably be eaten by the tribe of savages who set this trap. If we cut the net, we fall on our heads. Personally, I vote for falling on our heads. At least there's a chance we can get up and run away."

"I must agree with Bridget," said Babette, who was getting ready to whack.

"Hold it a second, Babette!" he yelled. "I admit your argument has its strong points, but I think you should give me time for a **rebuttal** before sending us on a dangerous free fall."

"This isn't a debate, Barnaby," said Bridget. "We're in a serious jam! We've got to get out of here on the double!"

Just then, a terrible, high-pitched, horsey laugh came from far below them.

"Oh, Father, aren't they quaint?" said a female voice in an odd, sort-of-British accent. "What is that **dialect** they speak? It sounds as though they come from the American colonies! Do let's cut them down!"

Barnaby, Bridget, Babette, and Beauregard heard a snap, and with that, they all came tumbling down.

"See," mumbled Bridget, rubbing her head. "We were going to fall on our heads one way or another."

The horsey laugh broke out again.

"Oh, look, Father, the girl is so **rustic.** Look at those heavy work pants of hers. She looks like she's straight out of the backwoods!"

Bridget looked around to find the source of the voice that had insulted her jeans. When she found it, she wished she hadn't bothered. Standing behind her was a large woman in a fluffy pink ball gown with a face so ugly it made Bridget shudder to look at her. Next to the woman was an old, fat man in a long purple robe. The man had a very fancy crown on his head.

"Hey, what do you mean by stringing us up like that? Who are you people, anyway?" growled Bridget.

"Dear me, that child is **uncouth**!" huffed the man in the crown. "Girl, were you not raised with any manners? Do you not know the proper way to address a king?"

"Please forgive us. It is just that we were taken by surprise. Good day, your majesties," said Barnaby with a little bow. The fall must have shaken up his hair, because as soon as he bent forward, a box of chocolates fell on the ground.

The woman's eyes grew very round, then very narrow, then she pounced on the box, opened it, and devoured every last chocolate.

"Oh, Father," she cooed, sucking caramel out from between her teeth. "I love him, I do! Did you see how he offered me this tribute? He is so **gallant**, so charming, like a knight in shining armor!"

"I see!" said the king, looking rather pleased. "Young knight, you have won my daughter's heart. What say you marry her? You will be my **heir,** and when I die you will **inherit** the throne and my entire fortune will be yours!"

"Things certainly do happen quickly around here," remarked Babette.

"Silence!" thundered the king. "Well, young knight?"

"Bu . . . but I . . . you don't . . . ," said Barnaby, **faltering** and hesitating over his words. "I don't even know her name."

"Ah, you are right. May I present Princess Equinia, daughter of Lyle the Great, King of Littledot," said the king with a wave of his hand. "And you are . . . ?"

Barnaby paused for a moment. These two people seemed genuinely crazy, and he didn't want to upset them. They might be dangerous. He decided on a bold strategy—stall them.

"Um, my name is Barnaby, Your Highness," he said. "I think I should point out that we hardly know each other. Shouldn't, er, Princess Equinia and I get acquainted before I **broach** the subject of marriage with her?"

"A courtship, eh?" said the king with a chuckle. "I've always thought that romance was a rather **provincial** custom. Good for the commoners, but we royals are much too sophisticated for all that hair-pulling and jumping about. Still, the idea has a sort of country charm, and it might please Equinia. Very well, Sir Barnaby. You have my permission to **woo** my daughter."

"Well, you know, it is important to develop a friendly relationship, a good **rapport** before going into marriage," said Barnaby.

"Fine, fine, fine," said the king. "All that will take care of itself."

"Oh, goody, goody!" cried the princess, clapping her hands and dancing around. "I have a new **suitor**. Barnaby's my boyfriend! Barnaby's my boyfriend!"

With that, the princess grabbed Barnaby's hand and pulled him after her into the woods. Barnaby tried to resist her yank, but Equinia was several times larger than he. He looked over at his friends desperately, and they tried to come to his aid, but just as they were about to run after him, they were stopped by the edge of a long, sharp blade.

"I wouldn't do that if I were you," said King Lyle, holding his sword out in front of them. "The romantic **liaison** between Equinia and Sir Barnaby is at a very delicate stage. You must leave them alone and not butt in or **interfere**."

"But he's not a 'sir' or a knight," said Bridget. "He's our friend, and we're very busy. He's nothing but a scientist."

"A man of science, eh?" said the king.

"Splendid. Well, I, too, am a very busy man. You two, I mean three, must come with me to the castle so I can keep watch over you."

The king gestured with his sword, and Beauregard, Babette, and Bridget reluctantly followed him through the woods. His castle was an odd building, more like a tower than a royal house. It was round, made of stone, and several stories high. Inside, it was filled with papers and pens. Books lined the walls from floor to ceiling.

"It looks as if you enjoy reading, Your Majesty," Babette commented.

"Actually, the enjoyment has faded," he sighed. "You see, as King of Littledot, it is my duty to make sure that all the reading material in the land is good for my people. New books are sent here, where they are stored **pending** my approval. I'm afraid many have been lying around for quite a long time. I must be so careful! I can't have people reading harmful or misleading material. No, I must personally read and approve everything—nothing goes out unless I **endorse** it."

Bridget opened her mouth to ask about these "people" the king supposedly ruled, but he started talking again.

"Of course, not every book is entirely bad or good. If that were the case, my job would be much easier. Instead, I must make changes when necessary. Sometimes books are too depressing, for example, so I do my best to change sad endings to happy ones.

"Sometimes a book means to be good, but it is just too long. In that case, I **condense** the text, boil it down to the essentials. People like short books, after all. I read one book in which a fellow commits a terrible murder early on. Then he worries about it for hundreds of pages, and finally turns himself in near the end. I thought it was much clearer without the middle part, so I decided it should be **omitted.** In my version, he commits the murder and goes directly to prison. Much better, don't you think?

"And sometimes it seems like the author's only purpose is to stir up people's emotions, to get them angry or excited. Believe me, **provocative** literature is the last thing I need in my kingdom. Kings prefer things to be as unexciting and **sedate** as possible. It's amazing how irresponsible authors are sometimes."

"But what you're doing is wrong!" said Bridget. "You're not making the books better, you're **censoring** them—taking out or changing anything that doesn't suit your personal and political goals!"

"Exactly, child!" boomed the king. "It is my royal right to decide what my subjects will read. What's wrong with that?"

"Nothing!" chirped Babette, who then turned and whispered to her friend, "Do not be upset. I strongly suspect the king and his daughter are the only people on this island, so he is harming no one. We should not anger him."

Bridget shrugged, and was silent.

"So, what are you working on today?" asked Babette.

"I'm glad you asked," said King Lyle eagerly, taking up his pen. "I'm working on a most frustrating book. It's about the French Revolution. Terrible war, I'm told. Many nobles were **decapitated.** That's right, the rebels had a machine that would chop their heads right off. Well, that just gave me the willies. The word 'decapitate' should not appear in decent literature. It gives people ideas. So I must go through and **obliterate** the word, wipe out any trace of it, every time it appears in the text—which is far too often, believe me."

King Lyle picked up a book, flipped to a marked page, and scribbled hard over one of the offensive words.

"Oh, there are so many of them!" he exclaimed, obliterating another one.

Babette, Bridget, and Beauregard decided to make themselves comfortable for the time being. It looked like they were in for a serious delay.

Things were much more interesting on the other side of the island, which wasn't far away, since it was very small. Barnaby, who was supposed to be wooing Equinia, found instead that it was he who was being wooed quite outrageously in a tiny beach bungalow.

"Darling, I adore you," purred the princess. "Your fluffy hair has such style, such oomph, such **panache**! Your concerned little face is so scholarly! I love men who study a lot. They are so . . . **studious**!"

Barnaby tried his best to ignore her, but that only seemed to spur her on. Equinia ran to a cupboard and pulled out a plate of cookies.

"Here, my love, I baked these for you myself," she cooed, offering him one.

Barnaby accepted. After all, he was very hungry. He tried biting into it, but it was so hard that he hurt his tooth.

"I can't eat them," he said.

"Why not?" asked the princess, looking hurt.

"It's **inedible**," replied Barnaby.

"What do you mean?" she gasped.

"I mean, it can't be eaten," he said, simply.

Equinia frowned a little, but she wasn't put off. She left the hut for a moment, and came back covered in tacky necklaces and gaudy earrings.

"Do you like me now?" she asked. "See? I have **adorned** myself with jewels to make myself even more attractive."

"There was no need," he replied.

"You mean, you thought I was already pretty without decoration?" she said, falling before him and putting her face near his as if waiting for a kiss.

Barnaby was not a **squeamish** person, not by a long shot, but the thought of kissing Equinia would have turned almost anyone's stomach. He was trying not to be rude, but he couldn't help noticing a huge, skin-colored growth that **protruded** about two inches from her right eyelid. It stuck out so far, in fact, that it seemed to block her line of vision.

"Doesn't that growth **impair** your vision?" he asked.

"What?" yelped Equinia, jumping up.

"That thing on your eyelid. It seems to be interfering with your ability to see," he said. "You should really have a doctor take a look at it. It's probably **benign,** which means there's nothing to worry about. But it could be **malignant.** That's bad. That means it's dangerous."

"How can you be so cruel?" she cried. "First you ignore me, sitting there so cold and **aloof,** and then when you do decide to talk to me, you're mean!"

Barnaby began to feel guilty.

"You don't love me anymore!" she moaned. "My heart is broken into a million pieces, and the damage is **irreparable.** I will never be happy again. I will **grieve** for your lost love forever! Boo hoo hoo!"

Equinia began to weep appallingly, which made her even more monstrous. Barnaby tried his best to **placate** her, but he didn't really have the knack.

"Don't cry, princess. This has all been a mistake. I never loved you in the first place," he said.

"You're lying. You gave me a box of chocolates on the beach!" she cried. "You're just **fickle,** just like the rest of them. Your feelings come and go like the tides you rode in on."

"What do you mean 'just like the rest of them'?" demanded Barnaby. He suddenly started feeling a little less guilty. There might be a way out of this situation after all.

Just as he was about to ask more, there was a knock at the door. It creaked open, and King Lyle poked his head in.

"Hello, children," he said cheerily. "Sir Barnaby, may I have a word with you?"

Barnaby was more than happy to have a **reprieve** from the terrible situation with Equinia, so he got up and followed the king.

"Well, how are things going, dear boy?" he asked, clapping his hand on Barnaby's shoulder. "Have you asked for her hand in marriage yet?"

"Um, no," replied Barnaby.

"What's the delay? Stop **procrastinating.** No sense in putting it off. The sooner you get done with it, the sooner we can plan the wedding," he said.

"I'm glad you brought that up, Your Highness," said Barnaby. "The marriage ceremony is a very important **rite,** almost as important as graduation. It shouldn't be taken lightly."

King Lyle looked at Barnaby carefully for a moment, then smiled broadly.

"You're a smart young man, I see," he declared. "You want some **incentive** to marry the princess, as if someday becoming King of Littledot weren't reason enough. Well, come on then. I'll show you what else you'll get in the bargain."

Barnaby was eager to get as far away from Equinia as possible, so he gladly walked with the king through the woods to a clearing where dozens of wooden barrels stood stacked.

"You see, Sir Barnaby, I am rich," he said.

"Um, I don't understand," said Barnaby. "What's in them?"

King Lyle motioned Barnaby close to one of the barrels. Then he cut a hole through its side with his sword. Water began pouring out into the sandy dirt.

"Ha ha! It doesn't even matter! I have plenty more. I have an endless supply!" he cried.

Barnaby stuck his hand in the stream of water and brought it to his mouth.

"This is seawater," he said, completely shocked at the utter senselessness of it. "Do you mean you've been **hoarding** barrels of seawater?"

"I don't have to hoard it! I have an endless supply! I hope that sweetens the marriage deal for you!"

Barnaby was at his wits' end. These people were absolutely mad. He was done being polite and wasting his time with them, even if it meant King Lyle might stick him with his sword.

"Look, the deal's off, Lyle," he said grimly. "Your daughter has had many suitors before me, and I'm not about to take their hand-me-downs. She's damaged goods, Pops."

"How dare you **tarnish** my daughter's reputation like that!" yelled the king. "Equinia is a charming, lively, **vivacious** girl. Naturally, she has had many admirers."

"Admirers you trapped for her!" snapped Barnaby.

"I would be **negligent** in my duties as father and king if I did not try to find my daughter a husband," explained the king. "I don't see why my method of doing so is **relevant**."

"It matters a great deal! Men are not animals to be caught and turned into pets!"

"I would have made you a king, not a pet!"

"Well, I'm happy to **forfeit** any claim to the throne in exchange for my liberty," declared Barnaby nobly.

Just then, there was a rustling in the bushes behind him, and looking over his shoulder, Barnaby was greatly relieved to see Bridget, Babette, and Beauregard.

"I wish we could stay and **mediate** between you two, and help you reach a friendly agreement, but I'm afraid we don't have time," said Bridget.

"Yes, Barnaby," said Babette. "We have thought about it for a long while, and we have come up with a plan."

"What is the plan?" he asked.

"Run to the beach as fast as you can!" she yelled.

Barnaby didn't have to be told twice. It sounded like a great plan to him, and he dashed through the woods after his friends. Of course, King Lyle came running after them, but he was not nearly as fast as they were. Bridget had plenty of time to blow her bubble boat and they were safely offshore by the time King Lyle even got to the beach. And there he stood, waving his sword and yelling at them, as they sailed off.

"What a pair of freaks!" panted Bridget. After a few minutes, she continued, "Gee, Barnaby, I thought you were the quiet, **reserved** type. I never realized you were such a heartbreaker," she said, giggling.

"I think this is a new **facet** of Barnaby's personality," said Babette. "Another side of him, yes?"

"That was my first experience with love," sighed Barnaby, who didn't think it was funny, "and it was a total **debacle**. What a disaster! I used to **covet** the good looks of my classmates who were popular with all the girls. Now I'm glad I don't have what they have. I don't envy them one little bit. Love is heck."

Bridget and Babette rolled their eyes and laughed to themselves. But Beauregard simply nodded his furry black head in silent agreement, and stared sadly out to sea.

✍ QUIZ #26 ✍
Relationships

Decide what relationship the following pairs of words have to each other. If they have similar meanings, write "S" next to the pair of words. If they have opposite meanings, write "O" next to the words.

1. benign :: malignant
2. reserved :: vivacious
3. endorse :: approve
4. condense :: expand
5. provocative :: sedate
6. impair :: improve
7. debacle :: disaster
8. uncouth :: gallant
9. passive :: active
10. tarnish :: polish
11. placate :: soothe

✍ QUIZ #27 ✍
Fill in the Blank

For each sentence below, choose the word that best completes the sentence.

1. The people in Smallville had
   _____ tastes, so they didn't
   appreciate the experimental theater group
   from New York that visited their town last
   month.

   a. squeamish **b.** diverse

   c. rustic **d.** provincial

2. In order to get into the club, Jim had to go
   through an initiation _____ that
   involved running through the campus in his
   underwear.

   a. dilemma **b.** liaison

   c. rite **d.** facet

3. During wartime, soldiers' letters are opened,
   read, and sometimes _____ to
   keep secrets from leaking out.

   a. mediated **b.** broached

   c. censored **d.** hoarded

4. Vince seemed to have a(n) _____
   athletic ability that made it easy for him to do
   well at any sport.

   a. innate **b.** pending

   c. irreparable **d.** relevant

5. When his grandfather dies, Manuel will
   _____ half of his great fortune—
   the other half goes to his sister, Amelia.

   a. inherit **b.** interfere

   c. decapitate **d.** obliterate

6. Clancey's strange _____ was
   hard to understand unless you came from the
   same Irish village as he.

   a. rapport **b.** incentive

   c. rebuttal **d.** dialect

✍ QUIZ #28 ✍
Matching

Match each word on the right with a word on
the left that has a similar meaning.

1.	hazardous	a.	at night
2.	nocturnal	b.	admirer
3.	flimsy	c.	weak
4.	heir	d.	inheritor
5.	faltering	e.	leave out
6.	woo	f.	scholarly
7.	suitor	g.	dangerous
8.	omit	h.	stumbling
9.	panache	i.	flair
10.	studious	j.	to romance

Matching

Match each word on the right with a word on
the left that has a similar meaning.

1. inedible   a. envy
2. adorned   b. not fit to eat
3. protrude   c. changeable
4. aloof   d. give up
5. grieve   e. cool
6. fickle   f. neglectful
7. reprieve   g. relief
8. procrastinate   h. decorated
9. negligent   i. stick out
10. forfeit   j. mourn
11. covet   k. delay

Chapter 7

The Cave of the Counterfeiters

Well, we hadn't eaten in a while and we still weren't exactly sure how to get back to France, but at least the weather was **temperate**—mild and dry, with a pleasant light wind blowing us westward. After all the delays and accidents, I was grateful for that much. That, and the fact that Barnaby was still a bachelor. The poor boy had a narrow escape.

I was kind of hoping we'd be picked up by an ocean liner—those cruise ships travel through the Greek islands all the time—but we didn't see anything but water. Everyone was very quiet, probably because we were so **weary** of traveling. But we all snapped out of it pretty quickly when we noticed that the boat had begun to **veer** sharply to the left and gain speed. We were headed straight toward a big, craggy rock that was sticking out of the ocean, and there was nothing we could do to change our course! I thought for sure that this was the end for us, but just before we crashed headlong into it, we were sucked down underwater. We didn't drown, though. No, instead we found ourselves in a

very strange cave beneath the surface of the
ocean . . . .

❧ ❧ ❧ ❧ ❧

A deafening siren **heralded** their arrival.
Speakers all over the cave announced:
"Intruder alert! Intruder alert! Intruder alert!"

All around them, people were scurrying to
hide what they were doing. Desks were
slammed shut. Work tables were covered with
sheets. Pieces of paper were being chewed up
and swallowed. Documents were being
shredded.

Suddenly, much to their displeasure,
Bridget, Barnaby, Babette, and Beauregard saw
that once again they had a gun aimed at them.
This time, it was an old man in a fancy antique
wheelchair who was threatening them. He was
a very proper and dignified-looking man, his
few gray hairs neatly combed, his red silk
jacket neatly pressed, and a fine wool blanket
thrown over his legs. He looked like someone
from another time and place. Even his gun, a
very **ornate** pistol made of polished wood and
covered in fancy brass decorations, looked like
some kind of family **heirloom,** passed down
by a soldier or duelist far back in his family's
past.

"Just what do you think you're doing here?"
he demanded. "How much did you see?"

"Nothing!" cried the travelers all at once. "We didn't see anything, honest!"

They all began talking at once, trying to convince the armed man of their harmlessness. But their talking did little to **allay** his suspicions. In fact, all it did was make matters worse.

"I don't believe you," he said simply. "I think this whole innocent kid thing is nothing but a clever act. Apart from his hair, you appear to be normal children, but I'm sure you have all the **guile** to be international spies. That's what you're here for, right?"

"I don't see much to spy on," replied Barnaby innocently, his right hand twiddling his hair nervously. He was trying to prove again that he and his friends hadn't seen anything important when they arrived. The man in the wheelchair, however, seemed terribly insulted by the comment.

"Oh, you don't see much, do you?" he yelled. "I'll have you know that this is the finest **counterfeiting** operation in the world! The finest in imitation jewels, fake money, **forgeries** of famous artworks, knockoffs of designer watches, wallets, purses, furs, and other **miscellaneous** items—they're all made right here in this cave! Not much, indeed!"

"Then we regret not seeing much of it, for we surely would have been impressed," said

Babette in the most **conciliatory** tone possible. After all, they seemed to be in a rather **precarious** position, considering that the old man had both a gun and a very short temper.

"I appreciate that, young lady," he said, apparently pleased with her compliment, "but I'm afraid you've caused us a great deal of trouble today. You see, we have daily **quotas** to satisfy. We're supposed to have at least one billion lira in thousand-lira notes ready this evening for some very important organizations in Italy. When you came in, these artists behind me were forced to destroy most of what they worked on so we wouldn't be caught with it."

"But why?" asked Bridget.

"My dear girl, because making your own money is highly illegal. That means it's against the law. Only governments are allowed to create money. Understand?" the man asked. He spoke very slowly and clearly. Bridget didn't like his tone. She felt that he was talking down to her, and being **patronized** was one thing she really hated.

"Yeah, I get it," she snapped. "Of course I know making fake stuff is against the law. I only meant that it's obvious we're not spies or police officers, so there was no reason to trash your whole day's work."

"It was not obvious to me what you were.

And it still isn't clear what you are doing here," he replied sharply. "Anyway, I don't have the time right now to decide what to do with you. We must catch up to make our quota. I suppose the most **expedient** thing would be to shoot you, throw you into the ocean, and let that be the end of it. Yes, that would be easiest, to be sure."

The old man paused for a brief, very tense moment, then, to the great relief of Barnaby, Babette, Bridget, and Beauregard, he yelled, "Leonard! Come take these children and this enormous cat to the conference room and make sure they don't get into any trouble until after we ship the lira! We'll decide what to do with them then."

A young man dressed in jeans and a paint-covered T-shirt came forward.

Still trying her best to act friendly, Babette decided to introduce herself and her friends. Leonard, though, didn't respond well. He just gave them a **curt** nod of his head and waved his hand to show that they should walk ahead of him toward a door marked "Conference Room."

The room looked pretty much like any other conference room you might find in a regular office building. There were no windows, the lighting was harsh and bright, and one lone lightbulb in the corner hummed away quietly, flickering every now and then. There were two pots of coffee slowly burning on the coffeemaker, filling the room with a bitter smell. There was a whiteboard on one wall and several dry-erase colored markers. Beauregard went to sleep right away, as do many people in conference rooms. Indeed, the only thing that was out of the ordinary was the beautiful white marble conference table.

"What a lovely table," remarked Babette.

Leonard smiled, walked over to the table, and rapped on it with his knuckles. Instead of hearing the solid sound of stone, the kids heard a hollow, cheap sound, as if he were knocking on an empty milk jug.

"That's right," said Leonard. "Plastic. It's a fake. Amazing, isn't it?"

They had to agree, it was an amazing likeness.

"It seems impossible," said Barnaby, "to **duplicate** the look and shine of marble so well with plastic. Did you create this?"

Leonard shook his head sadly. "No," he said. "I'm not nearly talented enough. Mr. Faux himself made this table."

"Mr. Faux is the guy with the gun?" asked Bridget.

"The guy with the gun, yes," said Leonard with a little laugh. "But in addition to having a gun, he is also one of the most **acclaimed** artists in the world. You can't imagine the praise, the **kudos** that have been heaped on him. I am proud to be his grandson."

He did look proud. But he looked troubled as well.

"If he's such a great artist, what's he doing hiding in a cave?" demanded Bridget.

"He isn't hiding," growled Leonard. "The public did not understand his genius. He was **persecuted** and **tormented** by the authorities. Police would follow him, arrest him on the flimsiest excuse, sometimes even **confiscate** his art equipment, saying it was 'evidence.' Ha! They just wanted to crush his spirit by taking away his supplies."

"He heard about this place from a friend of his in one of the terrible dungeons they threw him in. Apparently, the ancient Greeks found a small underwater cave hundreds of years ago, and they **excavated** it, removing sand and rocks and sometimes **gouging** through stone and silt to expand the living space. Since those days, it has been used by many different armies as a secret hiding place. So my grandfather came here, too—to be safe. Surely you can understand that."

"Right," said Bridget. "But why are all those other people here? Are they misunderstood artists, too?"

"Some are," said Leonard. "Most were drawn here by my grandfather's reputation. He is their boss, but he is also their **mentor.** He teaches and guides them. He's a very demanding teacher. Some of the new people here say he's too **didactic.** I have to admit, he does tend to lecture people, but only because he wants them to reach their 'personal **pinnacle,**' as he calls it. The highest point of their talent."

"Well, I guess that's **laudable** enough," said Barnaby. "I mean, you have to give a guy a little credit for pushing people to do their best. But what I want to know is how he got here all by himself. He's **paraplegic,** isn't he?"

"No, his legs aren't paralyzed," said Leonard. "That was just a model of an old Victorian wheelchair he made. He amuses himself with little projects like that. Like the pistol. It's an imitation of an eighteenth-century French dueling pistol."

Bridget and Babette exchanged a quick look, but Leonard was on to them. "It will shoot just as well as a real pistol, though," he added.

Leonard went and poured himself a cup of stale coffee. He blew into the foam cup and sighed.

"I came here with my grandfather when I was about your age, right after he escaped from prison," he said. "He told me he needed my help, and in exchange he promised to teach me to be a great artist. He knew I **aspired** to be a painter. It was my greatest wish. His offer held such a strong **allure** for me, I couldn't resist. I quit school and left with him on a dark, cold winter evening. I didn't even tell my parents where I was going. I haven't seen them since."

He took a sip of his coffee and looked thoughtfully into the cup. Bridget felt a little depressed, too.

"Well, did he?" she asked.

"Did he what?" said Leonard.

"Did he make you a great artist? Was it worth leaving your parents?"

Leonard shook his head and was silent for a while. If there had been a window in the room, he probably would have stared out of it.

"I am ashamed to say that I failed him," he said finally. "I tried my hardest to copy exactly everything he showed me. I learned to **discriminate** the finest details of a painting. Were the brush strokes made by a left-handed or right-handed person? Was the paint applied with a palette knife or with bare hands? Is that shade of brown burnt sienna or burnt umber? I practiced day and night, trying to **mimic** the styles in the paintings Grandfather showed me. I was absolutely **scrupulous.** But my careful attention to detail was absolutely to no **avail.**

"At first, Grandfather told me my work had some **merit.** He'd praise one little thing or another, but I noticed that none of it was ever shipped out. I thought if I **persevered** I might get better, but I could have stuck to it for ten years or a hundred—nothing would have changed. Finally, I asked him to give me a straight, **objective** opinion of my talent. I wasn't prepared for what he had to say.

"He was actually angry at me. He said I put too much of myself into the paintings. A good forgery, he told me, must be **superficial,** nothing but surface detail. My feelings and emotions should never show. I tried to argue with him, but he had caught me. You see, **unbeknownst** to me, he had sneaked into my workroom and discovered that I had been painting on my own. Not copies of anything, either, just whatever I felt like. I only did it for a change of pace, something different . . . making copies can be so **tedious.**"

Leonard kind of drifted off for a minute in

his own thoughts. Bridget, Babette, and Barnaby were too confused to offer any help.

"He **derided** my originals cruelly, making fun of them and scoffing at them. He said there was no challenge in painting something you thought up yourself because no one could tell if it was any good if there was nothing to compare it to. Originality, he said, is the **bane** of all good counterfeiters. The kiss of death, he said. He told me I must stop wasting my time painting. I cried and cried, but finally he calmed me down. He told me I could stay and help around the office, do little errands and things.

"That's what I've been doing ever since. It's been so **degrading.** The other counterfeiters know I'm a failure, and they treat me like dirt. But I have to put up with it. I'm not fit for anything else."

"That is absolutely **absurd,**" said Babette, stomping her foot.

"What?" said Leonard, as if shocked out of a dream.

"I mean, what your grandfather, Mr. Faux, said is completely ridiculous," she said, stomping her foot again. "I insist that we go see your paintings immediately."

Leonard was too startled to do or say anything for a minute. Then he objected mildly, saying that his grandfather had told him to keep them in the conference room. But

Babette wouldn't take no for an answer.

"You can watch us just as easily in your workroom. Leave a note on the whiteboard," she said.

"Back in five minutes," he wrote on the board. Then he showed them out another door and all of them, including Beauregard who had been awakened by Babette stomping on his tail, followed him down a long, damp, gray hallway. They came to a little door at the end, and Leonard pulled a key out of his jeans pocket, unlocked the door, and let them in.

The room was large and round, and had a big skylight high overhead. Leonard began explaining how they had built the skylight, but no one was listening. They were too busy admiring the amazing paintings that covered every wall. Even Bridget and Barnaby, who weren't big art fans, were impressed. Babette and Beauregard, who were obviously into that sort of thing, were studying the different paintings closely.

Leonard began to shuffle nervously from foot to foot. His paintings had never undergone such **scrutiny** before. He was scared he'd be laughed at again.

Finally, Babette came and looked him straight in the eyes. "Leonard," she said, "I think you are a very great artist. Your work is not only moving and powerful, it's **innovative.** You've created something entirely new!"

"That's the problem," said Mr. Faux, who had appeared suddenly in the doorway, without his wheelchair this time. "You see, I had a duty. I promised to make Leonard a great counterfeiter, and I failed to fulfill that **obligation.** Or rather, we failed. He just didn't have it in him. Pity, too, since I wanted to make this entire operation my **legacy** to him when I pass on.

"Unfortunately, he's a bad businessman as well as a bad counterfeiter. And one has to be **pragmatic** when it comes to business. You can't let emotions get in the way of faking money, if you'll forgive the pun. That's why I'm leaving everything to Ed. Boy, does he have a head for business. You'll never meet a **shrewder** man."

Leonard looked very pained. Babette looked very angry.

"Mr. Faux, you are a very bad grandfather!" she snapped. "And you are a very bad artist."

Mr. Faux actually looked upset at that, but because she couldn't tell which part of what she'd said had upset him, Babbette just kept talking.

"Why don't you encourage him instead of **undermining** his confidence and cutting him down? He is your own flesh and blood!"

Mr. Faux seemed unmoved.

"Leonard is a very talented painter. A great artist, even. Much better than you ever were or could ever hope to be! You're just jealous!" she cried.

Well, that seemed to hit home. Mr. Faux turned red in the face. Then purple. Then a sort of grayish-greenish shade. Veins started to pop out on his forehead. Barnaby was beginning to think he had suddenly been struck with a serious illness, but it turned out that Mr. Faux's reaction was more **psychological** than **pathological.**

"All right, all right!" he finally blurted out. "Yes, if you must know, I can't bear to look at these paintings. I knew when I brought him here that Leonard had a strong **aesthetic** sense. He could see and appreciate beauty in anything. But when I saw these paintings, I realized he was more than just a lover of beauty, he was an artistic genius. I almost hated him for that."

Bridget frowned.

"Oh, I see, you don't approve?" he said.

"How could you hate your own grandson, you ask? Well, I'll tell you. All I ever wanted as a boy, as a teenager, as a young man, and even as a not-so-young man, was to be an artist. I was so **resolute,** absolutely determined that nothing would stop me, not even starvation. I even left my wife and child because I thought they were **hampering** my career. A great artist, I thought, must **forgo** the comforts of home and family.

"I showed my first paintings in a gallery when I was twenty years old. I was so excited. Finally, I thought, the world would appreciate my work. I would get all the **prestige** and recognition I deserved. The critics, however, did something worse than attack me. '**Competent** but unoriginal,' they said. Basically, they meant I knew how to paint a horse that looked like a horse, but so what? It was nothing new or impressive.

"I didn't care, though. Their criticism only strengthened my **resolve.** I tried harder, put myself through a **rigorous** schedule of working as a waiter all day to earn a few dimes and painting all night to get ready for another show. A few months later I was ready. You know what the reviews in the papers said that time? '**Banal.**' '**Trite.**' That's right, boring and unoriginal. One critic said my work was '**insipid,**' which means more uninteresting than unoriginal, but you get the picture. The next show got the same reaction. In fact, all the subsequent shows got the same reaction. Banal, trite, insipid, unoriginal. Ergghh!!"

Mr. Faux started to turn red again, but calmed down before going purple.

"I took all sorts of lessons. I asked everyone for advice on how to improve. But they gave only the most **indefinite** answers, like, 'you've just got to feel it' or 'let yourself go'," he continued. "I've always been a person who likes things clear-cut, you know? Finally, after many years, I decided to give up. But not without a fight."

"My burning desire to be an artist turned into an **insatiable** desire for revenge against the entire artistic community, a desire that would never be satisfied! I had **squandered** my youth trying to impress them, but I would spend my older years destroying them. I started making forgeries of the most famous works of art in the world. My copies were so good that even experts had trouble telling the difference. Then I started copying other things, like clothing, money, jewels. I finally found my **niche** in the world of art. I am unoriginal, and good at being unoriginal. I make lots of money being unoriginal, and I don't intend to stop **reaping** the rewards just yet."

With that, Mr. Faux pulled his pistol out of the deep pocket of his red silk jacket and aimed it at the kids.

"Okay, that's enough, Mister," said Bridget, who was tired of hearing all this complaining and whining. "Face it, you're a flop as an artist. So what? I can't paint either. But it's not too late for you to be a good grandfather. Look at your choices: you can continue your life of crime, get caught eventually, because all criminals get caught eventually, and live out your days alone in a prison. Or you can give up your evil ways and try to **rectify** all the wrong you have done to your grandson. Get him out of this depressing dump, help him make something of himself, you know?"

Mr. Faux seemed torn and puzzled. He lowered the gun slightly, and seemed to be going through some emotional distress.

Babette chimed in, "Yes, Mr. Faux. Take him away from all this. Take him to Paris, so he can be truly appreciated as an artist. And through his success, you will have success."

Leonard looked longingly at his grandfather. "Could we?" he asked quietly. "Could we really go?"

Mr. Faux let the gun drop from his hand as tears flooded his eyes. "Of course, dear boy, of course," he said, holding out his arms to his grandson. At that, Leonard rushed to his grandfather and gave him a **hearty** embrace. The **calamity** had been avoided.

"Oh," said Babette, clapping her hands together. "It is so good to see that they have **reconciled** their differences."

"Yes, this is certainly a touching scene," said Barnaby.

But Bridget wasn't feeling as happy as her friends. She had wandered off into a corner and was lost in her own little world. When Beauregard came over and tried to nuzzle her hip, she was so **preoccupied** she didn't even notice him. When Babette saw her friend looking so troubled, she came over to help, too.

"Bridget, what is it?" she asked.

"Leonard has his grandfather back," she said, looking down at her high-top sneakers. "But I guess I'll never get my parents back, will I?"

Babette frowned and wrinkled her forehead in thought.

"Hmmm," she said. "I'm not so sure about that. I know you have every reason to be **pessimistic,** but I do think there is hope. Mr. Faux? Do you and Leonard plan to go to Paris right away?"

Mr. Faux, who was now beaming with joy, looked up and smiled widely. "Yes, of course!" he laughed. "Just as soon as we can arrange transportation."

"But I thought you shipped goods from

here," said Barnaby. "Don't you have a boat?"

"Oh, no," he said. "Our customers must pick up their orders personally."

"Oh, dear. You see, we have a problem," Babette explained. "We need to get back to Paris very quickly. Bridget's parents are there, and she needs to find them. Do you think we can start building a ship right away?"

"Well, I'm not sure I have all the materials I need," Mr. Faux replied, "but we could look into it. I'll do anything I can to help you kids. After all, you gave me back my grandson!"

Poor Bridget. I've never seen a child more depressed. I guess she'd put up a brave front as long as she could. Babette told her to go take a nap, get some rest, and I had to agree that was good advice. By the time she woke up, the situation looked much brighter. Leonard and Barnaby had worked together to draw up the plans for a small submarine. Mr. Faux was busy gathering maps and materials, and Babette was chopping sheet metal with her right hand (that girl packs a wow of a punch). Barnaby's amazing head of hair came in handy again. I swear I will never, so long as I live, forget how he pulled an entire periscope from behind his ear.

It didn't take long before all the pieces were ready. The only problem, it seemed, was how to hold them all together, but thanks to Bridget's resourcefulness that wasn't a problem for long. While everyone held the stuff up, Bridget pulled her gum out and wrapped it around and around the submarine until it was completely airtight and looked like a big pink ball of rubber bands. After packing up some food and art supplies, we were ready to go. Mr. Faux left all the keys with that fellow Ed, and we were off.

Of course, it being Leonard and Barnaby's first attempt at submarine design, there were some minor hitches. The controls were awkward and difficult to **manipulate,** and the whole vessel was clumsy and **unwieldy.** But all that aside, it looked as though we were headed for Paris at last.

✍ QUIZ #30 ✍
Relationships

Decide what relationship the following pairs of words have to each other. If they have similar meanings, write "S" next to the pair of words. If they have opposite meanings, write "O" next to the words.

1. counterfeit :: forgery
2. persecuted :: tormented
3. innovative :: insipid
4. banal :: trite
5. prestigious :: acclaimed
6. duplicate :: mimic
7. merit :: bane
8. kudos :: praise
9. confiscate :: donate
10. competent :: capable
11. resolute :: determined
12. squander :: waste
13. unwieldy :: graceful
14. pessimistic :: cheerful
15. temperate :: mild

✍ QUIZ #31 ✍
Fill in the Blank

For each sentence below, choose the word that best completes the sentence.

1. Lillian's ball gown was very
   _____; it must have taken
   weeks to sew on all those beads and
   decorations.
   a. miscellaneous **b.** ornate
   c. precarious **d.** conciliatory

2. Herman's silver belt buckle is a family
   _____, first worn by his great-
   great-great-grandfather Pete on his journey
   out to California many years ago.
   a. heirloom **b.** niche **c.** legacy **d.** guile

3. In order to keep up with the demand for their
   goods, the basket weavers set themselves a
   _____ of ten baskets a day each.
   a. mentor **b.** quota **c.** pinnacle **d.** scrutiny

4. As part of a(n) _____
   experiment, my roommate is forcing himself
   to go without sleep for five days to see how it
   affects his moods.
   a. psychological **b.** pathological
   c. aesthetic **d.** expedient

5. If you invest your money early, you will
   _____ great rewards later in life.
   a. preoccupy **b.** manipulate
   c. undermine **d.** reap

6. The other kids in the band _____
   my lame attempts to play "Melancholy Baby"
   on the tuba.
   a. patronized **b.** degraded
   c. derided **d.** discriminated
7. Lila's family loves to hear her sing and play
   the piano, but a more _____
   audience might not think she's as
   entertaining as her parents do.
   a. paraplegic **b.** insatiable
   c. didactic **d.** objective

✍ QUIZ #32 ✍
Matching

Match each word on the right with a word on
the left that has a similar meaning.

1. herald	a. shallow
2. weary	b. cut out
3. veer	c. hollow out
4. allay	d. announce
5. curt	e. lessen
6. excavate	f. careful
7. gouge	g. tired
8. laudable	h. usefulness
9. aspire	i. swerve
10. allure	j. brief
11. scrupulous	k. keep on
12. avail	l. praiseworthy
13. persevere	m. attraction
14. superficial	n. hope

QUIZ #33
Matching

Match each word on the right with a word on the left that has a similar meaning.

1. unbeknownst
2. tedious
3. absurd
4. obligation
5. pragmatic
6. shrewd
7. hamper
8. forgo
9. resolve
10. rigorous
11. indefinite
12. rectify
13. hearty
14. reconcile

a. crafty
b. reunite
c. not known
d. friendly
e. demanding
f. make right
g. duty
h. vague
i. tiresome
j. ridiculous
k. practical
l. determination
m. hold up
n. do without

Chapter 8

That's a Big Museum

All things considered, that submarine turned out to be pretty **durable,** especially for something held together with bubble gum. It proved to be more than tough enough to withstand our long trip underwater. Leonard and Mr. Faux **alternated** between steering and navigating. That is, while Leonard steered, Mr. Faux would plot the course, and **vice versa.** Which was fine by me. I was glad to have a chance to rest, and I know Bridget, Barnaby, and Babette were too.

In fact, I was forced to admit I didn't have the **stamina** I once had as a young cat. Our little adventures had emptied my saved-up energy **reserves,** if you know what I mean. I felt the need for a good long sleep, so I found a cozy little corner and was soon off in dreamland.

Next thing I knew, I was being awakened by all sorts of shouts and hand clapping. "Oh, no," I thought, "here we go again," but when I opened my eyes, I saw what all the racket was about. Believe it or not, we had made it! The submarine had surfaced in the Seine River—in Paris!

"Well, my friends, it is time for us to part," said Mr. Faux, as the travelers stood on the river bank. "I will always be grateful to you, but it is doubtful we will ever meet again. I am a wanted criminal, so I must travel **incognito** to avoid arrest. I will change my name, maybe even disguise my face! You would do well to forget you know me."

"We will never forget you," said Babette, "but we understand your point."

The friends hugged and waved good-bye to Leonard and his grandfather.

"Take care!" called Mr. Faux. "Come, Leonard, we are off to the Louvre."

Bridget jumped.

"The Louvre? Wait, wait!" she cried, running to catch up with them. "Um, I don't suppose we could share a taxi with you, could we?"

"Good idea," said Barnaby. "Let's start our search for your parents at the last place you saw them. Maybe we can pick up some clues."

"We should explain," said Babette to Mr. Faux. "Getting back to Paris was an important goal for us, but our **prime** goal is to find Bridget's parents."

"But of course!" said Mr. Faux. "It is the least I can do. But a couple of you will have to keep your heads down. I think you're only allowed four people in one taxi."

And with that, they walked up to the street to hail a cab.

It was a good thing Bridget was such a fast thinker, because they didn't have any money and the walk to the museum would have taken a very long time. After a lengthy ride, Mr. Faux paid the driver. Once again, it was time to say good-bye.

"We are going to overload our senses with art!" declared Mr. Faux, and he and Leonard walked into the museum.

Bridget, Barnaby, Babette, and Beauregard sat outside, trying to come up with a plan.

"The first thing we must do is **speculate** on every possible course of action your parents could have taken. Think hard," said Barnaby. "They may be in a nearby restaurant; they may be back at your hotel; they may be at the police station. We must **compile** a list of every possible option, then follow up on each one."

"That would take a very long time," said Bridget.

"That is a **gross** understatement, Bridget," said Babette.

"It would not just take a long time, it would take forever! Bridget's parents could be anywhere by now."

"I suppose you have a better idea," snapped Barnaby.

"Yes. I usually don't like calling on adults for help, but I think such action is **warranted** in a situation like this," said Babette. "I think adult assistance is definitely called for."

"What do you suggest, that I turn myself in to the lost and found?" asked Bridget.

"Well, no, I . . . hey, Bridget—those two people coming out the door," said Babette, pointing toward the museum. "They look a great deal like you, don't they?"

Bridget looked over her shoulder and squinted. She could see a man and a woman. The man was struggling with some big, **cumbersome** packages, and the woman was looking around anxiously. As they got a little closer, Bridget let out a yelp of happiness.

"Mom! Dad! Mom!" she called, waving her hands above her head.

The woman stopped and looked, then began running toward her full speed.

"Bridget!" she cried, as she scooped her daughter up in her arms. "Bridget, baby, here you are!"

Bridget's mother hugged and kissed her so **profusely** that her face was practically covered in pink lipstick prints. But her mother's **initial** happiness soon gave way to another reaction, which was definitely anger. She put her daughter down and looked her sternly in the eye.

"Bridget, didn't I tell you to wait by the information desk if we got separated?" she demanded. "What are you doing out here? Where have you been?"

Bridget's father finally managed to waddle over to them. He put down his many bags and packages and heaved a sigh.

"See?" he said. "I told you she was all right."

"How can you be so **complacent**? I can't understand how you keep from worrying about your own daughter. Anything could have happened to her! Kidnappings are so **prevalent** these days, and the problem is as widespread in Paris as it is in New York!"

"Well, I knew she couldn't have gone far," he said.

Barnaby and Babette giggled at the **irony** of that statement.

"Where have you been?" Bridget's mother repeated.

Bridget was too tired and hungry to give her mother a full **synopsis** of what she'd been up to. Besides, she thought, a summary like that might get her into more trouble. So she decided to answer her mother's question with a question of her own.

"Where have *I* been? I don't see how that's relevant. I'm the child, and it's your responsibility to keep up with me. I think a more **pertinent** question is where have *you* been? I've been waiting for you for days!" said Bridget. She felt quite pleased with herself. That gave her mother something to chew on.

But Bridget's mother only chewed on it for a couple of seconds before making Bridget sorry she'd ever even thought of talking back.

"My responsibility? I'll tell you about my responsiblity, young lady. I told you to wait by the information desk. You chose to ignore me. Based on that, I can only **conclude** that you have no respect for your mother, and it's my responsibility to punish you until you can learn to mind your parents!" she said in that low, scary voice she used whenever she was really mad.

"Wait just a minute, honey," said Bridget's father. "There's no sense locking her up and throwing away the key. Maybe she can be **rehabilitated,** you know? Reformed into a good citizen? Bridget, do you promise to be a good daughter from now on and wait where your mother tells you?"

Bridget nodded her head gratefully.

"There, see?" said her father. "Besides, honey, it does sort of seem like we've been in that museum gift shop for days." He looked down at all the packages around his feet.

"Your mother's been up to her **prodigal** gift buying again," he laughed. "I think she got a present for everyone on our block back home—even the folks she doesn't like!"

Bridget laughed. Her mother smiled and relaxed a bit.

"Well, it's okay to be extravagant when you're on vacation," she said. "But we're being rude. Bridget, it looks like you've made some friends."

"Yeah, Mom, these are my very best friends, Barnaby, Babette, and Beauregard," said Bridget.

"Well, since you are my daughter's very best friends, we'd be pleased if you'd join us for lunch. We're starved," she said. "That Louvre is one huge museum. You could spend days in there and not even notice the time passing."

Barnaby and Babette smiled at each other, and accepted her invitation. Then the whole group began walking to a nearby restaurant.

"That's a big black cat," said Bridget's dad, watching Beauregard's long tail swish back and forth ahead of him. "Careful he doesn't bring you big bad luck."

"That is one **superstition** I will never have again," said Bridget. "Beauregard is a great cat to have around when you're in trouble."

"Hmm," said Bridget's father, smiling with amusement, "maybe we'll have to buy him a big piece of fish, then, since he's such a good buddy."

"Definitely," said Bridget.

Beauregard's stomach rumbled softly in **anticipation** of the wonderful lunch he would soon be eating.

And it was a truly wonderful lunch. Babette, Barnaby, Bridget, and Beauregard all ordered huge plates of fish and french fries, and they were so hungry they even ate the parsley **garnish,** which was only meant for decoration, not for eating. In fact, they gobbled up everything they could lay their hands on.

"My, what little **gluttons** we have on our hands," said Bridget's mother, smiling. "Please have some dessert. We can't have you going away hungry!"

The children ordered chocolate mousse and ice cream and enjoyed it mightily, and they laughed and talked and told adventure stories for hours. Then they ordered more food, and told more stories. Bridget handed over her Yankees cap to Babette, who managed to look even more chic and mysterious with this new accessory. Everyone was having such a good time, in fact, that they didn't even notice the enormous black cat quietly slip out from under the table.

He knew his job was done. Bridget was safely returned to her parents, and Babette and Barnaby were back where they belonged, too. Beauregard took one last look at his human friends and smiled, thinking about all the fun they'd had. Then he walked out of the restaurant, down the block, and off into the beautiful Parisian sunset, perhaps to have a few little adventures of his own.

✍ QUIZ #34 ✍
Relationships

Decide what relationship the following pairs of words have to each other. If they have similar meanings, write "S" next to the pair of words. If they have opposite meanings, write "O" next to the words.

1. prodigal :: profuse
2. initial :: final
3. durable :: flimsy
4. prime :: main
5. pertinent :: relevant
6. garnish :: decoration
7. prevalent :: rare
8. cumbersome :: awkward
9. ironic :: literal
10. superstition :: fact

✍ QUIZ #35 ✎
Matching

Match each word on the right with the word on the left that has a similar meaning.

1. alternate
2. vice versa
3. stamina
4. reserve
5. incognito
6. speculate
7. compile
8. gross
9. warrant
10. complacent
11. synopsis
12. conclude
13. rehabilitate
14. anticipation
15. glutton

a. take turns
b. justify
c. in reverse
d. in disguise
e. endurance
f. large
g. think about
h. stored supply
i. put together
j. summary
k. overeater
l. expectation
m. decide
n. restore
o. self-satisfied

Cool Books
for Cool
Readers

Here's a list of books you may actually enjoy. You should know that reading is a surefire way to improve your vocabulary. But reading stories, novels, and poetry will help you do much more than improve your vocabulary. You can read for entertainment and for escape. You can also find out about the lives of young people like yourself who have grown up in places, cultures, or time periods different from your own. It's just like going on a trip, except that you don't have to worry about the driving.

The following list includes books recommended by teachers, librarians, and—most importantly—other young people. Check out the books in your library, and take home the ones that seem interesting to you. If you like a book, you can ask your parents, friends, teacher, or librarian to recommend others like it. But if you're not hooked after you've read a few chapters of a book, don't worry about it. Try something else. Nobody's grading you!

Adams, Douglas. *The Hitchhiker's Guide to the Galaxy.* (Science Fiction, Humor)

The first book in a series that includes *The Restaurant at the End of the Universe; Life, the Universe, and Everything; So Long, and Thanks for All the Fish,* and *Mostly Harmless.*

Alcott, Louisa May. *Little Women.* (Classic)

Block, Francesca Lia. *Weetzie Bat.* (Contemporary Fiction)

The first book in a series which has also been published in the volume *Dangerous Angels: The Weetzie Bat Books.*

Blume, Judy. *Tiger Eyes.* (Contemporary Fiction)

Blume has written many other popular books for young people, including *Blubber* and *Just as Long as We're Together.*

Burnett, Frances Hodgson. *The Secret Garden.* (Classic)

Carroll, Lewis. *Alice's Adventures in Wonderland.* (Classic)

Alice's adventures continue in *Through the Looking Glass.*

Creech, Sharon. *Walk Two Moons.* (Contemporary Fiction)

Creech has written other novels for young people, including *Chasing Redbird* and *The Wanderer.*

Cooper, Susan. *The Dark is Rising*. (Fantasy)

The first book in the series that includes *Greenwitch, The Grey King*, and *Silver on the Tree*. *Over Sea, Under Stone* is the prequel to this series.

Cormier, Robert. *The Chocolate War*. (Contemporary Fiction)

Dorris, Michael. *The Window*. (Contemporary Fiction)

Dorris also wrote about the main character of this novel, Rayona, in his debut novel, *Yellow Raft in Blue Water*.

Hinton, S. E. *The Outsiders* (Contemporary Fiction)

S. E. Hinton wrote this novel when she was a high school junior.

Fitzgerald, John. *The Great Brain*. (Historical Fiction)

The first book in a series that includes *More Adventures of the Great Brain, Me and My Little Brain, The Great Brain at the Academy, The Great Brain Reforms, The Return of the Great Brain*, and *The Great Brain Does it Again*.

George, Jean Craighead. *Julie of the Wolves*. (Contemporary Fiction)

George has written two other books about Julie, *Julie* and *Julie's Wolf Pack*, as well as *My Side of the Mountain*.

Hughes, Langston. *The Dream Keeper and Other Poems*. (Poetry)

Konigsburg, E. L. *From the Mixed-Up Files of Mrs. Basil E. Frankweiler*. (Contemporary Fiction)

Lee, Gus. *China Boy*. (Contemporary Fiction)

Also read the sequel, *Honor and Duty*.

LeGuin, Ursula. *The Wizard of Earthsea*. (Fantasy)

The first book in a series that includes *The Tombs of Atuan, The Farthest Shore*, and *Tehanu*.

L'Engle, Madeleine. *A Wrinkle in Time.* (Science Fiction, Contemporary Fiction)

L'Engle's series about the Murry family continues in *A Swiftly Tilting Planet, A Wind in the Door,* and *Many Waters.* Also try *A Ring of Endless Light,* a favorite in her series about Vicky Austin and her family.

Lewis, C. S. *The Lion, the Witch, and the Wardrobe.* (Classic, Fantasy)

The first book in the *Chronicles of Narnia.*

Montgomery, L. M. *Anne of Green Gables.* (Classic)

Anne Shirley's story continues in *Anne of Avonlea* and *Anne of the Island. Rainbow Valley* and *Rilla of Ingleside* are about her children.* Also try Montgomery's series about Emily Starr: *Emily of New Moon, Emily Climbs,* and *Emily's Quest.*

Myers, Walter Dean. *Hoops.* (Contemporary Fiction)

Myers has written dozens of books, including *Fallen Angels* and *Monster.*

Nye, Naomi Shihab. *Habibi.* (Contemporary Fiction)

Paterson, Katherine. *Bridge to Terabithia.* (Contemporary Fiction)

Other popular books by Paterson include *The Great Gilly Hopkins, The Master Puppeteer,* and *Jacob Have I Loved.*

Paulsen, Gary. *Nightjohn.* (Historical Fiction)

Paulsen has also written a sequel, *Sarny,* as well as many adventure books, including *Hatchet,* the first in a series.

Rawls, Wilson. *Where the Red Fern Grows.* (Classic)

Rowling, J. K. *Harry Potter and the Sorcerer's Stone.* (Fantasy)

The first book in a wildly popular series that includes *Harry Potter and the Chamber of Secrets, Harry Potter and the Prisoner of Azkaban,* and *Harry Potter and the Goblet of Fire.*

Salinger, J. D. *Catcher in the Rye.* (Classic)

de Saint-Exupery, Antoine. *The Little Prince.* (Classic, Fantasy)

Soto, Gary. *Baseball in April and Other Stories.* (Contemporary Fiction)

Also try Soto's novel *Crazy Weekend,* and *Neighborhood Odes,* a collection of his poetry.

Staples, Suzanne Fisher. *Shabanu: Daughter of the Wind.* (Contemporary Fiction)

Shabanu's story continues in *Haveli.*

Taylor, Mildred D. *Roll of Thunder, Hear My Cry.* (Historical Fiction)

Tolkien, J. R. R. *The Hobbit.* (Fantasy)

The prequel to the *Lord of the Rings* series, which includes *The Fellowship of the Ring, The Two Towers,* and *The Return of the King.*

Voigt, Cynthia. *Homecoming.* (Contemporary Fiction)

The first book about Dicey Tillerman's family and friends; others include *Dicey's Song, A Solitary Blue,* and *Seventeen Against the Dealer.*

Wojciechowska, Maia. *Shadow of a Bull.* (Fiction)

Yep, Laurence. *Dragonwings.* (Historical Fiction)

Also try Yep's other novels about Chinese-American life, *Child of the Owl* and *Dragon's Gate.*

Zindel, Paul. *The Pigman.* (Contemporary Fiction)

Glossary

ABDICATE (AB duh kayt) *v.* to give up the throne, or some other sort of right or power

King Edward VIII of England had to *abdicate* because he wanted to marry an American divorcée.

My social studies teacher made me *abdicate* my position as student council president in front of the whole class after she caught me cheating.

ABRUPT (uh BRUPT) *adj.* unexpected; quick

Susan was zooming down Pineapple Street on her bike, when a fallen tree in the middle of the road caused her to make an *abrupt* stop.

Aunt Gloria had been talking nonstop for at least an hour when I brought her endless yammering to an *abrupt* end by pouring ice water down her dress.

ABSTRACT (AB strakt) *adj.* not solid, like something you can touch or see, but more like an idea, thought, or theory

Our country's government is based on *abstract* concepts like "justice."

"Wishing me a happy birthday is fine," reasoned Whiny William, "but how about giving me something a little less *abstract*, like a five-pound box of taffy?"

ABSURD (ab SURD) *adj.* against common sense; ridiculous

The rumor that Jimi Hendrix was born with a guitar in his hand is *absurd*.

When I asked Gary why his cat Fluffy was shaved completely bald, he told me some *absurd* story about a dangerous gang of fur-cutting "cat whackers."

ACCLAIM (uh KLAYM) *v.* to show approval by cheering, praising, or applauding

I think Mr. Witherspoon will *acclaim* my latest book report as the greatest piece of writing he's seen since my essay on the joys of bubble wrap.

When the dinosaur movie *Jurassic Park* first opened in theaters, the special effects were *acclaimed* by both audiences and critics.

ACCOMPLICE (uh KAHM plis) *n.* someone who helps another person do something wrong or against the law

Police have arrested the jewel thief, but are still looking for his *accomplice*, who drove the getaway car.

ACQUAINTANCE (uh KWAYN tuhns) *n.* someone you know or have met, but who is not a close friend

Even though we have lived in this neighborhood for years, our neighbors seem more like *acquaintances* than friends.

Scott had several *acquaintances* at camp he was looking forward to seeing again.

ACUTE (uh KYOOT) *adj.* sharp; intense; keen

My sense of hearing is so *acute*, I can tell the ice cream man is coming from ten blocks away.

Jean's *acute* hunger pangs caused her to steal Cheezies from Bonnie.

ADAMANT (AD uh muhnt) *adj.* firm in one's position; stubborn

Tanya was *adamant* in her refusal to wear the frilly pink dress her grandmother picked out for her.

Lefty Lucas was an *adamant* supporter of the pitcher's rights in the pitcher/catcher baseball controversy of 1899.

AD-LIB (ad LIB) *v.* to make up something as you go along, without preparation

Wolfgang was supposed to play Ebenezer Scrooge in the play, but he forgot his lines and had to *ad-lib* the whole first act.

The president forgot to bring a copy of his speech to the rally, but he spoke so well that no one realized he was *ad-libbing*.

ADORN (uh DORN) *v.* to decorate

The queen *adorned* herself with diamond earrings and a ruby necklace.

He *adorned* himself with earrings, a boa, and a purple velvet hat.

ADVERSE (ad VURS) *adj.* not favorable; going against the direction you want

The snake oil I took to cure my baldness had some *adverse* effects—my toenails fell out and my face turned blue.

We were going to have a big barbeque out in the back yard, but *adverse* weather conditions forced us to stay inside and play Go Fish.

ADVOCATE (AD vuh kayt) *v.* to be in favor of

Charles won a landslide victory as student council president because he *advocated* longer lunch hours and a four-day school week.

Do you *advocate* using doggie biscuits as rewards when teaching puppies to do tricks?

AESTHETIC (es THET ik) *adj.* having to do with beauty or a sense of beauty

The reason Mario doesn't like the new race car was more *aesthetic* than practical; he just hates it because it's orange.

Even though the radish salad you made is *aesthetically* pleasing, I can't eat it because it tastes terrible.

AFFRONT (uh FRUNT) *v.* to insult or *n.* an insult

Bertha was *affronted* when Mary pointed at her feet and yelled, "Those things are as big as Buicks!"

When the waiter seated us in the kitchen, then ignored us all night, we took it as an *affront*.

AGENDA (uh JEN duh) *n.* a list of things to do

While we were traveling through Europe, our daily *agenda* was usually made up of shopping, visiting museums, and eating at famous restaurants.

Zach wanted to sleep all day Saturday, but his mother had a different *agenda* in mind. She made him wash the car, mow the lawn, and catch up on his homework.

AGHAST (uh GAST) *adj.* very shocked; horrified

Melissa was *aghast* at how much weight John had gained over the winter holidays.

Dad was *aghast* when he got an electricity bill for five hundred dollars.

AGITATE (AJ i tayt) *v.* to shake up; to upset someone or shake up their feelings

To make his famous "Flying Pickle Punch," Danny poured milk, cranberry juice, and pickle relish into his thermos, and *agitated* the mixture until it was completely blended.

We could tell the cat was *agitated* by the presence of two snarling German shepherds in the living room.

ALIAS (AY lee uhs) *n.* a fake name used to hide someone's identity

The train and bank robber Jesse James used the *alias* "Mr. Howard" in the small town where he and his wife lived.

Many criminals like to make up *aliases*, like "the Green Goblin" or "the Shah of Shoplifting," because their real names are too boring.

ALLAY (uh LAY) *v.* to lessen or calm

Carrie thought she could *allay* her little brother's fear of kindergarten by sitting in class with him every day.

Before aspirin was invented, people used to drink willow bark tea to *allay* headaches.

ALLEVIATE (uh LEE vee ayt) *v.* to relieve; lessen; allay

There are many medicines you can take to *alleviate* the symptoms of a cold, but the best cure is bed rest and daytime television.

In order to *alleviate* the stress she feels at work, Mom goes to the gym and lifts weights for a couple of hours before coming home at night.

ALLURE (uh LOOR) *v.* to attract or *n.* attraction.

The ads for the movie *Plot B from Outer Mongolia* were so *alluring* that I went to see it the day it opened.

Basil was supposed to be doing his algebra homework, but the *allure* of his Funboy handheld rocket-blaster game was too much for him to resist.

ALOOF (uh LOOF) *adj.* distant or removed, as if you were keeping yourself apart from things going on around you

We all tried to make friends with the French girl who moved to our neighborhood, but she acted so *aloof*—it was hard to talk to her.

Joey always gets crushes on girls who are *aloof*: the more they don't know he exists, the more he likes them.

ALTERNATE (AL tur nayt) *v.* to switch back and forth, or do in turns or *adj.* (AL tur nit) in place of another

Tallulah was such a great actress she could *alternate* between laughing and crying very easily.

I usually drive down Main Street to get to school, but I had to take an *alternate* route this morning because the St. Vitus Day parade was blocking that street.

AMATEUR (AM uh choor) *n.* a person who takes part in an activity for fun, not as a job or for money or *adj.* having to do with an amateur

Dr. Jensen has gotten so good at golf, even the professional players have a hard time believing he's an *amateur*.

After many discussions, the city council decided that an *amateur* bridge builders' competition was not such a good idea after all, and voted to hire a professional engineer for the job.

AMBASSADOR (am BAS uh dur) *n.* a high-ranking government official who represents his or her country in another country

Joseph Kennedy, President John F. Kennedy's father, was the American *ambassador* to England in the late 1930s.

People who have many years of experience at settling arguments and keeping peace between countries are usually the best *ambassadors*.

Note: An *embassy* (EM buh see) is the building where an ambassador and her staff work.

AMBIGUOUS (am BIG yoo us) *adj.* unclear in meaning

The directions we got from the man at the gas station were so *ambiguous* we wound up even more lost than we were before.

She wouldn't come out and say so, but I could tell Martha didn't like my new haircut because she was deliberately *ambiguous* when I asked her what she thought.

AMOROUS (AM ur us) *adj.* feeling love, or having to do with love

Michael almost died of embarrassment when his teacher read the class a very private, *amorous* note he was trying to pass to his girlfriend during class.

Of all the cartoon characters I have ever seen, there is none more romantic than Pepe le Pew, the *amorous* skunk who tries to seduce every female cat he meets.

ANARCHY (AN ar kee) *n.* the lack of any system of government or confusion caused by lack of authority or organization

During the French Revolution, the king and queen and many royal advisers were killed, which caused France to fall into a state of *anarchy*.

Although Russia has an official government, most people there feel they are living in *anarchy* because laws are not enforced and citizens must fend for themselves.

The substitute teacher left an orderly classroom to get a drink of water, and returned to find *anarchy:* spitballs were flying, desks were overturned, and loud screeching noises were coming from the back of the room.

ANCESTOR (AN ses tur) *n.* a family relation who came before you

Many scientists believe the *ancestors* of the Native Americans came to North America from Asia thousands of years ago.

The Jeffersons have lived in Virginia since their *ancestors* travelled here from England almost four hundred years ago.

ANESTHETIC (an is THET ik) *n.* a drug that causes the sense of touch to be numbed

The dentist injected an *anesthetic* into my gums before he started pulling out my teeth.

Polly wished that her mother had given her some kind of *anesthetic* before trying to dig the splinter out of her foot.

ANIMOSITY (an uh MOS i tee) *n.* open hatred

The *animosity* between the English and French, who were at war on and off throughout the Middle Ages, dates back to the Battle of Hastings in 1099.

There was much *animosity* between Bunny and Betty, even before Bunny set Betty's Barbies on fire.

ANTICIPATE (an TIS uh payt) *v.* to expect; see in advance; look forward to

Professor Zoltag did not *anticipate* such a large turnout for his slide-show presentation of "Those Amazing Leeches."

Note: The noun form of anticipate is *anticipation* (an tis uh PAY shun), which usually means happy expectation.

Sammy licked her lips in *anticipation* of the double scoop of Kandy Korn Krunch ice cream her grandfather was buying for her.

ANXIETY (ang ZYE uh tee) *n.* a feeling of worry about something

The thought of playing a tuba solo in front of the whole stadium caused Mort a great deal of *anxiety*.

I had a moment of *anxiety* before I jumped out of the airplane, but my parachute opened just fine.

APATHY (AP uh thee) *n.* lack of emotion or interest

Apathy is often blamed for low voter turnout.

When Marie Antoinette, queen of France, was told that her people were starving she supposedly said, "Let them eat cake." Her *apathy* in the face of such suffering sparked the French Revolution.

Note: The word *apathetic* (ap uh THET ik) is the adjective form of apathy.

It's hard to understand how people can be *apathetic* about pollution when their own drinking water might be filled with dangerous waste.

APPEASE (uh PEEZ) *v.* to calm or satisfy

The babysitter tried rocking, feeding, changing, and burping the crying baby, but nothing would *appease* him.

No amount of buried treasure would *appease* the pirate's lust for gold.

APPREHEND (ap ri HEND) *v.* to arrest or to understand

The police *apprehended* the person who was painting mustaches on all the city's statues.

Everyone thought the professor was brilliant, but few students could *apprehend* his theories.

APPRENTICE (uh PREN tis) *n.* a person who works closely with an expert in order to learn a trade or craft

The watchmaker's *apprentice* started out cutting glass for watch crystals, but is now learning how to make the tiny gears that run the hands.

Josh got a good job as an *apprentice* to a tailor.

APPROXIMATE (uh PROK suh mit) *adj.* nearly exact or *v.* (uh PROK suh mayt) to make a best guess

The famous diver plunged into the ocean from a cliff *approximately* six stories high.

The *approximate* speed of light is 186,000 miles per second.

Can you *approximate* the age of a person by listening to her voice?

APTITUDE (AP ti tood) *n.* a natural ability or quickness in learning

Keisha's *aptitude* for languages led her to become a translator at the United Nations.

Hakeem Olajuwon's *aptitude* for basketball helped him become a big star, even though he didn't start playing until he was seventeen.

AROUSE (uh ROWZ) *v.* to awaken or excite

Paul Revere *aroused* the sleeping minutemen by riding through town yelling, "The British are coming! The British are coming!"

We could tell the dog was *aroused* by the thought of getting leftover steak bones: he was drooling and whining.

ARRAY (uh RAY) *n.* an organized group or a very large number or *v.* to dress up

The *array* of studies linking smoking and lung cancer cannot be ignored.

When you graduate, you'll find an *array* of colleges to choose from.

The girls *arrayed* themselves in white dresses and floral wreaths for the spring dance.

ARTICULATE (ar TIK yuh lit) *adj.* spoken clearly, or able to speak clearly or *v.* (ar TIK yuh layt) to say or explain verbally.

The jury was impressed by the *articulate*, well-dressed lawyer.

Despite my *articulate* explanation of how space travel works, my grandmother still wouldn't believe that a man had walked on the moon.

Buster felt horrible about running over his sister's bicycle, but he couldn't seem to *articulate* his feelings to her.

ASCETIC (uh SET ik) *adj.* self-denying, rejecting the pleasures of life, often as a show of religious devotion

Cole never went to parties, never bought new clothes, never laughed, and insisted on sleeping next to the recyclables on the floor in the kitchen. For the son of a millionaire, he sure had *ascetic* tastes.

I paid the interior decorator thousands of dollars, and the only furniture he bought for my apartment was a single bed, a wooden stool, and a frying pan. He says the *ascetic* look is very popular in New York these days.

ASPIRE (uh SPYER) *v.* to desire strongly to achieve some goal

All her life, little Squeaky Fromme *aspired* to be a respected political activist.

"*Aspiring* to be wealthy is fine, Grover," said June, "but spending all your money on lottery tickets probably isn't the best way to achieve your goal."

Note: The noun form of aspire is *aspiration* (as puh RAY shun), and is usually used in the plural. He had *aspirations* of becoming a rocket scientist.

ASTONISH (uh STAHN ish) *v.* to fill with wonder, to amaze

Barney and Betty were *astonished* when their baby Bam Bam lifted the pet dinosaur over his head.

The Great Bardolini *astonishes* his audiences with magic tricks like escaping from handcuffs and pulling pigeons out of his hat.

ASTUTE (uh STOOT) *adj.* showing good judgment and quick understanding

Sherlock Holmes solved the crime by making the *astute* observation that the mud in the front yard was not the same color as the mud on the dead man's shoes.

Most people know that fortune tellers don't really see into the future. They are just very *astute* judges of character.

ATROCIOUS (uh TROH shus) *adj.* very evil; bad; cruel

More and more teenagers are being sent to adult prisons for *atrocious* crimes like murder and rape.

Note: The noun form of atrocious is *atrocity* (uh TRAHS suh tee).

After World War II, many Nazis were forced to stand trial for the *atrocities* they commited.

AUDACITY (aw DAS i tee) *n.* boldness, daring; sometimes a disrespectful boldness or outspokenness

Until that fateful day when the famous marshal Wyatt Earp rode into Tombstone, no one had the *audacity* to stand up to the fierce Clanton gang.

In the story "The Emperor's New Clothes," a little boy is the only one with the *audacity* to point out that the emperor is parading around town completely naked.

AUGMENT (awg MENT) *v.* to increase or make larger

The opera singer's weak voice had to be *augmented* with microphones.

Waiters rely on tips to *augment* their small salaries.

AUSTERE (aw STEER) *adj.* having a serious, stern appearance or personality; very plain and simple

Though life at the orphanage was *austere*, Little Orphan Annie kept her spirits up because she knew one day she would be rescued by an old bald millionaire who would spoil her rotten.

The children were a bit afraid of Miss Thumbscrew because her dark clothes and unsmiling face made her seem so *austere*.

AUTHORITARIAN (uh thor i TAYR ee uhn) *adj.* having to do with a system of government or power in which the freedoms of the people are threatened or taken away by one person or a small group of people who have all the control and who are not held responsible to the people (See *dictator*)

Under the former *authoritarian* government, the people of Haiti were often arrested, thrown in jail, or even killed with no explanation.

Even though it paid well and gave him a chance to travel, Elmer found life in the military too *authoritarian* for him.

AUTONOMOUS (aw TAHN uh mus) *adj.* self-ruling; existing independently

Many Native American reservations in the United States have *autonomous* governments, police forces, and legal systems.

"Now that you're out of college, in your own apartment, and are more or less *autonomous*," Mrs. March told her son, "it is time you learned to do your own laundry."

AVAIL (uh VAYL) *n.* use or advantage

Huey tried every argument he could think of to convince his parents, but to no *avail*—they refused to let him get his scalp tattooed.

"I hope you have more luck with this than I did," said Lucy. "I've been trying to untangle these necklaces for an hour, but to no *avail*."

AVERSION (uh VUR zhun) *n.* a strong dislike

While she was pregnant, Alicia had an *aversion* to chicken.

I have an *aversion* to men who wear pinky rings or berets.

AWKWARD (AWK wurd) *adj.* clumsy; embarrassing; hard to deal with

Ben has always been an *awkward* boy, constantly knocking things over and tripping over his own feet.

An *awkward* silence fell over the room when the chairman of the board got up to speak and everyone saw that his fly was unzipped.

BAFFLE (BAF uhl) *v.* to confuse

I am *baffled* by this jigsaw puzzle. All the pieces are the same color!

Your ability to stay up playing video games all night and still come to school in the morning is truly *baffling*.

BANAL (buh NAL) *adj.* humdrum; dull

"Aunt Flora," sighed Kit, "every time you come over, you make the same *banal* comment about how much I've grown. It's starting to bore me."

The parole board was not impressed by Stan's *banal* speech about how crime doesn't pay.

BANE (BAYN) *n.* a cause of ruin or harm

The unstoppable roaches were the *bane* of the otherwise spotless kitchen.

The actor's stuttering problem was the *bane* of his career.

BARRAGE (buh RAZH) *n.* an overwhelming quantity (usually having to do with words)

The president wasn't able to handle the *barrage* of questions from reporters.

Keanu didn't expect such a *barrage* of insults from the audience at his one-man show "I Am a Thespian Genius."

BASE (BAYS) *adj.* low; crude; without honor or decency

Some *base* thief stole the ring off the dead man's hand during the funeral.

"You will never win my heart with such *base* suggestions and bad language," said the young lady.

BECKON (BEK uhn) v. to signal with a nod or wave; to lure

Silently, the ghost *beckoned* Scrooge to look at his own tombstone.

Scarlett's smile seemed to *beckon* me to come over and introduce myself.

The beautiful cake practically *beckoned* me to dip my finger in the frosting.

BEHOLDEN (bi HOHL duhn) adj. indebted

The Clampetts didn't like to be *beholden* to anybody, but after their crops failed and they ran out of firewood, they finally accepted donations from the church.

Mike was *beholden* to his neighbors for taking care of his daughter while he was in the hospital.

BEHOOVE (bi HOOV) v. to be required or proper for; to be good or worthwhile for

It *behooves* young ladies and gentlemen not to use bad language unless they are very, very angry.

It would *behoove* you to learn to play the guitar early so you can get really good at it, join a band, and be extra-popular in college.

BELLIGERENT (buh LIJ ur unt) adj. warlike; fond of war or conflict; hostile

By repeatedly moving his troops near Iraq's border with Kuwait, Saddam Hussein showed that he had *belligerent* intentions.

As often happens when he's had too much pie for dessert, Hank became *belligerent* shortly after dinner.

BENEVOLENT (buh NEV uh lunt) adj. kind; full of goodness

The *benevolent* king opened his castle to people who needed shelter and gave bread to the hungry.

If it weren't for the *benevolent* donations from people across the country, Janet's parents wouldn't have been able to pay for the operation she needed.

BENIGN (buh NYNE) adj. harmless; gentle

The huge dog looked frightening, but the owner assured us it was completely *benign*.

Kurt went to the doctor because he had a weird lump on his neck, but it turned out to be *benign*.

BIGOT (BIG ut) *n.* a person who is intolerant of people who are different from him- or herself, in religion, race, or belief

While they were on their honeymoon in Acapulco, Jerry kept sneering at the language and customs of the Mexican people, and Midge realized she had married a *bigot*.

Note: The word *bigotry* (BIG uh tree) is used to describe the attitude or behavior of a bigot.

Since the Civil Rights movement of the 1960s, Americans have made great strides toward ending *bigotry* in our country; unfortunately, we still have a long way to go before all people are truly considered equal.

BINGE (BINJ) *n.* a period of excessive activity; a spree

Whenever Toby got depressed he would head for the mall and go on an all-day shopping *binge*.

To celebrate her birthday, Michelle treated herself and her friends to an all-you-can-eat ice cream *binge*.

BLACKMAIL (BLAK mayl) *n.* the act of forcing someone to give you money or other favors by threatening to expose some secret you know about him or her or *v.* to subject someone to blackmail

The butler immediately thought of *blackmail* when he found the box of pictures of Lord Periwinkle dressed as a ballerina.

The judge had been *blackmailed* for years by a woman he once had an affair with, but her demands for money finally got to be too much, and he confessed to his wife.

BLATANT (BLAYT unt) *adj.* totally obvious

Junior, who was standing with a slingshot in his hand, told a *blatant* lie about how his baby sister threw a rock through the neighbor's window.

In a *blatant* attempt to stay up past 11 o'clock, Tim made up a story about having to watch "Sports Center" for a grade in gym class.

BLEAK (BLEEK) *adj.* gloomy; dark and depressing

The cruise in the Caribbean was supposed to be fun, but bad weather made the whole week chilly and *bleak*.

The chances of Dad giving me thirty-five dollars for tickets to see Nine Inch Nails are *bleak*.

BLUNDER (BLUN dur) v. to make a big mistake or n. a big mistake

The lab assistant was worried the chemist would discover that his *blunder* in measuring the saline had ruined the year-long experiment.

David had almost convinced his mother to let him go to Jim's party when he *blundered* by telling her that Jim's parents were out of town.

BODE (BOHD) v. to be a sign of something to come

The rain clouds Steve and Debra saw during their drive to the campsite did not *bode* well for their trip.

The fact that Clark falls asleep whenever the lights are turned off does not *bode* well for his desire to be a film projectionist.

BOHEMIAN (bo HEE mee un) n. a person whose lifstyle is unusual or "on the edge"; often a person who has artistic or intellectual interests and doesn't share the same values as the rest of society or adj. having to do with the characteristics of a bohemian

The folks at the Glen Ridge apartment complex suspected that the people in 15J were a couple of *bohemians* when the woman who lived there told her neighbor she didn't believe in marriage, and the man said that organized religion was responsible for the greatest evils in history.

Clare tried to put up with her father's *bohemian* lifestyle, but the endless flow of poets and painters sleeping in the living room and the late-night shouting matches about philosophy got on her nerves so much that she went to live with her mother in Palm Beach.

Note: The word bohemian comes from Bohemia, a region in what used to be Czechoslovakia, and originally referred to the gypsies who lived there and their unusual lifestyle.

BOISTEROUS (BOY stur us) adj. rough; noisy and undisciplined

Minnie hated visiting her uncle's house because her *boisterous* cousins always wound up accidentally hurting her.

When the New York Rangers won the hockey championship, the *boisterous* fans throughout the city cheered and honked their horns.

BOVINE (BOH vyne) *adj.* cow-like; dull

Josh, who didn't have a clue what the teacher was talking about, just sat there with a *bovine* expression on his face.

BRISK (BRISK) *adj.* quick; lively; stimulating

I was practically falling asleep on my books, so I took a *brisk* walk around the block to wake myself up.

The old sea captain loved the salt air and the *brisk* wind off the waves.

BROACH (BROHCH) *v.* to bring something up for the first time

The police sergeant *broached* the theory that the fire that burned down the dry cleaners was started by someone with too much starch in his collar.

"I know in my heart that I must drop out of college to become a trapeze artist," confided Emo to his grandfather. "I just don't know how to *broach* the idea with my parents."

BUREAUCRACY (byoo ROK ruh see) *n.* an administration, as in a business or government, in which following strict rules and procedures becomes more important than the task at hand, and action becomes slow and complicated

All I wanted to do was transfer out of French class and into Spanish class, but the school's *bureaucracy* held up my request for a month.

After filling out six forms, waiting in five lines, and wasting three hours, I was beginning to believe that the company's *bureaucracy* was designed to keep people from returning items by wearing down their will to live.

CALIBER (KAL uh bur) *n.* quality or the diameter of a bullet

"No doubt about it," said the doctor, "the bullet that hit this clown's nose was a .22-*caliber*."

When I travel, I will only stay in hotels of the highest *caliber*.

Vinnie was the greatest quarterback in the state when he was in high school, but, as he quickly learned, the football players in college are of a much higher *caliber*.

CALLOUS (KAL us) *adj.* uncaring; unfeeling

Ike was finally getting used to his new hometown when his classmate's *callous* joke about his "funny accent" made him feel lonelier and more homesick than ever.

Old Man Jones is the richest landlord in town, and the most *callous*—he throws people out on the street even if they're only one day late on the rent.

CAMOUFLAGE (KAM uh flazh) *n.* the act of hiding yourself or your equipment, especially for military purposes, by making yourself blend in with the natural surroundings; a disguise or *v.* to hide or disguise through camouflage

Black and green face paint, palmetto leaves, and green uniforms are all part of the *camouflage* soldiers use when fighting in the jungle.

Brian tried to *camouflage* his magazines by putting notebook binders around them.

CANDID (KAN did) *adj.* open and straightforward

Mrs. Shields was determined to make her daughter a star, until a famous movie director was *candid* enough to tell her that acting was not one of her daughter's talents.

I would appreciate your *candid* opinion of my painting.

CANINE (KAY nyne) *adj.* of or like a dog, or having to do with dogs

The detective had an almost *canine* ability to track down criminals.

Suddenly, through the mist, a strange, *canine* creature, far too large to be a wolf, emerged and bared its bloody fangs to the unfortunate tourists.

CANNIBAL (KAN uh bul) *n.* a person who eats human flesh

The survivors of the airplane crash in the mountains became *cannibals* when they ate the dead passengers in order to survive.

Note: *Cannibalism* (KAN uh buh liz um) *n.* is the practice of being a cannibal.

The explorer was unaware that *cannibalism* was part of the tribe's tradition until he figured out he was to be the main course, not the guest of honor, at the feast that night.

CAPACITY (kuh PAS uh tee) *n.* the ability to hold or contain; ability to do something, mental ability

The stadium has a seating *capacity* of sixty thousand.

Elmo has no *capacity* for math of any kind.

The trunk of the car was filled to *capacity* with enough firewood to last all month.

CAPTIVE (KAP tiv) *n.* a prisoner or *adj.* held under restraint

Señorita Flores was held *captive* by the pirates after they attacked her father's ship and took her along with the family jewels.

The creative writing teacher tried to free the *captive* imaginations of her students.

CARCINOGEN (kar SIN uh jun) *n.* a substance that causes cancer

Chemicals called "nitrites," found in hot dogs and bacon, are known to be carcinogens.

Note: *Carcinogenic* (kar sin uh JIN ik) *adj.* means cancer-causing.

Nuclear radiation is highly *carcinogenic*.

CARICATURE (KAR i kuh choor) *n.* a picture of a person or thing in which certain features are exaggerated for comic effect

The *caricatures* of President Bush we see in the newspapers often make him look like a mouse with a big head.

CASUALTY (KAZH oo ul tee) *n.* a person killed or injured during an accident, or killed, injured, or taken prisoner during a military action

One reason the Vietnam War was so unpopular was that the number of civilian *casualties* was very high.

Officials say the number of *casualties* from last night's earthquake could be as high as three hundred.

CENSOR (SEN sur) *v.* to prevent from making public any material (such as movies, books, letters, or speech) that is considered harmful or *n.* a person who censors

In the early days of Hollywood, movie stars like Mae West and W.C. Fields were often in trouble with studio *censors* because their scripts were too "spicy."

In some situations, the military is allowed to *censor* soldiers' letters to protect national security.

CHAFE (CHAYF) *v.* to irritate by rubbing; to warm by rubbing

The criminal complained to the police that his handcuffs were *chafing* his wrists.

Bob's feet were bright red and stinging with cold after his day of sledding, so he *chafed* them with his hands.

CHAGRIN (shuh GRIN) *n.* a feeling of shame or regret

I was overcome with *chagrin* when I learned that my sister had been saving her allowance for months to buy me a Christmas present, and I hadn't even bothered to get her a card.

Much to my *chagrin*, I overslept the day I was supposed to take the SAT, which means I won't be able to apply to college this year.

CHAOS (KAY ahs) *n.* complete confusion and disorder

As the audience filed in for the opening night of the play, they had no idea that the backstage area was in a state of total *chaos*—the leading man was drunk and no one could find the severed head they needed for Act V.

We tried to find our friend Bruno at the Zombies concert, but since the club was in complete *chaos*, we didn't meet up until after the show.

CHIC (SHEEK) *adj.* stylish; fashionable

Shannon's new hairstyle is very *chic*.

Lance just got back from Paris with a French girlfriend and a *chic* wardrobe.

CIRCUMSTANCE (SUR cum stants) *n.* an event or occurrence

When the firemen arrived, they immediately determined the *circumstance* that led to the fire spreading.

CIVIL (SIV ul) *adj.* polite

If you can't be nice to your brother, at least be *civil*.

During the 1970s, relations between the United States and the Soviet Union were tense but *civil*.

CIVILIAN (si VIL yun) *n.* a person who is not in the military or *adj.* having to do with civilian life

After thirty years in the navy, the admiral was looking forward to being a *civilian* again.

I didn't recognize the major in his *civilian* clothes.

CLAMOR (KLA mur) *n.* loud, sustained noise or *v.* to make a clamor

The students were alarmed by the *clamor* coming from the teachers' lounge, where the faculty members were meeting.

After waiting for over an hour, the fans started *clamoring* for Ozzy Osbourne to come on stage and start his concert.

CLERGY (KLUR jee) *n.* a group of people whose job is to serve their religion (like priests, rabbis, or ministers)

In the Middle Ages it was common for sons of wealthy parents to enter the *clergy*, because priests could become very powerful.

In times of family trouble or confusion, many people turn to a member of the *clergy* for advice and comfort.

CLICHÉ (klee SHAY) *n.* an overused expression that has lost its original impact

After a crushing 72-0 defeat at the hands of the Paramus Pythons, the football coach told his team, "It's not whether you win or lose, it's how you play the game." The players didn't find much comfort in that *cliché*.

COMMEND (kuh MEND) *v.* to praise

The mayor *commended* the men and women for their work as volunteer firefighters.

COMPETENT (CAHM pi tuhnt) *adj.* capable; able to do something passably well

All the designers at La Boutique are *competent* dressmakers, but Sylvia is a fashion genius who can make anyone look good.

Mark is a *competent* drummer, and a pretty good bass player, but he really excels on the tuba.

COMPILE (kum PYLE) *v.* to put together into one set

Detective O'Reilly *compiled* a list of all the people who had entered or left the art museum on the day of the robbery.

The library managed to *compile* a complete collection of first-edition Ernest Hemingway novels.

COMPLACENT (kum PLAY sunt) *adj.* overly pleased with oneself

Ted Kennedy has been a senator for so long that he seems *complacent* even during election years.

Sportswriters claimed that the Cincinnati Bengals were able to beat Dallas because winning the Super Bowl two years in a row had made the Cowboys *complacent*.

COMPLIANCE (kum PLY uns) *n.* acting according to a rule, order, or demand

Compliance with a strict moral code is required of all students at Brigham Young University.

Note: The verb form of compliance is *comply* (kum PLY).

"Unless the city *complies* with my demands for a monster truck and a case of soda pop," cried the former city hall intern, "I will tell the press all about the mayor's plan to embezzle money from the city."

COMPREHEND (com pree HEND) *v.* to understand

Darius was speaking so quickly and waving his arms around so wildly, it was impossible to *comprehend* what he was trying to say.

Most Americans have read our country's constitution, but many do not truly *comprehend* it.

COMRADE (KOM rad) *n.* a friend who shares your activities

Dad went all out and bought imported beer and cashew nuts because his old army *comrades* were coming over.

CONCEAL (kun SEEL) *v.* to hide

Frank was jealous when he saw Josephine with her new boyfriend at the party, but he *concealed* his true feeling by cracking jokes and flirting with every girl he met.

The diamonds were *concealed* in a cooler full of ice.

CONCEIT (kun SEET) *n.* vanity; an exaggerated sense of your own worth, importance, or abilities

"Our band leader's *conceit* knows no limits," complained Ruth. "He criticizes us all the time, but he can't even play one instrument."

Note: *Conceited* (kun SEE tid) is the adjective form of conceit.

Nancy was beautiful and rich, but she was so *conceited* that no one could stand to be with her for more than a couple of hours.

CONCILIATORY (kun SIL ee uh tor ee) *adj.* tending to smooth over differences and calm hostilities

The little league coach used his most *conciliatory* tone of voice to stop the fight between the pitcher and the catcher.

After his son dropped out of medical school to become a clown, Mr. Hobnob refused to have any contact with him, but at the family reunion, he took a more *conciliatory* attitude and actually let his son make a balloon dog for him.

CONCLUDE (kun KLOOD) v. to bring to an end; to determine through reasoning

Every episode of the old television show "The Beverly Hillbillies" *concluded* with the words, "ya'll come back now, y'hear?"

After a thorough examination of the victim, Quincy *concluded* that a blow to the head with a blunt instrument was the cause of death.

CONDENSE (kun DENS) v. to shorten (usually referring to a book or story) or to make smaller or more concentrated

The author had to *condense* her short story so it could be published in the magazine.

The aluminum cans we brought to the recycling center were sent through the crushing machine and *condensed* to a fraction of their original size.

CONDONE (kun DOHN) v. to forgive or ignore

The police chief was accused of *condoning* the fact that his officers were taking bribes from local businesses.

"I may *condone* your talking in class and your tardiness," said the teacher, "but cheating is something I will never tolerate."

CONSPICUOUS (kun SPIK yoo us) adj. easily noticed; obvious

William was trying to spy on his sister at the fair, but by dressing all in black and wearing sunglasses, even though it was night, he made himself *conspicuous*.

The undercover cop was a bit *conspicuous* because everyone could see he had a gun stuffed down his pants.

CONSPIRACY (kun SPIR uh see) n. a secret plan or the act of creating a secret plan to do something illegal

Many people believe that Lee Harvey Oswald, the man accused of killing President John F. Kennedy, was part of a huge communist *conspiracy*.

The police discovered the doctor and his patients were involved in a *conspiracy* to get money from insurance companies by sending in claims for fake illnesses.

CONTAMINATE (kun TAM uh nayt) v. to pollute or make unclean

The Mississippi River has been *contaminated* for years by industries that dump waste into its waters.

The air around Bhopal, India, was *contaminated* by an accident at a nearby chemical plant.

CONTEMPLATE (KON tum playt) *v.* to think about carefully; to ponder

Raoul enjoyed sitting on the beach, *contemplating* the meaning of life.

When you hear about someone dying of a heart attack at the age of twenty-five, it makes you *contemplate* your own lifestyle and health.

CONTEMPT (kun TEMPT) *n.* scorn; a feeling you have for anything that is worthless, disgraceful, low

After she discovered that her boyfriend had lied to her about owning a Corvette, Melinda felt nothing but *contempt* for him.

Benedict Arnold, a traitor to the American Revolution, has been an object of *contempt* for over 200 years.

CONTENT (kun TENT) *adj.* happy, satisfied, or *n.* a feeling of happiness

Whiskers the cat was *content* just to lie in the patch of sun under the window for hours.

Grandpa told us he had the swimming pool put in his backyard so we could "splash around to our hearts' *content*."

CONVALESCE (kahn vuh LES) *v.* to get well after an illness

After a dangerous case of pneumonia last winter, Grandmother went to a warm beach resort to *convalesce*. She's been there ever since.

CONVENIENT (kun VEEN yunt) *adj.* easy to use; close by; well-suited to a particular purpose

Babs never used to eat ice cream, but since Milky Miracles opened a store right next to her office, it's just too *convenient* to pass up.

My friend Timmy says he doesn't recycle his bottles, cans, and newspapers because sorting his trash and taking it to the recycling center is not as *convenient* as just throwing everything into one bag and leaving it on the curb for the garbage collectors.

CORPSE (KORPS) *n.* a dead, usually human, body

The medical student fainted when the doctor began to dissect the *corpse*.

COUNTERFEIT (KOWN tur fit) *adj.* fake, made to look real in order to fool people or *v.* to fake or *n.* a fake

Paula was arrested for giving a *counterfeit* twenty dollar bill to the A & P supermarket.

The art dealer gave us a certificate that proved the painting we bought was a real Da Vinci, but both the certificate and the painting turned out to be *counterfeits.*

The beautiful widow *counterfeited* grief over the death of her very rich, very old husband, but the rest of the family knew she didn't really care.

COUP D'ETAT (koo day TAH) *n.* the overthrow of a government

Note: This phrase is often shortened to *coup* (KOO), which means either coup d'état or a successful, strong action.

The Cambodian government of Prince Sihanouk was overthrown in a bloody *coup d'état.*

Putting a person on the moon before the Soviets was seen as a major scientific *coup* for the Americans.

COVET (KUV it) *v.* to crave, often to crave something someone else has

The Academy Award is an honor *coveted* by most Hollywood actors.

CRISIS (KRYE sis) *n.* a dangerous or difficult event or situation, a turning point

The rash of burglaries, muggings, and assaults forced the mayor to admit that the downtown area was in a state of *crisis.*

Americans felt a *crisis* of faith in their government during the Watergate scandal, in which President Nixon was accused of ordering a burglary.

The American colonists had been unhappy for a long time with the taxes the British government was forcing them to pay, but the tea tax brought the situation to a *crisis,* and started talk of a revolution.

CULPRIT (KUL prit) *n.* a person guilty of a crime or fault

"We suspect our school mascot was kidnapped by students from our rival high school," announced the principal, "but we haven't yet found the *culprits.*"

The FBI said it was close to nabbing the main *culprit* in the counterfeiting ring that had made over two million dollars in fake bills.

CULT (KULT) *n.* a system of religion; a religious group that has an unusual lifestyle and set of beliefs, usually led by one person or a small group of people who demand the complete obedience of the followers; a strong devotion to something

Thousands of years ago, most people were part of nature-worshiping *cults* that paid tribute to the gods and goddesses of trees, water, and weather.

The leaders of religious *cults* are often very passionate and convincing, but are sometimes dangerous because they can use their influence to force their followers to do whatever they want.

The *cult* of physical perfection in the United States has caused many young girls and boys to think they need plastic surgery in order to be attractive.

CUMBERSOME (KUM bur sum) *adj.* hard to carry, bear, or manage

The luggage is too *cumbersome* for you to handle alone.

Hans complained that the Lincoln Town Car was too *cumbersome* for driving in the narrow German streets.

CURSORY (KUR suh ree) *adj.* quick and not thorough

The teacher got so behind in his grading, he only had time to give each paper a *cursory* reading.

It only took a *cursory* look under the hood for the mechanic to tell that the car had serious engine trouble.

CURT (KURT) *adj.* brief, sometimes rudely brief, in speech or action

Marvin gave his dinner guests a *curt* greeting, then went back to the den to watch the end of the hockey game.

On her last day of work, Claudia said a few *curt* good-byes, then hurried out of the building.

CYNIC (SIN ik) *n.* a person who believes that most people are selfish and no good

Harvey showed what a *cynic* he was when he commented that profits from the church bake sale would probaby be used to pay for the minister's vacation in the Bahamas.

Note: The adjective form of cynic is *cynical* (SIN i kul), which means distrustful.

Voters are *cynical* when the politicians they elect do not keep their campaign promises.

DABBLE (DAB ul) *v.* to splash around in water; to do some activity without serious intentions

The grown ups lounged on the lawn furniture while the kids *dabbled* in the kiddie pool.

"Before I became an accountant I *dabbled* in music," sighed Herb. "I was even in a band during one semester in college."

DEBACLE (di BAH kul) *n.* a disaster or downfall

The movie *Ishtar* was a *debacle* for the studio—it went millions of dollars over budget and was a flop in the theaters.

Springfield's production of the ballet *Swan Lake* was the worst *debacle* ever to hit the theaters: dancers tripped over each other, the set fell down, and the orchestra stopped playing twenty minutes into the show.

DEBAUCHERY (di BAW chuh ree) *n.* overindulgence in food, drink, or other pleasures

Nowadays, people do not tolerate *debauchery* in their public officials. They want politicians who are faithful to their spouses and don't stay out partying all night.

The Roman emperors led lifestyles of great *debauchery*, spending their days and nights feasting and drinking wine.

DEBRIS (duh BREE) *n.* the broken pieces of something that has been destroyed

Construction workers spent weeks clearing the *debris* of the condemned building after it was demolished.

The high winds from the hurricane scattered *debris* up and down the Florida coastline.

DECAPITATE (dee KAP i tayt) *v.* to cut the head off

Henry VIII, the King of England, accused his wife of treason and had her *decapitated*.

The townspeople were hopping mad when they found out that the statue of their founding father had been *decapitated* by some hoodlum.

DECEASED (di SEEST) *adj.* dead or *n.* the dead person or people

The travelling cat food salesman was unaware that the Smithereens' pet was *deceased*. If he had known, he wouldn't have knocked on the door and asked, "Is your cat as healthy as he could be?"

The church was filled with the friends and family of the *deceased*.

DECOY (DEE koy) *n.* person or thing used to lure someone into a trap

Police knew mobster Bruce "Buzzsaw" Parker was a big Madonna fan, so they hired her to act as a *decoy*, knowing he would try to meet her when his men told him she was in his favorite restaurant.

DEEM (DEEM) *v.* to hold as opinion, believe

Karen *deemed* Shelly's inability to throw a softball more than twenty feet a major problem for a third baseman.

I will do whatever the doctor *deems* necessary to recover from my flu.

Betty's short black dress was *deemed* inappropriate for the afternoon tea party at her great aunt's house.

DEFECT (DEE fekt) *n.* a flaw or *v.* (di FEKT) to abandon one country to take refuge in or become a citizen of another

The clothes the store sold had minor *defects*, but no one cared because they were so inexpensive.

Margaret's eyes had rare *defects* that made it impossible for her to cry.

Many famous citizens of the Soviet Union *defected* to the United States during the Cold War.

DEFERENCE (DEF ur uns) *n.* respectful submission to another person's wishes; respectful politeness

In *deference* to the guest of honor, who was a vegetarian, no meat was served at the party.

The Vargas family spoke English with each other most of the time, but at dinner they spoke only in Spanish, out of *deference* to their grandmother, who didn't understand English.

Cal almost never wore anything but ripped jeans and tank tops, but he would put on a shirt and tie went he visited home, in *deference* to his mother.

DEGRADE (di GRAYD) *v.* to disgrace or dishonor

Carmen was so stuck up, she wouldn't pump her own gas because she said it *degraded* her.

You only *degrade* yourself by spreading hurtful gossip about other people.

Pierre found it *degrading* to work behind a deli counter after he had been head chef at *Le Chat Pendu,* a fancy French restaurant.

DEJECTION (di JEK shun) *n.* depression, the condition of being in low spirits

The girls couldn't hide their *dejection* after failing to make the cheerleading squad.

DELIBERATE (duh LIB ur ut) *adj.* on purpose or *v.* (duh LIB uh rayt) to consider or think carefully about

Homer made a *deliberate* attempt to knock over the soda can castle I spent all day building.

The jury needed only ten minutes to *deliberate* before deciding that Sister Mary Margaret was not guilty of armed robbery.

Grant spent three days *deliberating* over whether sky blue or robin's-egg blue was a better color for his bedroom walls.

DELIRIOUS (di LIR ee us) *adj.* uncontrollably excited

Miss Burkina Faso was so *delirious* when she won the Miss World pageant, she ran around kissing the other 278 contestants, blew 500 kisses to her friends in Ouagadougou, and completely forgot to do the usual walk-and-wave down the ramp.

DENOUNCE (di NOWNS) *v.* to condemn openly or publicly

Prince Sergei Radzievsky was *denounced* by the members of high society when it was discovered that he was not actually heir to the Polish throne.

The principal called an assembly to *denounce* the use of violence in settling fights between students.

DENSE (DENS) *adj.* thick; crowded together

The cat had a hard time creeping through the tall, *dense* weeds around the house.

Because the population is so *dense,* pollution is usually worse in big cities.

DEPLETE (di PLEET) v. to use up or empty

By driving cars everywhere instead of walking or biking, we are *depleting* our supplies of gas and oil.

Irving developed a gambling habit late in life, and in two short years he managed to *deplete* the life savings he had spent fifty years accumulating.

DEPRAVITY (di PRAV uh tee) n. evilness; complete moral corruption

After he was fired as the minister at First Baptist, Reverend Foster just gave up on life—and the afterlife. His *depravity* knew no limits; there was not a sin he didn't commit.

When the teacher was arrested on armed robbery charges, the public was shocked at her *depravity*.

DERIDE (di RYED) v. to jeer at; to tease or laugh at in a mean way

The cruel students *derided* Jill for stuttering during her book report presentation.

Duke *derided* the French custom of kissing both cheeks as a form of greeting. He thought it was "sissified."

DESCENT (di SENT) n. the act of coming down; family background

Lillian found it easy to climb up Eagle Peak, but the *descent* was difficult and frightening.

My friend Ali O'Malley is of Iranian and Irish *descent*—his mother is from Tehran and his father is from Tipperary.

DESPICABLE (DES pik uh bul) adj. deserving contempt

The landlord's attempt to force tenants out of the apartment building by turning off the heat in the middle of January was *despicable*.

DETER (di TER) v. to prevent someone from doing something, usually through fear or doubt

Farmer Fred put up an electrified fence to *deter* cattle from wandering away.

When people go on vacation, they try to *deter* theft by using a device that turns the lights and the television on and off so it will look as though they are at home.

DETEST (di TEST) *v.* to hate

"I absolutely *detest* these fancy dinner parties," complained Mr. Vanderhooven. "There's never any ketchup for my steak!"

DEVOUR (di VOWR) *v.* to eat something completely and greedily

Kristin *devoured* the entire lasagna right out of the pan while her friends were in the kitchen looking for plates and forks.

After soccer practice, the boys and girls are so hungry they *devour* everything their parents give them at dinner, including the cauliflower.

DIALECT (DYE uh lekt) *n.* a variation in a language spoken in a certain location or by a certain group of people; a dialect has its own pronunciations for words and uses for words

In the *dialect* spoken in the South, people say they are "fixin' to do something" to mean they are about to do something.

Connor spoke in an Irish *dialect* I found hard to understand.

DICTATOR (DIK tay tur) *n.* an absolute ruler, especially one in control of a country without the free consent of the people

Adolf Hitler was a German *dictator* from 1934 to 1945, and leader of a depraved movement to kill off everyone he decided was "inferior" to the so-called "true Germans."

Gail was a great reporter for the school newspaper, but when she became editor-in-chief, the power must have gone to her head because she started acting like some kind of *dictator*—she even renamed the paper "Gail's Gazette."

DIDACTIC (dye DAK tik) *adj.* used for teaching purposes; inclined to teach too much, or in a preachy way

Aesop's fables are *didactic* stories that use animals as characters, but are meant to demonstrate human faults like vanity and greed.

"Whenever we go to an art museum, Ted becomes so *didactic*!" said Sid. "He gives a whole art history lecture on every painting and sculpture we pass, and bothers everyone around him."

DIGNITARY (DIG ni ter ee) *n.* a high-ranking person

The ambassador threw a big party for all the foreign *dignitaries* who had come to the conference.

DIGNITY (DIG ni tee) *n.* noble, honorable character; formal, noble action or speech

While the royal family has exposed all sorts of embarrassing secrets, Queen Elizabeth has tried to preserve the *dignity* of the British throne.

The governor took her defeat in the election with great *dignity*, and made a speech urging everyone to support the new administration.

DIGRESS (dye GRES) *v.* to stray from the main topic

Grandpa was trying to tell us about his cruise in the Carribean, but he kept *digressing* to talk about his days in the navy.

I was reading an article on the rise of tourism in Australia, but it was filled with *digressions* on the mating rituals of kangaroos and the eating habits of koalas, so I got bored and stopped reading.

DILEMMA (di LEM uh) *n.* a situation that forces a person to choose between two equally bad options

Norm was faced with a *dilemma*: if he went on strike with the other workers, he could lose his job, but if he didn't go on strike, the owner of the plant would probably never do anything about the dangerous working conditions.

When the teacher accused him of stealing hall passes from her desk, Lyle was faced with the *dilemma* of accepting the blame and being expelled, or telling her that he saw Rocky take them and being beaten up by Rocky and his gang after school.

DILIGENT (DIL uh junt) *adj.* painstaking; constant in effort to achieve something; hardworking

Vince realized that even after twelve years of *diligent* practice on the parallel bars, he could never hope to win an Olympic gold medal in that event.

Professor Hardihar rewarded her assistant's *diligent* research and record-keeping by giving him the weekend off.

DISCERNMENT (di SURN munt) *n.* sharpness of judgment and understanding

When Uma's fifth husband turned out to be a thief, just like the other four, her mother urged her to use a little more *discernment* the next time she decided to get married.

The basketball scout from Duke University showed great *discernment* in recruiting talented players.

DISCIPLINE (DIS uh plin) *n.* a branch of learning

History and art can be seen as related *disciplines* because most major events and advances in civilization are interpreted or reflected through art.

"I'm afraid I don't have an opinion on ancient Egyptian burial rites," said the physics professor. "My knowledge is limited to one *discipline*."

DISCLOSE (dis KLOHZ) *v.* to make known or to reveal

My mother refused to *disclose* the contents of any of the boxes under the Christmas tree.

It is considered impolite to ask a woman to *disclose* her age or weight, unless, of course, you work for the Department of Motor Vehicles.

DISCORD (DIS kord) *n.* disagreement; lack of harmony between people or things

The Barrett family house was filled with *discord* because no one could agree on where they should go for summer vacation.

It is hoped that the new peace agreement will end the decades of *discord* that existed between the Israelis and Palestinians.

DISCRIMINATE (di SKRIM uh nayt) *v.* to tell the difference between or to show prejudice

The skilled artist was able to *discriminate* between very similar shades of color.

When deciding how to sentence a criminal, a judge must *discriminate* different levels of guilt.

Some flight attendants have accused the airlines they work for of *discriminating* against people who are overweight.

DISDAIN (dis DAYN) *n.* a feeling of contempt for anything considered beneath oneself; scorn

The princess agreed to kiss the frog in order to get her golden ball back, but she did it with *disdain*.

Bridget gave me a look of *disdain* when I told her I'd give her five dollars if she'd let me copy her homework.

DISORIENT (dis OR ee ent) *v.* to confuse or cause to lose one's bearings

Right after he wakes up from a nap, Andrew is usually so *disoriented* that he bumps into things and isn't sure what time it is or where he is.

The long subway ride got me so *disoriented* that when I got up to the street I felt completely lost.

DISPARAGE (di SPAR ij) *v.* to try to discredit something or lower its importance; to belittle or speak of something as inferior

Environmental activists *disparage* the attempts of big business to avoid antipollution laws.

Ingrid is such a jealous person, she tries to *disparage* everyone else's work to make herself feel better about her own.

DISPARATE (DIS pur it) *adj.* completely different

When the cook found out that people from India, Ireland, Italy, and Israel were coming to the dinner, she was concerned that she wouldn't be able to come up with a menu to please their *disparate* tastes.

It's unusual to find someone with the *disparate* experiences of metal welding, professional balloon sculpting, and accounting on his or her resume.

DISPASSIONATE (dis PASH uh nit) *adj.* not affected by emotions

Child custody cases are difficult to decide, even for the most *dispassionate* judge.

The reporter wrote a *dispassionate* story about the mass murderer's gruesome death in the electric chair.

DISREGARD (dis ri GARD) *v.* to ignore or pay no attention to

If you choose to *disregard* the posted speed limit, you should be prepared to get a speeding ticket.

We *disregarded* the flash flood warning and wound up having to leave our car and run for high land as the street filled with water.

DISSENT (di SENT) *n.* disagreement

Until the bombing of Pearl Harbor, there was *dissent* in America over becoming involved in the war with Japan.

The demonstrators held up signs expressing their *dissent* with the government's civil rights policy.

DIVERSE (dye VERS) *adj.* different; of various kinds

The best way to stay healthy is to get plenty of exercise and make sure your diet is made up of *diverse* foods.

My taste in music is *diverse*; I like everything from country to rock to classical.

DOGMATIC (dog MAT ik) *adj.* characterized by holding to certain beliefs or principles in an arrogant or stubborn way

Pat spent so much of her time working for women's rights that she became rather *dogmatic* about it, and started calling all men sexist.

Copernicus, a Polish astronomer of the 1500s, believed the earth revolved around the sun, but his theory upset and enraged the *dogmatic* priests who had believed for hundreds of years that it was the other way around.

DOMAIN (doh MAYN) *n.* an area of control or authority; a field in which someone is skilled

The count's *domain* stretched from the Transylvanian mountains to the shores of Lake Blud.

"You're in luck!" cried Ernie the fix-it man. "Broken vacuum cleaners are in my *domain*."

DON (DON) *v.* to put on (clothes)

Cowboy Jake *donned* his hat and vest, kissed Maggie good-bye, and rode off into the sunset.

DORMITORY (DOR mi tor ee) *n.* a residence hall with living facilities for many people

Oliver stayed in the *dormitory* on campus his first year in college, but moved to an apartment off-campus when he got tired of having to walk all the way down the hall to use the bathroom.

DOTE (DOHT) *v.* to show excessive love or fondness

We tried to tell Willie that he was making a fool of himself by *doting* on Samantha so much, but he just shrugged and went off to buy her another dozen roses.

Lisa absolutely *doted* on her pony, Princess.

DUB (DUB) *v.* to make someone a knight by tapping him on the shoulder with a sword; to nickname

Sir Laurence Olivier was *dubbed* by Queen Elizabeth II.

The dog was named Theodore, but Ralph *dubbed* him "Hog" because of his fondness for bacon.

DUBIOUS (DOO bee us) *adj.* doubtful; inclined to doubt; questionable

Dad seemed *dubious* about letting me go on the field trip to the state prison.

Arthur was excited about his investment in Here Today Realty—he was sure he would triple his money in just a few months—but the whole set-up looked *dubious* to me.

DUPE (DOOP) *v.* to fool or trick or *n.* someone who is tricked

Thousands of people were *duped* into buying "gravity boots" because the ads promised that by hanging themselves upside down for an hour a day they could stop the aging process.

Carl was just a *dupe* the bank robbers used to take the fall for committing the crime.

DUPLICATE (DOO pli kayt) *v.* to make a copy of; to do again or repeat

The artist was asked to *duplicate* Leonardo Da Vinci's masterpiece, "La Gioconda."

Scientists have to *duplicate* their experiments in order to make sure their results are accurate.

DURABLE (DOOR uh bul) *adj.* sturdy; tough; lasting

"I just can't find jeans that are *durable* enough for Tony," whined Mrs. Vance. "He wears them out as fast as I can buy them."

The doghouse Dad built wasn't the most stylish structure, but it was *durable* enough to withstand ten years of rain, heat, and snow.

DUSK (DUSK) *n.* that point in the evening just before dark, when the sky has almost gone black; near darkness

Mom told us to be home by *dusk.*

I could barely see the raccoon in the forest at *dusk.*

EARMARK (EER mark) *v.* to set aside for a certain purpose

The funds raised by the bake sale were *earmarked* for new uniforms for the school band.

Lyle had *earmarked* the money he won in the lottery for a down payment on a private jet.

EARNEST (UR nist) *adj.* showing seriousness and sincerity

Mark showed an *earnest* desire to patch things up with his brother, who hadn't spoken to him in five years.

The kids made an *earnest* attempt to train the stray dog, but finally had to admit that it would never make a good pet.

EAVESDROP (EEVS drop) *v.* to listen secretly to a private conversation

Tommy hid in the closet to *eavesdrop* on the conversation his parents were having about what to get him for his birthday.

Ilsa caught her sister with her ear against the bathroom wall, *eavesdropping* on the telephone conversation their brother was having in the next room.

EBB (EB) *v.* to fade away; to flow back

Only after the high tides from the storm began to *ebb* were we able to figure out how much damage had been caused.

As the day dragged on and his strength began to *ebb,* the marathon runner began to wonder what point there was in running twenty-six miles when he had a perfectly good car.

ECCENTRIC (ek SEN trik) *adj.* odd or out of the ordinary in appearance, behavior, or action

Mr. Farmer was pretty normal except for his *eccentric* habit of dressing in a long black robe and wizard's hat, and riding his motorcyle through town early in the morning.

We all complimented the hat Susie had made out of staples and empty toilet paper rolls, but in truth we thought it was kind of *eccentric.*

ECSTASY (EK stuh see) *n.* overwhelming joy

Oliver was in *ecstasy* over the fancy dessert selection at the restaurant.

The Arizona Diamondbacks were in *ecstasy* after beating the New York Yankees in the ninth inning of game 7 of the World Series.

Note: The adjective form of ecstasy is *ecstatic* (ek STAT ik).

Cole was *ecstatic* when he found out that he had passed chemistry.

EGO (EE go) *n.* awareness of yourself as an independent person; self-confidence, sometimes to the point of arrogance

Babies are very attached to their mothers because they have not yet developed *egos*.

The little boy hurt my *ego* by saying my new hairdo made me look like Ronald McDonald.

Even though everyone thinks he's a brilliant piano teacher, I had to quit taking lessons from Mr. Legato because his *ego* was so huge he would only let me play music he had written himself.

ELOQUENT (EL o kwent) *adj.* having the power of forceful, persuasive, or elegant speech or writing; marked by persuasive or masterful expression

Martin Luther King, Jr. was an *eloquent* leader in the civil rights movement who gained support for his cause through his speeches and actions.

Abraham Lincoln's Gettysburg Address, given to honor the soldiers who died in the Battle of Gettysburg, is one of the most *eloquent* speeches in American history.

ELUDE (ee LOOD) *v.* to escape or avoid through skill or cunning; to escape the understanding

The spy *eluded* his attackers by cleverly disguising himself as former British Prime Minister Maragaret Thatcher.

Yvette was winking and gesturing at her father to let him know he had a long strip of toilet paper stuck to his shoe, but he just stared at her and said, "I'm afraid the meaning of all that head jerking *eludes* me, dear."

Elmer *eluded* his creditors by always answering the phone with a thick Hungarian accent and pretending not to understand English.

EMBARGO (em BAR go) *n.* an order by a government forbidding the shipment of certain goods or all goods to another country

The trade *embargo* on the country is ruining the economy and causing the common people to go without food and medicine, while the upper class still lives in high style.

In the 1980s, many countries used trade *embargos* on South Africa to compel that country to give up its racist practices.

EMERGE (i MURJ) *v.* to rise up (from under water, usually); to come forth or come into existence

The divers finally *emerged* from the dark waters after several hours of looking for the sunken treasure supposedly left by the pirate known as "Swamp Rat."

Eleanor Roosevelt *emerged* as a strong political force in her own right.

After repeated questioning and threats, the truth about how all the pots got covered in melted plastic began to *emerge*.

ENDORSE (en DORS) *v.* to give approval or support

The school board does not *endorse* the use of physical punishment.

Celebrities are often used to *endorse* products in television commercials.

ENGROSS (en GROHS) *v.* to absorb the complete attention of

At first, Marlon didn't want to watch the nature show about the insect world, but he was soon *engrossed* by the close-ups of a spider sucking the blood out of a fly.

Valerie was so *engrossed* by the detective novel she was reading, she didn't even notice that the kids she was supposed to be babysitting were setting fire to the curtains.

ENIGMA (i NIG muh) *n.* a person or occurence that is puzzling or hard to explain

The disappearance of Amelia Earhart's airplane over the Pacific Ocean has remained an *enigma* for almost sixty years.

Mr. Jones is a bit of an *enigma*—either he doesn't remember his past, or he refuses to tell any of us about it.

How the ancient monument of Stonehenge was made is an *enigma*.

ENSUE (en SOO) v. to come after; to result from

When the manager told the crowd that supermodel Cindy Crawford would not be appearing at the bookstore to sign her latest calendar, a riot *ensued*.

"We must not let anger *ensue* from our defeat," said the coach. "We must be good sports."

EN ROUTE (ahn ROOT) adv. on the way

The car ran out of gas *en route* to the fishing hole.

We'll pick up some chips and ice cream *en route* to the party.

ENVY (EN vee) n. jealousy over someone else's possessions or accomplishments or v. to be jealous of someone else's possessions or accomplishments

When I saw Anne's beautiful new car I was filled with *envy*.

I don't *envy* famous people because everybody wants something from them and they can't go anywhere without being chased by photographers.

EPHEMERAL (i FEM ur ul) adj. lasting a very short time

Bilbo enjoyed the *ephemeral* beauty of his garden at twilight.

For Ned, Yolanda was nothing but an *ephemeral* attraction, a short and sweet summer romance—but Yolanda was convinced that Ned was the man she would marry.

EQUILIBRIUM (ee kwuh LIB ree um) n. balance or stability

The medicine Walt was taking affected his *equilibrium*, making it difficult for him to walk.

Husbands and wives keep *equilibrium* in their relationships by sharing household chores.

The stock market crash of 1929 upset the country's financial *equilibrium* for over ten years.

ERADICATE (i RAD i kayt) v. to wipe out; destroy completely

I believe Dad would would stop at nothing to *eradicate* the stinkweed in our yard.

Genghis Khan refused to stop fighting until the enemy army was completely *eradicated*.

ESSENCE (ES uns) *n.* the basic, necessary part of something; the thing that makes it what it is

"Good music is the *essence* of a successful party," claimed the DJ.

"The *essence* of good eggnog is plenty of nog, and very little egg," insisted Ms. Tippler, rather confusingly.

ESTIMATE (ES tuh mayt) *v.* to make a rough calculation or *n.* (ES tuh mit) a rough calculation

Dan *estimated* that dinner for four at Taco Fandango would cost about thirty-five dollars.

The mechanic gave me a written *estimate* of what it would cost to repair the brakes on my car.

ETIQUETTE (ET i ket) *n.* the accepted rules of polite behavior

According to Malaysian *etiquette*, it is very rude to expose the soles of your feet to another person.

Good *etiquette* requires you to send a thank-you note if someone has given you a gift or done you a special favor.

Thirty years ago, *etiquette* required men to stand up whenever a woman entered a room or came to a table, and remain standing until she was seated.

EUPHONY (YOO fuh nee) *n.* pleasant sounds (usually in speech or writing, a pleasant sounding of words)

People said Mike Donohue had the gift of the gab because of the *euphony* of his speech.

Many people rely on the *euphony* of the poetry of Keats to win their sweethearts.

EVADE (ee VAYD) *v.* to escape or get around something through cleverness

Trudy tried to *evade* her parents' questions about her grades by changing the subject whenver they brought it up.

During the Vietnam War, many men *evaded* the draft by moving to Canada.

EXCAVATE (EX kuh vayt) *v.* to dig out, remove by digging out, or form a hole by digging

When Joey found a dinosaur bone behind his house, scientists came and *excavated* the entire back yard, looking for any more prehistoric remains.

A huge lot behind the hotel was *excavated* to make room for an Olympic-size swimming pool.

EXCEPTION (ek SEP shun) *n.* an instance of not sticking to rules or conditions; someone or something for whom rules or conditions are not applied or do not apply

"I don't usually eat dessert," Madge claimed, "but since it's my birthday, I'll make an *exception* and have the chocolate cake."

Most people think that lizards aren't very lovable, but my pet iguana Bobo is an *exception.*

EXCURSION (ek skur zhun) *n.* a short trip made for fun or a certain purpose

We stuck to the main highways for most of our cross-country drive, but we made an *excursion* to Memphis to see Graceland, the former home of Elvis Presley.

Val was from a small town in Missouri, but she was always dressed in the latest fashions because she and her mother went on monthly shopping *excursions* to St. Louis.

EXHAUST (ek ZAWST) *v.* to use up or wear out completely

The overuse of cars will eventually *exhaust* the world's supply of fossil fuels.

"All this bickering is beginning to *exhaust* my patience, boys," said Dad.

Note: People often say "exhausted" (ek ZAW stid) to mean very tired.

He was *exhausted* after the football game.

After a long week at work, I'm too *exhausted* to go out.

EXODUS (EK suh dus) *n.* the departure of a lot of people

The story in the newspaper about a leak at our town's nuclear power plant caused an *exodus.*

Neighboring countries had a hard time providing shelter for the *exodus* of refugees fleeing the war in Rwanda.

EXPEDIENT (ek SPEE dee unt) *adj.* suitable for a certain purpose; serving one's own desires

The swimmer decided that cutting her hair very short was more *expedient* than wearing a swimming cap or having to wash and style it all the time.

Oscar was not a popular manager because when it came time to make decisions, he always did what was *expedient* rather than what was best for the department in the long run.

EXPEDITE (EK spuh dyte) *v.* to speed up the progress of

Mr. Johnson's teaching assistant alphabetized the papers from all his classes in order to *expedite* the grading process.

Paying by credit card often *expedites* the delivery of orders you make over the phone.

EXPEDITION (ek spuh DISH un) *n.* a trip made by a group for a purpose

The explorer Ponce de Leon led an *expedition* to the Bimini Islands in search of the Fountain of Youth.

Ernest went on a hunting *expedition* through northern Africa.

EXPLICIT (ek SPLIS it) *adj.* clearly shown or said, with nothing left out

We weren't allowed to see the movie about the witch trials in school because the scenes of women being burned at the stake were too *explicit*.

Ronald is a good worker, but he doesn't really think for himself, so you have to give him *explicit* instructions.

EXPLOIT (ek SPLOIT) *v.* to use something to the greatest advantage; to use selfishly or wrongly

Graham *exploited* the unlimited supply of blackberries on his land by starting a major blackberry shipping company.

Illegal immigrants are often *exploited* by companies that want very cheap labor and know they can control immigrants by threatening to send them back to their country.

EXTOL (ek STOHL) *v.* to praise very highly

Joan of Arc, a young peasant girl who led the French into battle against the English and was burned at the stake for her trouble, was *extolled* for her courage and devotion to the church, and was declared a saint after her death.

I saw a well-known senator on a late-night television show *extolling* the health benefits of turnip juice.

EXTRAORDINARY (ek STROR duh ner ee) *adj.* out of the ordinary; remarkable

After the afternoon showers had ended, I saw the most *extraordinary* thing—a triple rainbow!

Angie has the *extraordinary* ability to add up long columns of numbers in her head.

FACET (FAS it) *n.* one way of looking at an issue or one piece of an issue; a flat surface on a cut gemstone

We must consider every *facet* of this problem before deciding what to do.

A marquise-shaped diamond has many *facets*, which makes it glisten in the light.

Mike's quick temper is not one of the best *facets* of his personality.

FACTION (FAK shun) *n.* a group within a larger group, usually a group that has interests or goals that aren't shared by the rest of the organization

One *faction* of the student council was in favor of starting a student strike, but the rest of us knew it wasn't a good idea.

FALTER (FAWL tur) *v.* to hesitate in action; to lose confidence or drive; to move unsteadily or stumble

My faith in the accuracy of my car's speedometer began to *falter* after I got my third speeding ticket.

The old professor *faltered* as he walked onto the stage to accept his award.

Wilma's desire to become an ambassador *faltered* when she learned that only two percent of U.S. ambassadors are women.

FAMINE (FAM in) *n.* a widespread, extreme shortage of food

In the mid-1980s, a large group of popular musicians got together to raise money to help the victims of *famine* in Ethiopia.

The repeated failure of potato crops in Ireland in the 1840s led to what's known as the Irish potato *famine*, which caused many people to starve to death and led many others to leave their homeland to come to America.

FANATIC (fuh NAT ik) *n.* a person who is completely, unreasonably devoted to a cause, person, or belief

Some people think the Buddhist monks who set themselves on fire to protest war are *fanatics*.

When it comes to the New York Giants, Lee is a complete *fanatic:* he knows every player, goes to every game, and regularly fights with people who say the team will never make it to the Super Bowl again.

FATIGUE (fuh TEEG) *n.* extreme tiredness or *v.* to tire out

Tom digs ditches for a living, so *fatigue* usually keeps him from wanting to go out after work.

After boxing up everything I owned, loading it into my car, driving for three days, then unloading everything in my new apartment, I felt very *fatigued*.

FEIGN (FAYN) *v.* to pretend or give false appearance

Brian found the mountain bike in his parents' closet a month before his birthday, but he *feigned* surprise when they gave it to him.

Mary *feigned* a stomachache to get out of going to school.

FELINE (FEE lyne) *adj.* cat-like

There was something *feline* and mysterious about her slanting green eyes.

My little sister has an almost *feline* ability to sneak up on people.

FERVOR (FER vur) *n.* great warmth or strength of feeling

Our country's 200th anniversary was celebrated with patriotic *fervor*.

Even at a young age, Margaret showed great *fervor* when discussing the subject of women's rights.

FEUD (FYOOD) *n.* a bitter, sometimes long-lasting quarrel or *v.* to have a feud

During the Middle Ages, the counts of Europe were constantly *feuding* with each other over land or money, probably because they had nothing better to do since television hadn't yet been invented.

The Hatfields and McCoys had a famous family *feud* that lasted for generations.

FICKLE (FIK ul) *adj.* having changeable or inconstant feelings

Loren is a *fickle* friend: one day she stands up for you, the next day she's gossiping behind your back.

Don Juan was a famous Spaniard whose *fickle* heart and romantic skill led him from one love affair to another throughout his life.

FIDELITY (fi DEL i tee) *n.* loyalty; faithfulness

When two people get married, they swear an oath of *fidelity* to each other.

No one questioned the soldier's *fidelity* to his commanding officer.

FINESSE (fin NES) *n.* delicacy and skill in performing a task

The grandmother had enough *finesse* to change her sleeping grandson out of his clothes and into his pajamas without waking him up.

A good brain surgeon must have patience and *finesse*.

FLIMSY (FLIM zee) *adj.* weak; not effective; thin; light

The construction of those beach houses was so *flimsy*, it's no wonder they were torn apart by the first storm that hit them.

Tanya, who was freezing to death in her *flimsy* evening gown, wished she'd checked the weather report before going out.

FLIPPANT (FLIP unt) *adj.* disrespectful; showing a lack of seriousness

George used to anger his boss by passing notes and making *flippant* remarks during the weekly departmental meetings.

"This is no time to be *flippant*, Vinnie," said Irene. "Losing the cable television will be the least of our worries if we don't get out of here before the hurricane hits."

FOE (FOH) *n.* enemy

On the television show "Star Trek," the Klingons are the *foes* of Captain Kirk and his crew.

In many of Arthur Conan Doyle's detective novels, Sherlock Holmes must match wits with his old *foe*, Professor Moriarty.

Sugar and sticky desserts are the *foes* of healthy teeth.

FORBEARANCE (for BAYR uns) *n.* restraint; tolerance

I praised Hal for his *forbearance* in not punching the bully who was calling him names.

When the two kids were found guilty of stealing a car and running it into a tree, their parents begged the judge to show some *forbearance* by giving the boys a light sentence.

FORFEIT (FOR fit) *v.* to give up a right or possession as a penalty for a mistake or offense

We need at least eight players to show up before six o'clock, or we *forfeit* the softball game and the other team wins.

If he can't pay back his bank loan, the farmer will have to *forfeit* his land.

FORGERY (FOR juh ree) *n.* a fake or copy or the act of making such a fake or copy

The theft at the art museum wasn't discovered for weeks, because the thieves had replaced the paintings they stole with clever *forgeries*.

Izzy made a *forgery* of his report card and replaced all the Ds with Bs so he wouldn't get in trouble with his parents.

FORGO (for GO) *v.* to do without or give up

Barbara and Bernie decided to *forgo* their usual summer vacation so they could use the money to buy a motorcycle.

Uncle Evan had to *forgo* his after-dinner cigar because the restaurant didn't allow smoking of any kind.

FORSAKE (for SAYK) *v.* to give up, leave, or renounce someone or something

No one could believe that Mr. Holden would *forsake* his wife and children to follow his dream of being a circus clown.

Mrs. Richter said she wouldn't take her husband back unless he quit gambling and hanging around the pool halls and swore to *forsake* his sinful ways.

FOUL (FOWL) *adj.* offensive to the senses; disgusting; unclean; evil

There was a *foul* smell coming from Shawn's gym locker.

The mass murderer was sentenced to the electric chair for his *foul* crimes.

Don't use *foul* language in front of your teacher.

FRAUD (FRAWD) *n.* a trick or other dishonest action used to gain something; an impostor or swindler

The woman who dressed as a nun and called herself "Sister Margaret" had managed to collect almost ten thousand dollars in donations for the so-called Holy Mother of Munificence Orphanage, when it was discovered that the whole thing was a *fraud*, and that she was actually an escaped convict named Maggie "the Ax" McGill.

The government tries to protect citizens from *fraud* by monitoring advertisements to make sure false claims are not made.

FRIGID (FRIJ id) *adj.* very cold in temperature; lacking warmth of feeling; without enthusiasm

Dad's proposal that we get rid of the television so that we would all use our time more productively got a *frigid* response from the rest of the family.

There was an unusual wave of *frigid* weather in late April last year.

FUTILE (FYOOT ul) *adj.* having no effect; useless

The fly made several *futile* attempts to get out of the spider's web.

All our efforts to get the engine started again were *futile:* it was dead and we were stuck.

GALLANT (GAL unt) *adj.* stylish and dashing; brave and noble

All the girls were shocked to see Pam, the class brain, with such a *gallant* escort at the prom.

The Polish people put up a *gallant* resistance to the much stronger German forces.

GALLIVANT (GAL uh vant) *v.* to wander around looking for fun things to do

David was always out *gallivanting* instead of doing school work, so no one was surprised when he failed eighth grade.

GALLOWS (GAL ohz) *n.* a stucture or framework with two uprights and a crossbeam, built for the purpose of executing people by hanging

As he stood on the *gallows* before being executed by the British, Nathan Hale said, "I only regret that I have but one life to lose for my country."

"You'd better get back on your horse and ride on," said the gambler to the gunfighter. "If the sheriff sees you here, you'll be swinging from the *gallows* by sundown."

GAPE (GAYP) *v.* to stare with an open mouth

The audience *gaped* at the amazing performance of the trapeze artists.

Tourists in New York City often *gape* at the strange people and sights they see on the streets.

GARNISH (GAR nish) *v.* to decorate, usually food

The cook *garnished* the plate of fish with bright lemon slices and parsley.

My mother *garnished* my birthday cake with strawberries and cream.

GAVEL (GAV ul) *n.* small mallet used by a judge to call a court to order

The judge pounded his *gavel* when a fight broke out in the courtroom.

GENETIC (juh NET ik) *adj.* having to do with heredity or physical traits inherited from parents and relatives

Our physical features—from the color of our eyes to our height—are largely decided by our *genetic* makeup.

Folks here in Harrisonburg think it must be something *genetic* that makes all the Clampett boys grow up to be plumbers.

GENOCIDE (JEN uh syde) *n.* the deliberate attempt to kill off an entire group of people

During World War II, the Nazis killed at least six million Jews—one of the most horrible acts of *genocide* in modern history.

Many people consider Christopher Columbus a great explorer and a great man, but others point out that he and his men were guilty of the brutal *genocide* of the Arawak Indians, the friendly, peaceful natives that greeted him after his first journey across the Atlantic.

GEYSER (GYE zer) *n.* a hot spring in the earth that sprays boiling water and steam into the air

Old Faithful is a famous *geyser* located in Yellowstone National Park.

GHOSTWRITER (GOHST ryte ur) *n.* a person who writes something for another person, but who doesn't take credit for writing it

The baseball star hired a *ghostwriter* to write his life story.

Most presidents have *ghostwriters* who create their speeches.

GLOAT (GLOHT) *v.* to show great pleasure, sometimes in a mean-spirited or unkind way

Lydia *gloated* about her promotion so much that her co-workers began to hate her.

It's not good sportsmanship to *gloat* over your victories.

GLUTTON (GLUT un) *n.* someone who eats way too much

When she found him with mustard all over his tie and his hand stuck in the candy machine, Marge decided she'd better duck out the back door before people found out that the *glutton* was her date.

GOATEE (goh TEE) *n.* a small beard that doesn't cover the cheek area and is trimmed to a point below the chin

Spike Lee has a *goatee*.

GORE (GOR) *v.* to stab with a horn or tusk or *n.* blood from a wound

The toreador was *gored* to death by the bull.

There's too much blood and *gore* in horror movies nowadays.

GORGE (GORJ) *n.* a narrow passage between high cliffs or *v.* to stuff yourself with food or eat greedily

Some of the oldest human remains known to scientists were found in Olduvai *Gorge*, in the African country of Tanzania.

After sticking to his diet for two months and losing fifteen pounds, Ira *gorged* himself on spaghetti and meatballs every night for a week, and gained every pound back.

GOUGE (GOWJ) *v.* to scoop out or cut out

Henrietta was suspended from school for trying to *gouge* out her classmate's eye with a ballpoint pen.

The bandit used a stick to *gouge* out a little hole in the ground in which to bury his loot.

GOUT (GOWT) *n.* a disease in which uric acid salts are deposited in the joints of legs, feet, and hands, causing pain and discomfort

When you read old British novels, you will find many characters, usually rich old men, who complain of having *gout*.

GRAVE (GRAYV) *adj.* serious, somber; important; critical

The *grave* expression on the doctor's face as he came out of the operating room told us that the news wasn't good.

"The situation is *grave*, guys," said Bob. "We're out of cheezy doodles already, and it isn't even halftime."

Note: the noun form of grave is *gravity* (GRAV i tee).

No one understood the *gravity* of Lyle's condition until doctors told us that even though he seemed healthy, he was slowly going blind.

GRIEVE (GREEV) *v.* to cause to be sad or to feel sad; to mourn

The news of his parents' planned divorce *grieved* Paul terribly.

"So what if you lost the tennis championship?" said Mo the coach. "There's no sense *grieving* like this."

GRIMACE (GRIM is) *n.* a twisted sort of expression on the face caused by pain or disgust or *v.* to make a grimace

I tried to sing "Happy Birthday" to my boyfriend, but I was so off-key he *grimaced* in spite of himself.

Daniel tried a bite of liver in order to please his mother, but as soon as it hit his tongue, his face twisted up into a *grimace* and he had to spit it out.

GROSS (GROHS) *adj.* without deductions; very easy to see

Chris's *gross* pay is two thousand dollars a month, but after all the state and federal income taxes are deducted, he's only left with $1,400.

When Marie handed in her algebra test, she was sure she had done well, but when she got it back she was shocked at the number of *gross* errors she had made.

GRUFF (GRUF) *adj.* rough; harsh; unfriendly

When football coach Paul "Bear" Bryant barked out orders in his *gruff* voice, no one dared disobey.

Miranda was put off by her grandfather's *gruff* manner and stern face.

GUILE (GYLE) *n.* skillful trickery; cunning

The spy used her *guile* to persuade enemy officers she was in love with them, then tricked them into telling her military secrets.

The travelling salesman had enough *guile* to sell ice cubes to the Eskimos.

GULLIBLE (GUL uh bul) *adj.* easy to fool or mislead

The charming saleslady actually convinced the *gullible* woman that her special thigh cream would "melt the pounds away."

On the first day of junior high, Wally had his lunch stolen because he was *gullible* enough to give it to a kid who said he was the student council lunch inspector.

GUST (GUST) *n.* a sudden, strong wind; a sudden, strong burst of something like rain, smoke, or even an emotion

A *gust* of wind blew the umbrella out of my hands.

Mr. and Mrs. Hutchins thought they had their daughter calmed down, but when they tried to leave her with her kindergarten teacher, she let loose another *gust* of tears and protests.

GUSTO (GUS toh) *n.* great enjoyment, usually in eating or drinking

The Thanksgiving dinner smelled so good we ate with *gusto.*

GYRATE (JYE rayt) *v.* to move in a circular motion or circular path

Elvis Presley was a rock 'n' roll singer who drove teenage girls crazy by *gyrating* his hips when he sang.

The earth *gyrates* on its axis.

HALLOWED (HAL ohd) *adj.* seen or respected as holy

Jerusalem is a very important city for Jews, Christians, and Muslims, all of whom think of it as a *hallowed* place.

In his Gettysburg Address, President Lincoln said that the battlefield outside Gettysburg was *hallowed* ground because of the brave sacrifices made by the soldiers who fought and died there.

HALLUCINATE (hah LOO suh nayt) *v.* to see, hear, or sense things that aren't really there

Irene's fever was so high she began to *hallucinate,* screaming that there were bats in her bedroom and spiders crawling on her arms.

Note: The noun form of hallucinate is *hallucination* (hah loo suh NAY shun).

On Halloween night, Oscar claimed he saw a ghost, but we think it was just a *hallucination* brought on by eating too much candy.

HAMPER (HAM pur) *v.* to prevent the progress of; hold back; interfere with

The prisoner tried to escape by running across the field, but he was *hampered* by the fifty-pound iron ball attached to his leg with a chain.

Clara couldn't climb the tree because she was *hampered* by her high heels, her tight dress, and her fear of bark.

HARASS (HAR us) or (huh RAS) *v.* to bother or attack repeatedly

It turned out that some crazy fan of actress Erin Moran was the one *harassing* actor Scott Baio with phone calls and threatening letters.

The confused activist for vegetable rights was arrested for *harassing* people in the supermarket.

HAUGHTY (HAW tee) *adj.* proud in a snobby way

The rich girl was so *haughty* she wouldn't dream of going to the dance at the public school or hanging out with people who didn't come from her neighborhood.

HAZARDOUS (HAZ ur duhs) *adj.* risky; full of danger

Many of the settlers didn't survive the *hazardous* journey through the desert and across the mountains.

Only the bravest skiers attempt the *hazardous* course at Icicle Canyon.

HEARTY (HAR tee) *adj.* friendly and cheerful; nourishing and satisfying; strong

When Ron saw his old grade-school friend, he greeted him with a *hearty* handshake and a pat on the back.

After a day of sledding, there's nothing like a *hearty* bowl of beef stew.

Life on the farm had made Olaf *hearty* and healthy.

HEATHEN (HEE thun) *n.* a term used mainly by Christians to describe someone who is not of their faith; a barbarian; an uncivilized person

The church sent missionaries to South America to convert the *heathens* to Christianity.

HEED (HEED) *v.* to give close attention to or *n.* close attention

Everyone we met told us not to drive up Mt. Slippy right after a snowstorm, but unfortunately we didn't *heed* their warnings.

You would be wise to *heed* the words of old Jedediah, because rumor has it he's over two hundred years old and knows how to talk to animals.

Lon paid no *heed* to his mother when she told him his eyes would stick that way if he kept crossing them.

HEIR (ayr) *n.* someone who is legally entitled to inherit the title or property of another

Prince Charles is *heir* to the British throne.

Marvin is *heir* to the Fluffo Marshmallow Company fortune, which his grandfather started building eighty years ago with one marshmallow cart on the Lower East Side of New York.

Note: A woman who is legally entitled to inherit a title or property is called an *heiress* (AYR is).

HEIRLOOM (AYR loom) *n.* a possession passed down from one generation to the next

The gold watch Neil got for his graduation was a family *heirloom* that had been bought by his grandfather's grandfather.

HERALD (HER uld) *v.* to announce the coming of or *n.* someone who announces the coming of something

When the new principal replaced recess with a required study hall, we knew it was the *herald* of a dark and joyless time for the students of Shadowvale Middle School.

The dogs' barking always *heralds* my father's return home from work.

HERESY (HER i see) *n.* an opinion that isn't in line with the accepted view on a subject, especially religion

In the Middle Ages, it was dangerous to challenge the teachings of the Roman Catholic Church because *heresy* was punishable by death.

Many gourmet cooks consider it *heresy* to put ketchup on steak or put ice cubes in wine.

Note: A person accused of heresy is called a *heretic* (HER uh tik).

HESITATE (HEZ i tayt) *v.* to pause in uncertainty before acting; to be slow in acting

Tom *hestitated* to call his father for money more than three times in one month.

When I got to the edge of the diving board, I *hesitated* because I had never jumped off the high board before.

HOARD (HORD) *v.* to gather and store for future use

My parents *hoard* canned foods in the cellar because if there's ever a war, they want to be sure they'll have enough to eat.

Squirrels *hoard* their nuts and berries so they can get through the winter.

HOAX (HOHKS) *n.* something designed to fool people; a deception

The circus claimed to have a three-headed horse in one of its tents, but it turned out to be a *hoax*.

The Piltdown Skull, supposedly the skull of a new kind of human, was "discovered" in England in 1911, but was later uncovered as a *hoax* perpetrated by a geology professor at Oxford University.

HOMAGE (HOM ij) *n.* special honor or respect

The Vietnam Memorial Wall is an *homage* to the veterans of the Vietnam War.

The school paid *homage* to the well-loved coach by naming the football field after him.

HONE (HOHN) *v.* to sharpen or make more effective

The camper *honed* his knife on a whetstone.

Many famous chefs have *honed* their skills at the Cordon Bleu cooking school in Paris.

HORIZONTAL (hor i ZON tul) *adj.* parallel to the ground; flat

The library was well stocked but hard to use because all the books were stacked *horizontally*, so you couldn't pull a book off the shelf without disturbing the books on top of it.

The Christmas tree was too tall to fit through the door upright, so we carried it through *horizontally*.

HOSTILE (HAWS tul) *adj.* showing ill will toward, as an enemy would

The unpopular governor didn't realize how *hostile* the audience was until they started booing and throwing rotten eggs at him.

Ever since Dad accused him of breaking our lawn mower when he borrowed it last spring, our neighbor, Mr. Hathaway, has been *hostile* toward our whole family.

Note: The noun form of hostile is hostility (haws TIL i tee).

The old ethnic *hostility* between the Serbians and the Bosnian Muslims erupted into a bloody war.

HUMBLE (HUM bul) *adj.* modest; meek; not boastful or proud

Even after all the Olympic gold medals she won, Bonnie is still very *humble* and down-to-earth.

Janice was so *humble* when she found out she had won first place at the science fair, she kept saying she truly felt many of the other projects were more deserving than hers.

Note: The noun form of humble is *humility* (hyoo MIL i tee).

It is wise to show a little *humility* when you become rich and famous.

HYPOCHONDRIAC (hye poh KON dree ak) *n.* someone who imagines he is ill or worries about getting sick too much

Marcel was a *hypochondriac*: he wore a scarf all summer, was deathly afraid of drafts, and went to the doctor at least once a week, complaining of chills and aches.

HYPOCRITE (HIP uh crit) *n.* someone who tells other people what virtues or beliefs to have, but doesn't uphold or act on those beliefs herself; someone who doesn't "practice what she preaches"

Our English teacher, Mr. Unger, is such a *hypocrite*—he won't accept our papers after the due date, but he always turns in his lesson plans late.

Note: The adjective form of hypocrite is *hypocritical* (hip oh CRIT i kul).

We all thought it was *hypocritical* of the senator to push for school prayer when he hadn't been to church in years.

HYSTERICAL (hi STER i kul) *adj.* having extreme, uncontrollable, sometimes irrational emotion (often laughter or crying); having to do with such an emotion

The child became *hysterical* when we took his blanket away so we could wash it.

Hysterical laughing is sometimes a reaction people have when they get very bad news or become very upset.

IDEAL (eye DEEL) *adj.* seen as the standard of perfection; perfect

The sky was gray, the air was chilly, I had nothing clean to wear: it was an *ideal* day to stay in bed and read.

Moist, hot conditions are *ideal* for growing orchids.

"This light cotton dress is *ideal* for outdoor summer parties," said the sales clerk.

IDENTICAL (eye DEN ti kul) *adj.* exactly alike; exactly the same

Margery was embarrassed when she got to the prom and saw that three other girls were wearing dresses *identical* to hers.

"That's so weird," thought Paco. "Those two cake molds are *identical*."

IDIOM (ID ee um) *n.* a phrase or expression whose meaning cannot be understood from the meanings of the individual words; a phrase whose meaning has little to do with the literal meaning of the words

"To fly off the handle" is an *idiom* that means to lose one's temper.

Most languages have *idioms* that are hard to translate literally.

IDIOSYNCRASY (id ee oh SING kruh see) *n.* a unique trait or habit someone has

Ernie has this strange *idiosyncrasy* of always going to the bathroom before leaving any building.

Wearing a dyed green carnation on his coat was one of Oscar Wilde's *idioscyncrasies*.

ILLEGIBLE (i LEJ uh bul) *adj.* very hard or impossible to read

"My mother wrote me an excuse for being absent from school, but rain smeared the ink and made it *illegible*," said Clarisse. "Honest."

Doctors are known for having *illegible* handwriting.

IMMACULATE (i MAK yuh lit) *adj.* spotless; perfectly clean

The cook insisted on keeping the kitchen *immaculate*.

No one dared to accuse the police chief of planting evidence because his record was *immaculate*.

IMMORTAL (i MOR tul) *adj.* living forever; having fame that lasts forever

Elvis Presley may be dead (at least most people think so) but his legend is *immortal*.

As long as they get plenty of blood and avoid sunlight and wooden stakes, vampires are *immortal*.

IMMUNITY (i MYOO ni tee) *n.* ability to resist disease; freedom from certain restrictions or punishments

Once you catch the chicken pox, your body builds up a natural *immunity* to it, so you can never catch it again.

The district attorney granted Jimmy *immunity* from prosecution in exchange for his testimony against the crime boss known as "The Hammer."

IMPAIR (im PAYR) *v.* to lessen in strength or ability; to weaken

The bride's heavy veil *impaired* her vision and caused her to fall into one of the pews as she tried to walk down the aisle.

Cough and cold medicines can *impair* your ability to operate a wrecking crane, bulldozer, car, or other large machine.

IMPARTIAL (im PAR shul) *adj.* fair; not favoring one side over another

In the United States, you have the right to a fair and *impartial* jury if you must stand trial.

Umpires are supposed to be *impartial*, but many people think they give the benefit of the doubt to more famous pitchers.

IMPROMPTU (im PROMP too) *adj.* said or done without preparation

When we found out it was Gary's birthday, we threw together an *impromptu* celebration for him.

In the age of television, it is dangerous for political candidates to make *impromptu* remarks because any little mistakes they make can be broadcast on the news that night.

IMPUDENT (IM pyuh dunt) *adj.* disrespectfully or offensively bold

The *impudent* teenager laughed at the police when they arrested him, and boasted that he would never go to jail because he was a juvenile.

Note: The noun form of impudent is *impudence* (IM pyuh dens).

Barney got a slap on the face for having the *impudence* to call his father an old gas bag in front of several dinner guests.

INADMISSIBLE (in ad MIS uh bul) *adj.* not permitted to enter; not admissible; often used in court to describe information or evidence that will not be allowed in the trial

The judge decided that the bloody knife was *inadmissible* as evidence because it was discovered during an unlawful search by the police.

The accused murderer's confession was *inadmissible* because he was not informed of his rights at the time of his arrest.

INCENTIVE (in SEN tiv) *n.* something that promotes action or provides motivation

As an *incentive* for finishing the term papers early, the teacher promised five extra-credit points on each paper that was handed in before the due date.

The speed with which I lost weight and developed muscle was all the *incentive* I needed for continuing my exercise program.

INCESSANT (in SES unt) *adj.* unending; continuous

Woody found it hard to sleep in the country because of the *incessant* chirping of the crickets outside his window.

"I could never live in Seattle," said Tex. "I hear the rain is almost *incessant* up there."

INCOGNITO (in kog NEE toh) *adv.* or *adj.* having one's identity hidden to avoid notice; with one's indentity hidden to avoid notice

The prince learned a great deal about his country by traveling *incognito* for a year.

Rumor has it that Mick Jagger made an *incognito* appearance at this nightclub yesterday to see his friend's band play.

INCOHERENT (in coh HEER unt) *adj.* confused, not logically put together; unable to think or express yourself clearly

Mrs. Meyer, who was abducted by aliens last week, used to write long letters to the military about spaceships landing in her backyard; unfortunately, the letters were so *incoherent*, no one knew what she was saying until it was too late.

After the seventh brutal sack of the game, the quarterback was dazed and *incoherent.*

INDEFINITE (in DEF uh nit) *adj.* not clear; not clearly defined; vague

Our plans for our summer vacation are still pretty *indefinite*—all we know is we want to go some place warm and sunny.

If you look hard enough, you can see the *indefinite* outlines of reindeer hoofprints in the snow on the roof.

INDICT (in DYTE) *v.* to accuse of wrongdoing; in law, a formal accusation based on the findings of a grand jury

The article in *The Daily Gazette indicted* the entire airline industry for endangering passengers by lowering safety standards.

Harry "the Horse" Hooperman was *indicted* thirty-six times for crimes ranging from fraud to grand theft, but he was never convicted.

INDIFFERENT (in DIF ur unt) *adj.* not caring or having an interest

The cat seemed *indifferent* to the can of tuna we opened for her.

Eleanor was *indifferent* to the flowers and candy her boyfriends kept sending her.

INEDIBLE (in ED uh bul) *adj.* not fit to be eaten

The pot roast was burned so badly it was *inedible.*

Note: The opposite of inedible is *edible* (ED uh bul).

There are many varieties of *edible* mushrooms in these woods, but be careful—some of the mushrooms you'll find are poisonous.

INEPT (in EPT) *adj.* awkward; lacking skill

Clancey did his friend a favor by hiring his son as a file clerk, but the boy kept losing things and was so *inept*, in general, that he had to be let go two weeks after he started.

Kate was such an *inept* cook, she never failed to burn or break something every time she was in the kitchen.

INEVITABLE (in EV i tuh bul) *adj.* unavoidable, inescapable; certain to happen

For most people, falling down a lot is an *inevitable* part of learning to ski.

Taxes and death are both *inevitable*.

INFAMOUS (IN fuh mus) *adj.* having a terrible reputation; shocking or shamefully bad

Nero was an *infamous* Roman emperor known mostly for playing his lyre and reciting poetry while watching a fire, which he caused, burn down most of Rome.

Jesse James was an *infamous* train and bank robber in the late 1800s.

Japanese pilots began their *infamous* bombing attack on the U.S. Pacific fleet in Pearl Harbor at 7:53 on a Sunday morning.

INHABIT (in HAB it) *v.* to live in

Many different kinds of plants and animals *inhabit* the world.

We have yet to discover any other *inhabited* planets in our solar system.

INHERIT (in HER it) *v.* to receive from someone else

When his uncle died, Pat *inherited* his valuable stamp collection.

Colleen *inherited* her red hair from her mother's side of the family.

INHIBIT (in HIB it) *v.* to hold back; restrain

Tina's braces *inhibited* her from smiling.

The giant centerpiece *inhibited* the dinner conversation because no one could see across the table.

INITIAL (i NISH ul) *adj.* first; having to do with the beginning

The astronauts landed successfully on their *initial* attempt.

The *initial* results of our poll show that most people prefer chocolate over vanilla ice cream, but more opinions must be gathered before we can draw any definite conclusions.

INNATE (i NAYT) *adj.* inborn; possessed since birth; existing as a necessary part of something

Martha has an *innate* musical ability. She can pick up almost any instrument and play it without ever taking lessons.

Cats have an *innate* dislike of being thrown into water.

INNOVATE (IN o vayt) v. to do or introduce for the first time

For years, scientists have worked on *innovating* new, safer, cleaner sources of energy to help us stop polluting the environment.

Note: The noun form of innovate is *innovation* (in o VAY shun), which is either the act of introducing something new, or the new thing itself.

The electric can opener was an *innovation* that helped millions of left-handed people open cans more easily.

INSATIABLE (in SAY shuh bul) *adj.* impossible to satisfy

The student had an *insatiable* desire to learn.

I have an *insatiable* appetite.

The pirate had an *insatiable* thirst for rum.

INSIPID (in SIP id) *adj.* lacking flavor; dull or uninteresting

Grandma's "oatmeal" was actually more like an *insipid*, watery mush.

The movie about a figure skater who falls in love with a hockey player was so predictable and *insipid* that I left in the middle.

INSTIGATE (IN stuh gayt) v. to provoke; to stir up

The surprising verdict in the much-publicized trial *instigated* a riot in the streets that lasted for several days.

The deadly fire at the Coconut Grove nightclub *instigated* the development of many new fire safety practices and laws.

INSUBORDINATE (in suh BOR duh nit) *adj.* disobedient; not obeying orders

The *insubordinate* employee, who talked to the press even after strict orders not to, was fired.

Insubordinate behavior is not tolerated in the military.

INTERROGATE (in TER uh gayt) v. to examine a person by asking questions, especially for official reasons

The police *interrogated* the suspect for two hours before they managed to get any information out of her.

INTERFERE (in tur FEER) v. to get in the way as if to block or stop something; to meddle

Donny and Daisy were having an ugly argument, but I didn't try to do anything about it because I think it's best not to *interfere* in fights between brothers and sisters.

When I told the man in the seat in front of me that his talking was *interfering* with my enjoyment of the movie, he dumped his popcorn on my head.

INTERVENE (in tur VEEN) *v.* to come between two things or events; to come between two things to change the course of action

A stranger on the street was brave enough to *intervene* in a struggle between a mugger and a woman who was fighting to keep her purse from being stolen.

The United States sometimes sends its military to *intervene* in foreign wars.

INTOXICATE (in TOK sl kayt) *v.* to make someone lose full control over their mental or physical abilities, especially through chemicals or alcohol; to fill with excitement

The driver of the car that hit the cyclist was so *intoxicated* he could barely stand up straight.

The ocean breeze and the clear, starry night *intoxicated* the romantic young girl.

INTROVERT (IN tro vurt) *n.* a person who keeps to him- or herself; a shy person

Kelly is such an *introvert,* she would rather sit in her room and read than go out to the movies or hang out with friends.

Ben goes out to parties with us, but he's too much of an *introvert* to meet new people or get involved in conversations.

IRK (URK) *v.* to annoy; to bother

Nothing *irks* me more than people who hum when they chew their food.

Karen was *irked* when the customer service person at Toast-o-Matic put her on hold for the third time.

IRONY (EYE ruh nee) *n.* using words to express something different from or opposite to the literal meaning of the words used; when what you say is the opposite of what you mean; a conflict between what is expected and what actually happens

Saying "What a dump!" when entering a huge, beautiful mansion is an example of *irony.*

When Megan came home covered in mud with holes in her jeans, her mother said she was "pretty as a picture," but the *irony* of the statement was lost on Megan.

Note: The adjective form of irony is ironic (eye RON ik).

It's *ironic* that Gayle, who has no sense of smell, got a job selling perfume.

IRRELEVANT (i REL uh vunt) *adj.* having nothing to do with the matter at hand

We were having a great class discussion about the play *Hamlet,* when Joey asked an *irrelevant* question about Danish cooking.

A person's race or sex is *irrelevant* to how smart he or she is.

Your height, weight, and marital status are considered *irrelevant* pieces of information on a resume.

IRREPARABLE (i REP ur uh bul) *adj.* impossible to repair

The accident caused *irreparable* damage to the car.

The broken wing on the statue of the angel was *irreparable*.

ITINERARY (eye TIN ur rer ee) *n.* a schedule of places to visit on a trip

While we were in Italy, our *itinerary* was mostly made up of trips to cathedrals and museums.

Cleavon and Patricia spent a month in Southeast Asia without any sort of *itinerary*—they just drifted around and did whatever they felt like doing.

JEOPARDY (JEP ur dee) *n.* danger; risk of harm

Frequent hurricanes put Howard's beach house in *jeopardy*.

Note: The verb form of jeopardy is *jeopardize* (JEP ur dyze), meaning to put at risk or endanger.

Howard *jeopardized* his whole life savings by betting everything he owned on a horse race.

JURISDICTION (joor is DIK shun) *n.* the power to interpret or enforce the law in a certain area; range of power or control

A police officer from New York could not arrest someone in California because California is not under her *jurisdiction*.

The Supreme Court of Alabama has *jurisdiction* over the entire state.

"The yard is not under my *jurisdiction*," said the housekeeper when his employer told him the grass needed cutting. "You should speak to the gardener."

KOWTOW (KOW tow) v. to kneel and touch your forehead to the ground to show respect; to show exaggerated respect or obedience

The insecure manager expected all his employees to fetch his coffee, do personal favors for him, and basically *kowtow* to him in every way.

In China, it was customary to *kowtow* before any member of the royal family.

KUDOS (KOO dohs) n. praise, glory (seen as singular)

The children received *kudos* from their parents for getting straight As.

LABYRINTH (LAB uh rinth) n. a maze; something confusing in design or construction

According to Greek mythology, the Minotaur, a creature half-man and half-bull, was kept in a *labyrinth* on the island of Crete.

"This town is like some kind of *labyrinth*," huffed Charles, after trying for two hours to find his hotel.

LACERATION (las uh RAY shun) n. a jagged tear or wound

Rene fell off her skateboard onto a broken drain pipe and got a nasty *laceration* on her leg.

The tree branch whipped back unexpectedly in the wind and gave Charlie several *lacerations* on his face and neck.

LAMENT (luh MENT) to grieve over or regret deeply

The children all *lamented* the end of summer vacation.

Some people spend so much time *lamenting* the state of our country that they don't have enough time left over to vote.

LANGUISH (LANG gwish) v. to become weak or feeble; to be neglected

In the book *The Count of Monte Cristo*, Edmond Dantès is thrown into a terrible prison and is left to *languish* there for many years.

The poor dog *languished* in the dry heat of the Arizona desert.

LAPSE (LAPS) v. to fall back into worse or lower conditions; to become invalid or inactive

After going almost a month without so much as saying "ain't," Moe *lapsed* into his former bad grammar habits.

It seemed like my cold was getting better, but then I *lapsed* into pneumonia.

Dad let the insurance policy on the car *lapse* because he wanted to sell it.

Note: Lapse can also be used as a noun to mean a slip or failure.

"I must be having a memory *lapse*," said George. "I can't remember my telephone number."

It must have been a *lapse* of good sense that caused Roger to leave the stove on when he left the house.

LAUDABLE (LAW duh bul) *adj.* praiseworthy

Your efforts to get the school to recycle paper and cans are *laudable*.

Sylvester made *laudable* improvements in his grades this year.

LAVISH (LAV ish) *adj.* very generous; very plentiful

There was a *lavish* buffet at the birthday party—so much food, in fact, that much of it was wasted.

When it came to his grandchildren, Grandfather was *lavish* with his money, and bought them practically anything they wanted.

LAX (LAKS) *adj.* not careful; not firm; loose

Max had been *lax* in his kitchen cleaning chores, and soon all sorts of gunk began to build up in the oven and in the vegetable drawer of the refrigerator.

When Arnold stopped lifting weights, his muscles became *lax* within a few months.

LEGACY (LEG uh see) *n.* something left to someone in a will; something passed on to future generations

Part of Howard's *legacy* to his granddaughter was a trust fund set up to pay for her college education.

Democracy as a system of government is our *legacy* from the ancient Greeks.

LENIENT (LEE nee unt) *adj.* tolerant; flexible where rules are concerned; permissive

The kids liked Rhonda as their sitter because she was more *lenient* than the others and would let them eat ice pops and stay up past ten.

"Since this is the first time you've been arrested, I've decided to be *lenient*," said the judge. "But if you're ever caught knocking over mailboxes again, you're going to jail!"

LEST (LEST) conj. for fear that

It is important to keep studying history *lest* we repeat our past mistakes.

Keep your voice down, *lest* your parents wake up and find us raiding the refrigerator.

Note: Don't worry. *Lest* is not used too much in conversation or writing anymore, but you will find it often in older books.

LEVEE (LEV ee) *n.* a high bank of earth, rock, or other material built up along the side of a river to keep it from flooding

We had a picnic out on the *levee* beside the Mississippi River.

After ten days of heavy rain, the river began to rush over the top of the *levee* and flooded over one-third of the town.

LIAISON (LEE ay zon) *n.* a contact person between two units of an organization; an improper romantic connection

Doug worked as a *liaison* between the advertising department and the budget department to make sure spending on commercials didn't get out of control.

The queen's *liaison* with the king's best general was the source of gossip around the palace.

LIMB (LIM) *n.* a part of an animal body that is not the head or trunk, like arms, legs, or wings; a large tree branch

Most ballet dancers have long, graceful limbs.

We hung the swing off one of the lower limbs of the tree.

LIMBO (LIM boh) *n.* in Roman Catholicism, a place between heaven and hell that serves as the eternal resting place of the souls of babies who died before baptism and of good people who died before the birth of Christ; a state of being neglected, forgotten, or put aside

The completion of the giant hotel has been in *limbo* for ten years, ever since the construction company ran out of money.

We were making arrangements to go on a vacation in the Bahamas this June, but the plans are in *limbo* now because Dad might not be able to get off work.

According to Catholicism, on the Day of Judgment, the souls of the prophets, like Moses, will be accepted out of *limbo* and into heaven.

LISTLESS (LIST lis) *adj.* without energy or interest

The school usually overheated the classrooms during the winter, which made the teachers and students sleepy and *listless*.

The rainy, dark day made me *listless* and depressed.

LITERAL (LIT ur ul) *adj.* sticking to the exact meaning of a word or words, as in a translation; sticking to the exact meaning of a word or words, rather than a hidden or implied meaning

Sometimes it's hard to give a *literal* translation of foreign phrases because there isn't always an exact match for the words in English.

You'll miss the meaning of many songs and poems if you stick to the *literal* meaning of every word.

Note: The word literally (LIT ur uh lee) is the adverb form of literal, and it means exactly literal, or without exaggeration.

There were *literally* hundreds of thousands of protesters in front of the capitol building in Washington, D.C.

"You shouldn't take me so *literally*," said Billie's father. "When I said dinner would be ready in a minute, I didn't mean exactly sixty seconds."

LOAF (LOHF) *v.* to be lazy; to spend time doing nothing, or very little

"I can't believe you just *loafed* around the house all day when you were supposed to be painting the kitchen," huffed Maggie.

Dad loves to spend the weekends *loafing* around the yard in his cut-off shorts.

LOATHE (LOHTH) *v.* to hate intensely; to despise

I *loathe* the sight of water beetles, but my cat thinks they're fun to play with.

Mom keeps making me eat fried liver, even though she knows I *loathe* it.

When Barney found out his best friend had snitched on him, a feeling of *loathing* swept over him.

LOCALE (loh KAL) *n.* a place, especially having to do with events related to it; a setting

A dark alley is probably not a good *locale* for a birthday party.

Boston is the *locale* in the television show *Cheers*.

LONGEVITY (lon JEV i tee) *n.* long life; the length of a life

Tortoises, which can live for over a hundred years, are famous for their *longevity.*

Humans have an average *longevity* of seventy-five years.

I had no idea when I bought this toaster fifty years ago that it would have such amazing *longevity.*

LOOT (LOOT) *v.* to rob by open force, as in a war, raid, or riot or *n.* the stuff stolen through looting

During the electrical blackout, thieves broke shop windows and *looted* stores throughout the city.

For some reason, crowds celebrating the Chicago Bulls NBA championship got carried away and starting *looting* the stores in their own hometown.

The pirates returned to their ship with bags of *loot* after their midnight raid on the island town.

Note: *Loot* is also a slang term for money.

LUCID (LOO sid) *adj.* clear and easy to understand; rational and mentally sound; clear and bright

Captain Dan, the airplane pilot, gave the passengers a *lucid* explanation of how air travel works.

Lottie had witnessed the burglary, but because she was so old and her memory failed so often, the judge decided she was not *lucid* enough to give testimony.

The night sky was so *lucid,* you could see millions of stars.

LUCRATIVE (LOO kruh tiv) *adj.* profitable

Poker can be very *lucrative* for people who know what they're doing; unfortunately, most people don't.

Even though Sasha dreamed of being a violinist, he took a job as a banker because it was more *lucrative.*

LULL (LUL) *v.* to cause to sleep; to soothe and calm

The mother *lulled* her baby by rocking it and softly humming a song.

The sound of the waves *lulled* the sunbather to sleep.

Note: *Lull* can also be used as a noun to be a period of calm or quiet.

Most businesses experience a *lull* between Christmas and New Year's Day because a lot of people are on vacation.

LUMINOUS (LOO muh nus) *adj.* shining, full of light

The reflection of the moon made the lake *luminous*.

Elizabeth's eyes were *luminous* in the candlelight.

LURCH (LURCH) *v.* to move suddenly and unsteadily

As I was coming to a stop at a red light, my foot slipped off the brake, and the car *lurched* forward and almost hit a woman in the crosswalk.

We shot the monster three times and thought it was going to fall down, but instead it *lurched* toward us, so we screamed and ran.

LURE (LOOR) *v.* to attract or tempt or *n.* an attraction or temptation

The trainer *lured* the dog into the cage with a steak bone.

Old Salty the sailor tried to settle down and lead a normal life, but in the end, he couldn't resist the *lure* of the sea.

The *lure* of Lee's meatball sandwich was too much for Kristin to stand, so she sneaked over and took it while he was out of the room.

LYNCH (LINCH) *v.* to execute someone by hanging without benefit of a trial

The accused horse thief was captured by an angry mob, who *lynched* him before the sheriff could get there to stop them.

MACHO (MAH choh) *adj.* having an exaggerated sense of manliness; overly aggressive; virile; dominant

John was so *macho*, he wouldn't be caught dead cooking because he considered it "women's work."

I don't like going to the gym anymore because it's full of all those *macho* men flexing their huge muscles and talking about sports.

In his movies, Clint Eastwood usually plays very *macho* characters, like gun-fighting cowboys and tough detectives.

MALICE (MAL is) *n.* bad will toward others; the desire to hurt others

Holly told everyone her sister Polly was a bed-wetter out of *malice*.

I know a kid who was so full of *malice*, he would shove a firecracker into a turtle's shell just to watch it explode.

Note: The adjective form of malice is *malicious* (ma LISH us).
Polly was angry at her sister for spreading the *malicious*
rumor that she wet her bed.

MALIGNANT (ma LIG nunt) *adj.* having ill will, malicious; deadly

Cal was having *malignant* thoughts about running over
his brother's bike with a car.

Diabetes can be a *malignant* disease if it is not treated.

MANIPULATE (muh NIP yuh layt) *v.* to control with skill; to influence in a clever way

Years of practice made it easy for Victor to *manipulate* the
complex controls on the wrecking crane.

Rasputin was a Siberian monk who used his personal and
religious power to *manipulate* the last monarchs of Russia to
suit his evil purposes.

MANSLAUGHTER (MAN slaw tur) *n.* the crime of killing a person without meaning to, as through negligence

Rich was convicted of *manslaughter* for killing a person
while driving drunk, and is serving five years in prison.

In certain cases of extreme emotional distress, a person
who shoots or stabs someone to death may be charged with
manslaughter instead of murder because it could be argued that
the person didn't know what he or she was doing at the time.

MANUAL (MAN yoo ul) *adj.* having to do with the hands or
being operated by hand

Gregory had such *manual* skill, we knew he would either
be a great surgeon or a great magician.

Most of the controls in the car are electric, but you have to
roll down the windows *manually*.

In a car with a *manual* transmission, you have to shift
gears yourself; an automatic transmission shifts gears for you.

MARTIAL LAW (MAR shul LAW) *n.* military rule over a civilian
population in times of emergency, such as during a war or after
the collapse of the civilian government

The country was still under *martial law* after three
attempts at democratic elections had failed or resulted in
bloody riots.

The general overthrew the president, declared himself the
supreme ruler, and declared *martial law* over the entire country.

MARVEL (MAR vul) *n.* a thing of wonder or *v.* to be filled with wonder

The laptop computer is a *marvel* of modern technology.

The audience *marveled* at the juggler's ability to juggle a bowling ball, a flaming torch, a knife, and a live chicken all at the same time.

MATERNAL (muh TUR nul) *adj.* motherly; having to do with the mother or motherhood

One of the strongest *maternal* instincts is the desire to protect children from harm.

"Stop being so *maternal*," snapped Jim at his girlfriend. "I can pick out my clothes without your help."

All the neighborhood kids loved Mrs. Wallace, a kind, *maternal* woman who always gave them cookies, and who always smelled of cinnamon and vanilla.

MATRIARCH (MAY tree ark) *n.* a woman who rules a family, clan, tribe, or other organization

Isadora, the founder of the first theater in Greenville, was the *matriarch* of the town's artistic society.

In ancient times, many tribes were ruled by *matriarchs*, who passed their power on to their daughters and granddaughters.

MECCA (MEK uh) *n.* the center of a certain interest or activity

New York City is a *mecca* for people who want to be stage actors.

Hollywood is the international movie *mecca*.

Silicon Valley is a *mecca* for innovators in the field of computer technology.

MEDIA (MEE dee uh) *n.* plural of medium (MEE dee um), a way of giving information to large numbers of people

Movies are a good *medium* for telling stories.

The Internet is a *medium* that gives computer owners access to huge amounts of information.

Note: The plural, media, is used to refer to those groups that usually report news events—radio, television, newspapers, and magazines. Remember, the word media is plural (even though it doesn't have an "s" on the end of it), so make sure you use the right verb with it.

The *media* were tracking the senator like bloodthirsty lions, waiting to pounce on any mistake he might make.

The *media* were accused of turning the trial into a circus.

MEDIATE (MEE dee ayt) *v.* to settle an argument by working with all sides; to bring about an agreement between different sides

President Jimmy Carter *mediated* an important peace treaty between Egypt and Israel.

Former president Jimmy Carter *mediated* the dispute between the U.S. government and the government of Haiti, and helped us avoid a war.

My big brother Ned *mediated* a fight I was having with my friend over who could play the video game first, and helped us work out a way to share it.

MEDITATE (MED i tayt) *v.* to think deeply about something

Albert Einstein spent a lot of time *meditating* about the nature of time and space.

Carol couldn't figure out why the model plane she put together didn't fly as it was supposed to, so she sat in her room to *meditate* on the problem.

MEDLEY (MED lee) *n.* a mixture; a musical arrangement that uses pieces of different songs

The restaurant makes a dish called "seafood *medley*," which is a mixture of shrimp, scallops, mussels, and lobster.

The pianist played a *medley* of songs by Cole Porter.

MELEE (MAY lay) *n.* a confused fight among a number of people

There was some kind of *melee* in the school cafeteria this afternoon, but no one is sure what it was about.

Sara, who was on her way home from the market, got hit in the head with a brick when she stumbled onto a *melee* that had broken out over who had the right to use a certain parking space.

MEMENTO (muh MEN toh) *n.* something that serves as a reminder of something past; a souvenir

Valerie bought a pair of mouse ears as a *memento* of her trip to Disneyland.

The whole time he was stationed in Korea, Sgt. York kept a pressed magnolia blossom in the front pocket of his uniform as a *memento* of his home in Mississippi.

MENACE (MEN is) *n.* something that threatens to cause danger or harm

The fire ants were a *menace* to all the people who were trying to have a picnic on the grass.

Armed gangs are a *menace* to the safety of our neighborhoods.

MENTOR (MEN tor) *n.* a wise teacher and adviser

When I first started working at Bumbleby & Bumbleby, I knew nothing about the honey business, but luckily my boss became my *mentor*, and she showed me all the ins and outs of the company.

My father's business partner was always a *mentor* to me. I'd turn to him for advice and support.

MERIT (MER it) *n.* excellence; something that entitles a person to a reward or recognition or *v.* to deserve

Her writing professor told Marcia her short story had *merit*.

Colin has many *merits*, but neatness is not one of them.

The actor's wonderful performance *merits* the praise of the critics and the applause of the audience.

METAMORPHOSIS (met uh MOR fuh sis) *n.* a complete change in appearance or attitude

When the wicked, selfish Grinch in Dr. Seuss's story sees that stealing all the presents in Whoville doesn't ruin Christmas, and that the Whos still seem happy even without gifts, he goes through a *metamorphosis*, and turns into a pretty nice guy.

In one weird short story by Franz Kafka, Gregor Samsa goes to sleep as a human, goes through some *metamorphosis* in the night, and wakes up as a giant insect.

MILITANT (MIL uh tunt) *adj.* fiercely aggressive or warlike, especially for a cause

Millicent was *militant* about her objection to testing products on animals, and would go into stores and break as many bottles of perfume or hair dye as she could before security guards stopped her.

Militant protesters chanted slogans and held up signs calling for the Congress to repeal the Eighteenth Amendment.

MIMIC (MIM ik) *v.* to imitate; to copy closely in speech or expression

Wanda didn't realize she was doing it, but after about a week in Scotland she started to *mimic* the accents of Scottish people.

Sam can *mimic* the calls of birds so well, they sometimes answer him or fly close to him.

MIRAGE (mi RAZH) *n.* an illusion usually seen in the desert that looks like a body of water or a city; something that has no substance or isn't real

After being stranded in the desert for three days without water, Baldwin saw a pool of water up ahead of him and went running toward it, but it turned out to be nothing more than a *mirage*.

Blanche's beauty was a *mirage* created with clever lighting, makeup, and memories.

MISCELLANEOUS (mis uh LAY nee us) *adj.* made up of different things, subjects, or qualities

The book entitled *Reading Matter* is made up of *miscellaneous* poems, stories, songs, and observations.

His shelves are filled with books, compact discs, and *miscellaneous* knicknacks.

"You have such a *miscellaneous* collection of CDs," remarked Judy when she noticed Evan seemed to have every sort of music imaginable.

MODERATE (MOD ur it) *adj.* not extreme; medium; not severe; mild

The new Chinese restaurant charges *moderate* prices, but the food is fantastic!

Most of the year, the accountants have a *moderate* workload, but they get really busy in the spring.

"We can expect *moderate* temperatures for the rest of the week, with a chance of rain on Friday," said Buff Shiney, our local meteorologist.

MODEST (MOD ist) *adj.* not like a show-off, not overly proud; not too large or fancy

"Wilma was just being *modest* when she said her grades were okay," boasted her mother. "She's made straight As since she was in first grade."

All the other girls wore bright gowns with beads and sequins and bows to the prom, but Eula preferred her *modest* white dress.

The Jones family lives in a *modest* home in a nice part of town.

MOMENTUM (moh MEN tum) *n.* speed of motion

The steam engine started out slowly, but gradually built up *momentum.*

When we headed down the hill on our bikes, it was as though we were flying, but we lost *momentum* as the ground leveled out.

MONOTONY (muh NOT uh nee) *n.* boring repetition; lack of variation

I usually pass the time by looking out the car window when we take trips, but the *monotony* of the flat, treeless North Dakota landscape had me bored and restless in five minutes.

"Every day for the past six months we've had candy for breakfast, ice cream for lunch, and waffles for dinner," cried Lyle. "The *monotony* is driving me crazy!"

MONSOON (mahn SOON) *n.* a seasonal wind of the Indian Ocean and southern Asia

The intense *monsoon* brought heavy rains that flooded most of southern Thailand.

MORBID (MOR bid) *adj.* overly interested in death and decay; gruesome

Harold was a *morbid* little boy who liked to visit funeral parlors.

We thought using a coffin as a coffee table was kind of *morbid.*

Barbara got some sort of *morbid* enjoyment out of pretending to drown herself in the swimming pool.

MOTIVE (MOH tiv) *n.* something that causes or leads someone to act a certain way

It seems greed was Mrs. Boswell's *motive* for killing her husband, who had left her several million dollars in his will.

Mr. Creases said his love of children was his only *motive* in donating all the money needed for a new youth center.

MUTATE (MYOO tayt) *v.* to change form

In the movie *The Thing*, aliens take over the bodies of humans, and just when you least expect it, people who look normal start to *mutate* into horribly disgusting, slimy monsters.

Exposure to gamma rays caused Dr. Bruce Banner to *mutate* into the Incredible Hulk.

Note: A *mutant* (MYOOT unt) is a living thing that has gone through mutation.

The petting zoo at the circus was full of *mutants*: two-headed horses, a hippopotamus with wings, and goats with six legs.

MUTINY (MYOOT un ee) *n.* rebellion against authority, especially on a ship at sea

In the late 1700s, Fletcher Christian, an officer aboard *H.M.S. Bounty*, led a famous *mutiny* against the cruel Captain Bligh.

Rumor has it the girls at the Sylvia Smithers Academy staged a *mutiny* against the outdated dress code, and all showed up to class in jeans on Monday.

MYTH (MITH) *n.* a traditional tale usually used to explain why the world is the way it is, or how the world was created; a story that is not really true, but is often repeated

The existence of the Loch Ness monster in Scotland is thought of as a *myth* by most people, although many others have spent years trying to prove the existence of the giant beast.

According to an ancient Roman *myth*, Echo was a young girl who loved a very handsome, but vain, young man who didn't return her love, so she wasted away until nothing was left of her but her voice.

NAIVE (neye EEV) *adj.* inexperienced; innocent in the ways of the world

Kelly's brother told her someone had put poison in the Halloween candy and that she better give hers to him so he could get rid of it, and she was so *naive* she didn't realize he just wanted her candy for himself.

"Don't be so *naive*," said Mrs. Woolard to her husband as the hitchhiker drove away in their car. "We're in the middle of nowhere. I doubt he's just gone to run an errand."

NAVIGATE (NAV i gayt) *v.* to plan a course and steer through it

It takes an expert kayaker to *navigate* the rough waters of this river.

Hundreds of years ago, sailors used to *navigate* their ships using the stars to guide them.

NEGLIGENT (NEG li junt) *adj.* not showing proper care or concern; neglectful

Jack was a *negligent* pet owner: he never bathed his dogs, and sometimes let them go for days without food.

Samantha was supposed to take care of her friend's sea monkeys while she was on vacation, but she was so *negligent*, most of the sea monkey tribe died by the time her friend returned.

NICHE (NICH) *n.* a hollowed out space in a wall; a place or position that suits someone or something well

The little statue of Peter Pan was displayed in a *niche* in the entry hall of the theater.

Nelson the shoemaker had a lot of competition until he found his *niche* as a maker of ballet slippers.

Pauline had a hard time settling into college and making friends until she found her *niche* in the art department.

NOCTURNAL (nok TUR nul) *adj.* having to do with night; most active at night; happening at night

Witches are known for their *nocturnal* meetings in groups which are called covens.

The moon is best seen in the *nocturnal* sky, but sometimes you can see it during the day as well.

My cat is a *nocturnal* animal: she sleeps all day, and scampers around the house all night.

NOMAD (NOH mad) *n.* a person who wanders from place to place; a person who belongs of a group of people who move around to find food for themselves and their livestock

Danny's mother wondered when her son would give up being a *nomad* and find himself a nice girl to settle down with.

Most of the Native Americans who lived in the North American plains were *nomads* who moved from season to season.

Note: The adjective form of nomad is *nomadic* (noh MAD ik).

The Gypsies are a *nomadic* group of people who first came to Europe from India 600 years ago.

NOMINATE (NOM i nayt) *v.* to propose someone as a candidate for an elected office

I *nominated* Betsy as our student council representative.

NONCHALANT (non shuh LAHNT) *adj.* cool and unconcerned

George didn't want Melanie to know he liked her, so whenever she spoke to him, he tried to act as *nonchalant* as possible.

Trey, who was dressed up as a giant lizard, realized a moment too late that this wasn't a costume party after all, but he somehow managed to be completely *nonchalant* as he strolled toward the punch bowl, dragging his tail behind him.

NOTORIOUS (noh TOR ee us) *adj.* having a bad reputation that is widely known

Mrs. Jacobsen was *notorious* for falling asleep at dinner parties, sometimes even before the main course arrived.

Doc Holiday was a *notorious* gambler of the Old West.

NOVEL (NAH vul) *adj.* new and different

Adam had a *novel* approach to mopping: he strapped sponges to his feet and skated across the kitchen floor.

Millions of empty plastic milk jugs were going to waste until someone came up with the *novel* idea of using them as planters.

NOVICE (NAH vis) *n.* a beginner

The ski resort has small hills called "bunny slopes" for *novices*.

After Luigi dropped the fourth batch of dough on his head, he was forced to admit that he was a *novice* in the art of pizza crust twirling.

OASIS (oh AY sis) *n.* a small area in the desert that has plants and water; a place or thing that is a pleasant change or relief

The weary travellers decided to rest themselves and their camels at the *oasis*.

Sandra's office was an *oasis* of calm in an otherwise tense and frantic company.

OBESE (oh BEES) *adj.* very overweight

According to her doctor, Kim is *obese,* and must lose weight if she wants to avoid health problems.

The man was so *obese* he had to be buried in a piano crate because a regular coffin wasn't big enough for him.

OBJECTIVE (uhb JEK tiv) *adj.* not influenced by emotion or personal opinion

Mothers are rarely *objective* about their children's abilities, and usually think their sons and daughters are the smartest, cutest, most talented kids in the world.

Elaine was *objective* enough about her appearance to realize she would never be Miss America.

OBLIGATION (ahb li GAY shun) *n.* a duty, or something you've promised to do; a debt owed for a favor

"After all your grandfather has done for you, you have an *obligation* to go see him in the hospital," scolded Jim's mother.

When Iggy broke Pop's electric can opener, he felt an *obligation* to buy him a new one.

OBLITERATE (uh BLIT u rayt) *v.* to destroy completely

The sand castle was *obliterated* by the rising tide.

Kelly completely *obliterated* her opponent when she checkmated him at chess in five minutes.

OBLIVIOUS (uh BLIV ee us) *adj.* unaware; unmindful

The substitute teacher was *oblivious* to the whispering and note-passing that was going on in his classroom.

Sharon was madly in love with Stan, but he was *oblivious* to her affection.

OBSCURE (ahb SKYOOR) *adj.* hard to see or understand; not well known

The scientist found a stone tablet with ancient writing on it, but many of the letters were too *obscure* to make out.

Shawn has an irritating habit of quoting *obscure* movies and books none of us have ever heard of.

OBSOLETE (ahb suh LEET) *adj.* out of date, no longer useful; no longer in use

When the light bulb was invented, oil lamps became *obsolete*.

Because our language changes and grows, new words are always being added to the dictionary, while other words become *obsolete* and are dropped.

OBTRUSIVE (uhb TROO siv) *adj.* forced and obvious

Cal kept clearing his throat and coughing in the most *obtrusive* way, trying to get his girlfriend, who was sitting in the front of the theater, to turn around and see him.

The president's daughter wanted, more than anything, to have a normal birthday party, but it was hard to have fun with two huge, *obtrusive* security guards at every door.

OMEN (OH mun) *n.* something that is believed to be a sign of events to come, or sign of good or bad luck

Many cultures consider the appearance of a raven to be a bad *omen* that predicts death or bad luck.

When the general tripped and fell on his face getting out of his jeep, the soldiers took it as a bad *omen* for the battle they faced the next day.

OMIT (oh MIT) *v.* to leave out

When my high school did a production of the play *A Streetcar Named Desire,* we had to *omit* certain scenes that our parents and teachers thought were too adult for us.

"Please tell me all about the party, and don't *omit* a single detail," said Jeannie, who was eager to hear some good gossip.

OMNIPOTENT (ahm NIP uh tent) *adj.* having the ability to control everything

In the George Orwell book *1984,* the people's lives are ruled by an *omnipotent* dictator named "Big Brother."

Christians, Jews, and Muslims all believe in the existence of one *omnipotent* god.

OPAQUE (oh PAYK) *adj.* not letting light pass through; not transparent

Betty prefers *opaque* tights to sheer stockings because she has a lot of freckles on her legs.

We decided the windows in the bathroom should be *opaque* so no one could look in and see us taking baths.

OPTIMISM (AHP ti miz um) *n.* an ability to look on the bright side of things and believe that everything will work out for the best

The *optimism* and excitement Frank felt on the opening of his restaurant, Frank's Fry House, soon faded as days went by with no customers.

Note: The adjective form of optimisim is *optimistic* (ahp ti MIS tik).

Even though it looked as though she would lose the election, Anne stayed *optimistic* and refused to give up until all the votes were counted.

ORATOR (OR uh tur) *n.* someone who gives a formal speech; a public speaker

The Reverend Martin Luther King, Jr. was a gifted *orator* whose speeches on civil rights moved many people to take a stand against bigotry.

We had no idea Damon was such a good *orator* until we saw him at the city council meeting, where his speech on homeless puppies brought tears to the eyes of many in the audience.

ORNATE (or NAYT) *adj.* decorated excessively, showy

Bill's *ornate* jacket had dozens of flashy pins, gold buttons, and a silver lapel.

ORTHODOX (OR thuh dox) *adj.* sticking to traditional, accepted beliefs or expectations

The wedding was completely *orthodox*, except for the fact that the couple wrote their own vows.

The critic's taste in art was a bit too *orthodox* for him to appreciate the new paintings at the modern art gallery.

OSTRACIZE (OS truh syze) v. to banish or cut off from a group or society

People with AIDS are often *ostracized* by neighbors and friends who are ignorant about the nature of the disease.

Mr. Weltkrieg was *ostracized* by the town when it was discovered he was a notorious war criminal.

OVERT (oh VURT) adj. open and obvious

After weeks of trying to get Cindy to notice him, Elmo decided more *overt* steps were necessary, so he sent her a dozen roses and asked her on a date.

Horace made an *overt* attempt to walk out of the lunchroom with an entire tray of desserts, but he was stopped before he got to the door.

OVERWHELM (oh vur WELM) v. to overpower; to affect deeply

Tulane University's football team was simply *overwhelmed* by Florida State, and they lost the game 72 to 3.

Myra was *overwhelmed* with gratitude when she found out her whole neighborhood had chipped in some money to help her pay her hospital bills.

OZONE LAYER (OH zohn LAY ur) n. a layer of the gas ozone high above the surface of the earth; it helps shield the world from too much radiation from the sun

Scientists say that our overuse of chemicals called chlorofluorocarbons has caused holes in the *ozone layer* above the arctic poles.

PACIFIST (PAS uh fist) n. someone who is against violence as a way of settling problems; someone who refuses to fight in a war because of the belief that war and killing are wrong

William is a *pacifist* who spent time in jail for refusing to report to the draft board during the Vietnam War.

Some religions, such as the Society of Friends, require their members to be *pacifists*.

PALLOR (PAL ur) n. extreme paleness of the skin, as from fright or sickness.

Macbeth's face took on such a *pallor*, you would think he had seen a ghost.

Years of working long hours in the city gave Cindy bad headaches and a sickly *pallor*.

PANACHE (puh NAHSH) *n.* grand, dramatic style or manner

The count always leaves a room with great *panache*: he kisses the hand of his hostess, bows deeply, turns into a bat, and flies out the window.

Bela always wore a cape—even during the summer—because he thought it gave him some *panache*.

PANDEMONIUM (pan duh MOH nee um) *n.* a wild uproar

What started as a minor food fight between two students turned into a *pandemonium* of flying cakes and clattering trays before teachers could do anything about it.

When the football team won its first game in five years, the fans rushed onto the field and the whole stadium was in a state of *pandemonium*.

PANTOMIME (PAN tuh myme) *n.* face and body gestures used to express a message or *v.* to make face and body gestures to express a message

When we were on vacation in China, we had to communicate mainly through *pantomime*, since the only things we knew how to say in Chinese were "I am an American" and "Where is the embassy?"

My grandfather flapped his arms at the Italian desk clerk and pretended things were stinging his behind in an attempt to *pantomime* the fact that there was a nest of wasps in his hotel room.

PARALLEL (PAR uh lel) *adj.* running in the same direction, but never crossing; similar or along the same lines

Main Street is usually so full of traffic that I often take Second Street, which runs *parallel* to Main, whenever I want to go downtown.

PARANOID (PAR uh noid) *adj.* abnormally concerned about one's safety or security; having the feeling that everyone is against you or "out to get you"

My great aunt was so *paranoid*, every night she made me check in all the closets and under the bed to make sure a crazy killer was not hiding, waiting for her to go to sleep.

General Augusto was convinced that all his conversations were being recorded through hidden microphones, that his food was being poisoned, and that secret police were following him, but his doctor told him he was being *paranoid*.

PARAPLEGIC (par uh PLEE jik) *adj.* having the lower half of the body paralyzed, usually through injury to the spinal cord or *n.* a person who is paralyzed from the waist down

Since his terrible car accident Bud has been *paraplegic.*

Bud had a hard time adjusting to life as a *paraplegic* because he was so active and athletic before his accident.

PASSIVE (PAS iv) *adj.* not active; receiving action, but not returning any; giving no resistance

It amazed me that Amy could stay completely *passive* while her brother tried to tickle the soles of her feet.

The dog was *passive* as the children tied its ears above its head and dressed it up in their dolls' clothing.

PATHOLOGICAL (path uh LOJ i kul) *adj.* having to do with, or caused by, a disease or mental disorder

Steve is a *pathological* liar, which means he can't control his tendency to lie.

Sylvia's mood swings are so extreme they might be considered *pathological.*

PATRIARCH (PAY tree ark) *n.* the father or leader of a tribe, family, or group; an old, respected man

Old Mr. Jenkins, one of our town's founders and certainly its *patriarch*, was much more powerful than the mayor and town council combined.

PATRONIZE (PAY truh nyze) *v.* to be a supporter or customer of; to talk down to someone

Eva *patronized* only the most exclusive, expensive stores on Rodeo Drive.

"Don't *patronize* me," my grandmother yelled at the waiter. "I may be old, but that doesn't mean I'm stupid."

Note: A *patron* (PAY trun) is a person who supports a group or activity, or a regular customer.

Isabella Stewart Gardner was a *patron* of the arts.

PAUPER (PAW pur) *n.* a very poor person

Nothing makes rich people into *paupers* faster than a bad gambling habit.

PENDING (PEN ding) *adj.* not yet occurring or happening soon or *prep.* while awaiting

The *pending* peace talks brought an air of optimism to the war-torn country.

His *pending* meeting with the principal made Jimmy nervous.

Pending a full safety inspection of its rides, the carnival was closed down.

PENSIVE (PEN siv) *adj.* in deep, serious thought or showing deep thought

Harold was a *pensive* and quiet boy who would spend hours just staring out a window.

Even though my mother said nothing was wrong, I could tell by the *pensive* expressive on her face that she was worried about my father's plane landing safely in the snowstorm.

PERCEPTIVE (pur SEP tiv) *adj.* having sharp insight, or the ability to notice small details

The detective Hercule Poirot was *perceptive* enough to notice that the candlestick holder had been moved about one foot to the left since the last time he had been in the study.

Her parents thought they were being very sneaky, but Clara was a *perceptive* girl, and realized right away they were planning a surprise party for her.

PERJURY (PUR juh ree) *n.* the unlawful act of lying while under oath

Mr. Thompson knew his wife was guilty, so to protect her he committed *perjury* by telling the jury he was the one who had shot the stranger.

PERPENDICULAR (pur pen DIK yuh lur) *adj.* crossing or meeting at a right angle

Church Street is *perpendicular* to Varick Street.

The table legs are *perpendicular* to the tabletop.

PERSECUTE (PUR suh cyoot) *v.* to bother, harrass, or attack regularly

All the popular kids at school *persecuted* Warren terribly by stealing his lunch money, calling him a geek, snapping his suspenders, and generally making his life a nightmare.

Many immigrants came to the United States because they were being *persecuted* for their religious beliefs in Europe.

PERSEVERE (pur suh VEER) *v.* to hold on or keep on in a course of action or a belief

In spite of harsh weather and food shortages, the pioneers *persevered* and made it to their destination.

If you want to be a famous writer, you must *persevere*, no matter how many times your work is rejected.

PERTINENT (PUR tin int) *adj.* related to the matter at hand; relevant

Clancey irritated his teacher by always asking questions that weren't *pertinent* to the class discussion.

Weather and traffic conditions are *pertinent* factors to consider when planning a car trip.

PESSIMISM (PES uh miz um) *n.* a tendency to stress the bad side of things

Our coach was always so full of *pessimism* about our chances of winning that it was hard for us to get fired up, and we usually lost.

Note: The adjective form of pessimism is *pessimistic* (pes uh MIS tik).

Geraldine was *pessimistic* about her chances of becoming president.

PHILANTHROPY (fi LAN thruh pee) *n.* a love of humankind that is often shown through generosity and charity

The fact that Mr. Moneybags left most of his money to charity is a great example of his *philanthropy*.

Note: Someone known for philanthropy is a *philanthropist* (fi LAN thruh pist).

The princess was widely known as a *philanthropist* and activist for the underprivileged.

PINNACLE (PIN uh kul) *n.* the peak or highest point of something

Mike Tyson was at the *pinnacle* of his career as a heavyweight boxer when he was thrown in prison for attacking a young beauty queen.

I planted a little American flag at the *pinnacle* of the mountain.

PIOUS (PYE us) *adj.* showing religious devotion, commitment and respect

Mary was a *pious* woman who would never think of skipping church on Sunday.

We always knew William was *pious,* but we never thought he would decide to become a priest.

PITTANCE (PIT uns) *n.* a very small amount of money

It was hard for Bob Crachit to take care of his family on the *pittance* Mr. Scrooge paid him.

"One million dollars is a *pittance* to him," said the kidnapper. "I'm sure he'll pay much more for the return of his daughter."

PLACATE (PLAY kayt) *v.* to calm the anger of, especially by giving something

Bonnie screamed and cried when her mother left the room, so the babysitter *placated* her by letting her play with her special squeaky bunny toy.

The angry townspeople were not *placated* by the police chief's vow to bring the hoodlums to justice—they wanted immediate action.

PLAINTIVE (PLAYN tiv) *adj.* sorrowful

Wanda finally gave in to the dog's *plaintive* whines and gave her some table scraps.

The streets were filled with the slow, *plaintive* song of the saxophone player.

PLATONIC (pluh TAHN ik) *adj.* not physically passionate; mainly friendly or spiritual

"My relationship with Candace is strictly *platonic!*" Martin insisted to his jealous girlfriend.

Everyone thought that Chris and Marie were boyfriend and girlfriend, but it turned out they just had a very intense *platonic* relationship.

PLEA (PLEE) *n.* an urgent request; in law, the accused criminal's answer to the charges

Sandra's *plea* for a raise in her allowance was ignored.

Herman's lawyers encouraged him to enter a *plea* of "not guilty."

PLIGHT (PLYTE) *n.* a dangerous or difficult situation

Quentin was moved by the *plight* of the wounded bird, so he took it in and nursed it back to health.

The *plight* of the baby whale which had accidentally wound up in the Delaware River was broadcast on the news every night until it was rescued.

POLYGAMY (puh LIG uh mee) *n.* the crime of being married to more than one person at the same time

It took ten years for Eldridge's wives, one living in Utah, one in Kentucky, and another in Oregon, to realize they were married to a *polygamist.*

POMPOUS (POM pus) *adj.* self-important; overly full of a sense of importance or dignity

It's a shame that winning the Little Miss Apple Blossom beauty contest turned Margery into such a *pompous* girl.

The student council president's speech at graduation was so *pompous* that all the seniors rolled their eyes and giggled.

POTENT (POHT unt) *adj.* powerful

The doctor gave me a very *potent* medicine for my insomnia—two pills put me to sleep in ten minutes.

European settlers often faced *potent* opposition from the Native Americans who were being forced off their land.

PRAGMATIC (prag MAT ik) *adj.* practical

Mom had a *pragmatic* solution to our fight over the last piece of pie: she sliced it in half.

PRECARIOUS (pri KAR ee us) *adj.* dangerously unstable

The way Mona had the tray of glasses balanced on her head looked pretty *precarious.*

The peace between the two countries was *precarious* at best: one false move on either side, and the war could start up again.

PREDOMINANT (pri DOM uh nunt) *adj.* strongest or greatest; most common or most represented

During the 1980s, the San Francisco Forty-Niners were the *predominant* football team.

Tulips are the *predominant* flowers in my garden.

Note: *Predominantly* (pri DOM uh nunt lee) means mostly. His hair is *predominantly* black, with a few flecks of gray.

PREJUDICE (PREJ uh dis) *n.* a judgment made about someone or something before the facts are known; unfair judgments or beliefs about a race, religion, or group

Melvin had a *prejudice* against opera music because his father always made fun of it, so he refused to go on the field trip to see *Carmen*.

Zoe's belief that all used-car salespeople are dishonest is an example of *prejudice*.

PREMATURE (pree muh TYOOR) *adj.* too early; happening before the usual time

When Edson failed his English exam and wound up getting an "F" in the course, his father realized that his sending out graduation invitations had been *premature*.

Don't you think that deciding you hate a book after reading only two pages is a little *premature*?

PREOCCUPIED (pree OK yuh pyed) *adj.* distracted or caught up in thought

Olivia was so *preoccupied* with thoughts of her weekend trip to the beach that she didn't even hear her teacher call on her. "I apologize for not giving you my full attention," said Beth's piano teacher, "but I'm a little *preoccupied* with problems of my own today."

PRESTIGE (pre STEEZH) *n.* honor or high standing

Being the football quarterback gave Penn great *prestige* among his classmates.

Note: The adjective form of prestige is *prestigious* (pre STEE jus).

The Congressional Medal of Honor is one of the most *prestigious* awards an American can receive.

PREVALENT (PREV uh lunt) *adj.* common; in wide existence

Blond hair is *prevalent* in the Scandinavian countries.

Tuberculosis is a disease that is much more *prevalent* in cities than in the country.

PREVIOUS (PREE vee us) *adj.* coming before in order

Ms. Spurlock went back to the *previous* day's lesson to review some topics that gave the students difficulty.

In the *previous* episode of *Star Trek,* Mr. Spock had been kidnapped, but this time it was Captain Kirk who was in danger.

PRIME (PRYME) *adj.* first in quality, value, or degree

"My *prime* concern is the safety of the children," said the fire chief.

Dr. Jonas Salk's *prime* accomplishment was the development of a polio vaccination in the 1950s.

PRIOR (PRY ur) *adj.* coming before in time or order

"I'm afraid I can't come to your dance recital," said Dinah. "I have a *prior* engagement."

Note: *Prior to* means before.

Prior to the game, Troy tripped and reinjured his thumb, so he was unable to play.

PROCRASTINATE (proh KRAS tuh nayt) *v.* to delay or put off doing something

Emily would use any excuse to *procrastinate* when it came to doing her homework.

Every year, Andy said he wanted to go to clown school, but he *procrastinated* until it was too late to send in an application.

PRODIGAL (PROD i gul) *adj.* reckless; wasteful; overly generous

Roy made *prodigal* use of the money he won in the lottery; he went to the racetrack and lost it all in one day.

Mrs. Finney was *prodigal* when it came to buying gifts for her children and grandchildren.

PROFOUND (pruh FOWND) *adj.* deep; thorough; deeply felt

Ever since she was bitten by a dachshund at the age of three, Lillian has had a *profound* dislike of dogs.

Voltaire was a philosopher known for his *profound,* but sometimes cynical, observations on life.

PROFUSE (pro FYOOS) *adj.* plentiful; extravagant

My eyes began to water as I stood in the elevator with Dennis because he had made rather *profuse* use of aftershave that evening.

The neighbors were annoyed by the crowds attracted to the *profuse* display of Christmas lights on Mr. Kringle's lawn.

PROPAGANDA (prop uh GAN duh) *n.* material or information distributed to a large number of people, often repeatedly, for the purpose of winning them over to a certain belief; this information is usually one-sided, often unfair, and sometimes untrue

During times of war, most countries use *propaganda* to keep the civilian population supportive.

Many extreme political groups use *propaganda*—scary television commercials, alarming speeches, and sometimes outright lies—to push people into voting a certain way without knowing all the facts.

PROSAIC (proh ZAY ik) *adj.* dull and unimaginative

Cameron's attempts at romance are so *prosaic*, it's no wonder he can never keep a girlfriend.

Up until the time he met the magician and learned to turn himself into any animal he wanted, Lorenzo led the *prosaic* life of a small-town paper boy.

PROSE (PROHZ) *n.* ordinary speech or writing, as opposed to poetry

The language in Zola's novels was so beautiful it sounded more like music than *prose*.

The exciting story of the battle at the Alamo was made boring by the book's dull, straightforward *prose*.

PROTRUDE (proh TROOD) *v.* to stick out

The man's shoe *protruded* from under the curtain he was trying to hide behind.

Stella's tongue *protruded* every time someone said hello to her, which was quite rude on her part.

PROVINCIAL (pro VIN shul) *adj.* not sophisticated, as if from a small town; narrow-minded

It was easy to see Jeb was not from the city because of his country accent and his *provincial* clothing.

Antoinette was embarrassed by her date's *provincial* habit of asking for ketchup with his steak.

The French think Americans have *provincial* attitudes about showing nudity on television.

PROVOCATIVE (pruh VOK uh tiv) *adj.* tending to stir up feeling, excitement, or action

The new scientific evidence showing that eating a pound of chocolate a day will make you live to 100 was so *provoca-*

tive that sales of chocolate skyrocketed the day after the research was made public.

PROXIMITY (prok SIM i tee) *n.* the state of being near; nearness

The *proximity* of Jacob's apartment to his job made it possible for him to walk to work.

At the air show, we saw several planes flying in close *proximity* to each other.

The *proximity* of the beautiful beach made it hard for Matthew to stay inside and study.

PSEUDONYM (SOOD uh nim) *n.* a false name used by an author

In the 1800s, female authors sometimes chose male *pseudonyms*. George Eliot's real name was Mary Ann Evans, and George Sand's real name was Lucie Dudevant.

PSYCHOLOGICAL (sy kuh LOJ i kul) *adj.* having to do with the mind and emotions or the study of the mind and emotions

After many tests proved that there was nothing wrong with her legs, doctors decided that the Mary's illness was *psychological,* not physical.

Dr. Skinner conducted several *psychological* experiments on dogs to learn more about human behavior.

QUALM (KWAHLM) *n.* a sudden, disturbing feeling; a pang of conscience. This word is usually used in the plural

I'm having *qualms* about leaving the kids all alone for five days.

Cody had no *qualms* about feeding his sister's prized fish to the cat.

QUANDARY (KWAHN dree) *n.* a state of uncertainly or doubt

Celeste was in a *quandary* as to what to do with all the leftovers from last night's dinner.

QUERY (KWIR ee) *n.* a question

The vice president was caught off guard by *queries* from the press about his policy on war in Burkina Faso, a country he had never heard of.

The grandfather was embarrassed by his four-year-old granddaughter's *query* about where babies come from.

QUIRK (KWURK) *n.* some odd part of a person's behavior

Ian always mixes together all the food on his plate before he eats it. It's just one of his *quirks*.

QUOTA (KWOH tuh) *n.* a number or amount set as an acceptable standard

When Sunny worked at the basket weaving factory, each weaver had a *quota* of twenty baskets a day.

The government sometimes sets *quotas* on the number of immigrants the United States will accept from different countries.

RADICAL (RAD i kul) *adj.* extreme; revolutionary

Justine made a *radical* change in her appearance by shaving her head and losing 150 pounds.

Ross had proposed a *radical* method for keeping the U.S. out of entaglements in messy foreign wars: he suggested we build a huge wall all the way around the country and cut off all long-distance telephone communication with outside countries.

RAPPORT (ruh POR) *n.* a good relationship or connection

It's important for a teacher to develop a *rapport* with his or her students.

Everyone in the department thought Jane should bring their complaints to the boss since she had the best *rapport* with him.

REAP (REEP) *v.* to gain as a result of effort

If you start exercising when you are young, you will *reap* the health benefits later in life.

The inventor had no idea that he would *reap* such riches from his simplest creation, the paper clip.

REBUTTAL (ri BUT ul) *n.* a counterargument; presentation of a side of an issue different from one already presented

In the debate, Mike made an angry *rebuttal* to the accusation that he had stolen public funds.

The newspaper article attacking Mr. McBain for poor management of the strained-banana disaster at the baby food plant was unfair because the reporter had never called Mr. McBain for a comment or a *rebuttal*.

RECLUSE (REK loos) *n.* a person who lives alone, away from society

The once-famous movie star gave up her career at the age of thirty and became a *recluse,* living in a small house on a faraway island.

RECONCILE (REK un syle) *v.* to bring friendship or good relations back; to settle or bring into agreement

On yesterday's episode of the "Susie Snoop Show," a mother and daughter who hadn't spoken in ten years were *reconciled.*

The two countries decided to give up war and *reconcile* their differences through negotiation.

Note: The noun form of reconcile is *reconciliation* (rek un sil ee AY shun).

Mr. and Mrs. Semper made several attempts at *reconciliation,* but finally decided it was best if they got divorced while they still had some unbroken dishes.

RECOUNT (ri KOWNT) *v.* to tell in detail

The tribal storyteller can *recount* the entire history of his clan, all the way back to its beginning several hundred years ago.

The book *I, Claudius recounts* the final years of the corrupt Roman Empire.

RECTIFY (REK tuh fye) *v.* to correct or make right

When the president of the college noticed that the plaque under the statue of the founder had a spelling error on it, he decided to *rectify* the mistake, and ordered a new plaque immediately.

The children thought the Sun revolved around Earth until their astronomy teacher *rectified* their mistake.

RECUR (ri KUR) *v.* to happen again; to happen repeatedly

After the playoffs, I had a *recurring* nightmare about a sad-faced clown dressed in a Los Angeles Lakers uniform.

Selena showed me the meadow where the reported alien visitations had *recurred* over the years.

REDUNDANT (ri DUN dunt) *adj.* made up of more words than necessary; unnecessarily wordy; unnecessarily repetitive

When Mrs. Flipper yelled, "I want an immediate explanation and I want it right now!" no one had the guts to tell her she was being *redundant*, since "immediate" and "right now" mean the same thing.

The editor removed several *redundant* paragraphs from the textbook.

Asking someone to repeat something again is *redundant*.

REFUGE (REF yooj) *n.* a place of safety or shelter

Several African countries set aside land as a *refuge* for the elephants, which were being killed off by hunters who wanted their tusks for ivory.

For Sarah, the attic was a *refuge* from her loud, rough brothers.

REGIME (ray ZHEEM) *n.* the ruling system of government

Many Romanians died at the hands of their own government during the cruel *regime* of Nicolae Ceausescu, the former communist ruler.

The arts flourished and England prospered during the Queen Elizabeth I's *regime*.

Albania is still under the control of a strict, communist *regime*.

REHABILITATE (ree huh BIL i tayt) *v.* to restore to health or usefulness

Supposedly, the aim of our prison system is to *rehabilitate* criminals so that when they get out, they can be productive members of society.

The athlete spent months doing special exercises, hoping to *rehabilitate* his knee.

REIMBURSE (ree im BURS) *v.* to pay back

"If you pick up a pizza on the way here to watch the game, I'll *reimburse* you for it," offered Pete.

Sid wanted to be *reimbursed* for the cost of the long distance phone calls he made on behalf of the company.

RELENTLESS (ri LENT les) *adj.* harsh; severe; unending

We were lost at sea for days, our boat tossed and battered by *relentless* wind and rain.

The police officer was *relentless* when it came to hunting down criminals; he wouldn't rest until he got his man.

RELEVANT (REL uh vunt) *adj.* having something to do with the matter at hand

I think Mary's age is *relevant* to the question of whether or not she would be a good trapeze artist, but everyone else disagrees with me.

It seems as though some of my classmates like to raise their hands and make comments even if they have nothing *relevant* to say.

RELINQUISH (ri LING kwish) *v.* to give back; to give up; to abandon

Endless bombing raids forced the army to *relinquish* its camp and retreat.

When a new Miss America is selected, the old Miss America must *relinquish* her crown and title.

RELUCTANT (ri LUK tunt) *adj.* unwilling

The magician asked Otto to come up on stage and assist him, but Otto was shy and *reluctant*.

Ernie was *reluctant* to leave the beach because he was only halfway through building his sand castle.

REMINISCE (rem uh NIS) *v.* to remember and tell stories about past events

When we moved back to Alabama, my parents were eager to spend time *reminiscing* with their old friends.

I don't mind the fact that my grandmother likes to *reminisce*, but she tells the same stories over and over again.

RENDEZVOUS (RAI IN day voo) *n.* a meeting at a certain time and place or *v.* to meet at a certain time and place

Colette and Pierre decided that the café by the river was the perfect spot for a *rendezvous*.

The spies decided to *rendezvous* at midnight under the bridge so they could exchange the secret information.

RENOUNCE (ri NOWNS) *v.* to give up formally; to reject

Claude *renounced* his father when it was discovered he had sold secret military information to the enemy.

Mrs. Evans told her husband she would only take him back if he *renounced* gambling forever.

RENOWNED (ri NOWND) *adj.* famous

Natalia is a *renowned* concert pianist.

Jimmy Carter is *renowned* for his diplomatic negotiation skills.

Tracy is *renowned* throughout school for being able to blow gigantic bubbles with her gum.

REPENT (ri PENT) *v.* to regret or feel bad about

Irving *repented* after cheating on the test.

Elizabeth *repented* her mean treatment of the new girl at school.

REPRIEVE (ri PREEV) *n.* temporary safety from danger; cancellation of punishment

Calvin awoke with a sense of doom because he realized he'd forgotten to study for the big test, but nature granted him a *reprieve* in the form of a huge snowstorm that caused school to be cancelled.

Theodore was about to be executed by the firing squad when his life was saved by a last-minute *reprieve* from the governor.

REPRIMAND (REP ruh mand) *v.* to scold or *n.* a strong scolding

Hugo, the bus driver, was sternly *reprimanded* by his boss when he was found sleeping in the baggage compartment.

Mr. Philips, the chemistry teacher, received a written *reprimand* from the principal for teaching his students how to combine potentially explosive chemicals.

REPULSIVE (ri PUL siv) *adj.* disgusting, off-putting

That dog is cute from a distance, but it has a *repulsive* odor.

Nick makes a really *repulsive* face by flipping his eyelids inside out and rolling his eyes back into his head so all you can see are the whites.

RESERVE (ri ZURV) *v.* to save for later; to order for use later

I want a glass of milk before bedtime, but I'll *reserve* enough so you can have it with your cereal for breakfast.

That restaurant is so popular you have to call and *reserve* a table two months in advance if you want to eat there.

Note: When people say a person is *reserved*, that means the person holds back, or is shy and says little. A person who is *reserved* has *reserve*.

RESIGNATION (rez ig NAY shun) *n.* the act of quitting or a notice that one is quitting; acceptance of something difficult

Nancy's boss refused to accept her *resignation* and offered to double her salary if she would stay and keep working.

Brian was so upset by the vice president's unfair accusations that he went back to his desk, typed up his *resignation*, left it on his boss's desk, and went home.

After fighting about it for two weeks, Harvey sighed with *resignation* and said, "Okay, we'll sell the television."

The soldiers could hear the *resignation* in the general's voice as he announced that the president had relieved him of duty and put another general in charge.

RESOLUTE (REZ uh loot) *adj.* firm and determined

In a calm and *resolute* voice, Mindy said, "Give me a full refund right now, in cash, or I will have the police in here to arrest you so fast it will make your head spin."

Ted had grown from a shy little boy into a confident man: his head held high, his step *resolute*, his handshake firm, and his smile warm.

RESOLVE (ri ZOLV) *v.* to commit oneself, or make a firm decision; to find a solution

In an effort to make better grades, Linda *resolved* to spend no less than two hours every night doing homework.

It's a sign of maturity to be able to *resolve* problems on your own.

Note: The word *resolution* (rez uh LOO shun) means a firm agreement you make with yourself. When people talk about making New Year's *resolutions*, they are promising themselves that they will start or stop doing something.

RESUME (ri ZOOM) *v.* to start again

After I came back from the restroom, we *resumed* our discussion.

Our game of chess had dragged on so long we decided to quit for the day and *resume* tomorrow.

RETORT (ri TORT) *v.* to make a quick and witty answer or *n.* a quick, witty answer

When the man in the restaurant asked, "What's this fly doing in my soup?" his waiter *retorted*, "It looks like the backstroke."

Winston Churchill, the former prime minister of Great Britain, was known for his clever *retorts* as well as his leadership.

REVEL (REV ul) v. to take great pleasure; to have noisy, festive fun

Will *reveled* in the millions of dollars he won in the lottery.

Jealous Joan *reveled* in the misfortune of her coworker.

When the Detroit Red Wings won the Stanley Cup, all of Detroit *reveled* for days.

Note: *Revelry* (REV ul ree) is loud partying.

Marco is so rich he can afford not to work and to spend his days and nights in endless *revelry*.

REVERE (ri VEER) v. to respect highly; to honor

Before the end of World War II, the Japanese people *revered* their emperor as a god.

The Chief Justice of the Supreme Court is *revered* for his fairness and wisdom.

Note: To be *reverent* (REV uh runt) is to be respectful. To be *irreverent* (i REV uh runt) is to be slightly disrespectful.

It was *irreverant* for Joey to call the eighty-year-old bank president "gramps."

RIGOROUS (RIG ur us) adj. strict; harsh

Actress Demi Moore hired a personal trainer and started a *rigorous* exercise schedule to get into top shape for her next movie.

When Tina found out that she had to go to practice three times a week, she decided that the life of a cheerleader was too *rigorous* for her.

RISQUÉ (ris KAY) adj. very close to being shocking or indecent

The school board wouldn't let us see the 1960s movie version of *Romeo and Juliet* because they thought some of the love scenes were too *risqué*.

Grandpa was about to tell a story about an exotic dancer he knew during the war, but, much to our disappointment, Mom told him it was too *risqué* for us kids to hear.

RITE (RYTE) a ceremony; an act or series of acts performed by custom

Many different cultures have *rites* of passage that boys and girls must go through in order to be considered men and women.

The tradition of dancing around a maypole on the first day of May is an ancient *rite* of spring.

RUSTIC (RUS tik) *adj.* having to do with the country or country life

Even though he was a rich big-city lawyer, Harold liked having *rustic* furniture and decorations in his apartment.

The restaurant was brand new, but it was built to look old-fashioned and *rustic*—the wooden tables looked faded and weather-beaten, drinks were served out of mason jars, and there were a lot of antlers hanging on the walls.

SABOTAGE (SAB uh tahzh) *n.* an attempt to slow down or stop a cause or activity by destroying property or disrupting work or *v.* to commit sabotage

When Dad discovered that some important parts of the lawn mower were missing, he immediately accused us of *sabotage*.

Jake dreaded going back to boarding school so much that he tried to *sabotage* the family car.

Computer viruses are a dangerous form of *sabotage*.

SARCASTIC (sar KAS tik) *adj.* ironic, sneering, or intended to hurt someone's feelings

Ian's *sarcastic* sense of humor upsets lots of people, but I think he is very funny.

When Bonnie admitted she didn't know the capital of California, Les made the *sarcastic* comment, "I'm sure you'll make the state a fine senator some day."

SCANTY (SKAN tee) *adj.* barely sufficient or not enough in terms of amount

Sally's father wouldn't let her out of the house in such a *scanty* dress.

The supply of apples on our tree is so *scanty* this year, I doubt I'll have enough for more than a couple of pies.

SCOFF (SKOF) *v.* to express contempt; to mock

The children *scoffed* at my idea that we should turn the television off and go outside to play.

"You've done nothing but *scoff* at every idea I've had so far," said Lillian to Mick. "Since you're so smart, why don't you go get that elephant off our car by yourself?"

SCRUPULOUS (SKROO pyuh lus) *adj.* extremely careful

Eugene was *scrupulous* in keeping his room clean; he never so much as left a sock on the floor.

Ferns are delicate plants that need *scrupulous* care and attention.

SCRUTINY (SKROOTn ee) *n.* close observation; careful watching or study

Simon's room appeared neat at a glance, but closer *scrutiny* would show that he had just shoved everything under his bed.

The editor was known for his *scrutiny*; he never missed a single mistake.

SECT (SEKT) *n.* a number of people that form their own special group within a larger group

The Baptist church can be considered a Protestant *sect* because it shares many beliefs with other Protestant churches, but has some of its own practices, too.

The Hasidim are the members of a Jewish *sect* that stresses the power of mysticism and prayer.

SEDATE (suh DAYT) *adj.* calm and dignified; quiet

Nothing—not even loud noises, big dogs, or squirts from my water gun—could disturb the fat, *sedate* cat.

The principal was scared our prom would get too wild and out of hand, but it turned out to be so *sedate* you could have mistaken it for a meeting of the bridge club.

SEDENTARY (SED un ter ee) *adj.* requiring a lot of sitting; used to sitting a lot and not getting much exercise

Even though Kristin eats constantly and has a *sedentary* lifestyle, she is as skinny as a toothpick.

If you don't like *sedentary* work, truck driving is not for you.

SERENE (suh REEN) *adj.* peaceful and calm

The lake looked so beautiful and *serene* in the early morning light.

Even though children were yelling and fighting all around her, Mrs. Dolittle looked happy and *serene*.

SERVILE (SUR vyle) *adj.* like a slave or servant; submissive

Mona was alarmed by the *servile* attitude her boyfriend's mother had toward him and her husband. She did all the laundry, cooked all the meals, and fetched them something to drink whenever they wanted.

Veronica was a beautiful but mean-spirited girl who demanded *servile* obedience from her boyfriends.

Note: The noun form of servile is *servility* (sur VIL i tee).

Mona told her boyfriend he'd better not expect *servility* from her.

SHREWD (SHROOD) *adj.* clever

Clara is a *shrewd* shopper; she always finds the best bargains and never pays full price.

Shrewd poker players can tell whether or not you have a good hand by the look on your face.

SIESTA (see ES tuh) *n.* a nap taken after the midday meal

In Spain and Italy, many stores are closed for a couple of hours in the afternoon while the owners take their *siestas*.

I wish *siestas* were a common practice in America.

SIMILAR (SIM uh lur) *adj.* alike but not exacty the same

Spanish and Italian are *similar* languages because they both came from Latin.

Larry's car is *similar* to Mo's: they both drive blue Ford Mustangs, but Larry's is a couple of years older than Mo's.

SIMULTANEOUS (sye mul TAY nee us) *adj.* happening at the same time

The flash of lightning and the crash of thunder were almost *simultaneous*.

The umpire had a hard call to make: the runner slid home and *simultaneously* the catcher tagged him.

SKEPTIC (SKEP tik) *n.* a person who doubts the truth of something

"I'm afraid I'm a skeptic when it comes to so-called true love," said Ida.

Note: A skeptic is *skeptical* (SKEPT ti kul).

The rest of the town was convinced that the Magnificent Mario could predict the future, but Saul was *skeptical*.

SKIRMISH (SKUR mish) *n.* a minor battle between small groups

Except for a few *skirmishes*, the town was finally peaceful after three years of war.

Several *skirmishes* between rival gang members broke out during the Icy Dogg concert.

SLANDER (SLAN dur) v. to spread false, bad rumors about some-one; to tell lies about someone publicly or n. a false statement spread publicly to damage a person's reputation

The coach *slandered* his quarterback by calling him a shoplifter on national television.

The quarterback said he would not put up with such *slander*, and sued the coach for five million dollars.

SMIRK (SMURK) n. the annoying smile of a person who is too happy with him- or herself or v. to smile annoyingly out of self-satisfaction

Gregory *smirked* at the rest of the students when the teacher announced that he had received a perfect score on the test and the rest of them had failed.

Priscilla told Gregory he'd better wipe that *smirk* off his face or she'd do it for him.

SNIDE (SNYDE) adj. cruel and sarcastic

Sylvia was reduced to tears by Monty's *snide* comment that her dress looked like a tent.

SOLEMN (SAH lum) adj. very serious

I could tell by Mom's *solemn* expression that she was not pleased with my report card.

Police officers must take a *solemn* oath to uphold the law.

SOLICIT (suh LIS it) v. to try to get; to ask for repeatedly

Terry's mother found him *soliciting* donations of scrap metal from the neighbors for a time travel machine he planned on building.

Pamela *solicited* her parents and grandparents for contri-butions to the class party.

SOLITARY (SOL i ter ee) adj. existing or living alone; being the only one

Jed lived a *solitary* life in the backwoods of Kentucky.

There was a *solitary* tree left standing after the storm.

SOPHISTICATED (suh FIS tuh kay tid) adj. having experience, education, upbringing to be worldly; pleasing to the tastes of worldly people

Lena left the farm an innocent young girl and came back six months later a *sophisticated* movie star.

Her taste had become so *sophisticated*, she no longer liked hot dogs and soda, but preferred champagne and caviar.

Lena traded in her simple cotton dress for a *sophisticated* silk gown and expensive furs.

SPAT (SPAT) *n.* a small argument

Jill and Jackie had a *spat* over what kind of toast to make with breakfast; Jill wanted wheat, but Jackie wanted rye. By afternoon, they had both forgotten about it.

SPECULATE (SPEK yuh layt) *v.* to wonder or think deeply on

The neighbors were forced to *speculate* about what the giant pile of mud was doing in Mr. Sampson's backyard; he refused to tell them what it was for.

Note: The noun form of speculate is *speculation* (spek yuh LAY shun), which mean the act of speculating or the opinion formed after speculating.

Everyone had *speculations* about Mr. Sampson's mud pile, but I knew he was using it to hide a giant dinosaur egg.

SPONTANEOUS (spon TAY nee us) *adj.* happening without apparent cause; sudden and impulsive

When something just bursts into flames without any noticeable reason, it's called *spontaneous* combustion.

After twenty years of driving to and from work the same way, Mr. Peabody, while pulling out of his driveway this morning, made a *spontaneous* decision to take the scenic route to the office.

Note: The noun form of spontaneous is *spontaneity* (spon tuh NAY i tee).

Going to school at the convent, with all its rules and schedules, was hard for Peggy. She longed for more freedom and *spontaneity*.

SPOUSE (SPOWS) *n.* a husband or wife

Everyone in the company was invited to bring his or her *spouse* to the office holiday celebration.

SQUANDER (SKWAWN dur) *v.* to spend or use up wastefully

Danny *squandered* his huge inheritance on fast women and slow horses.

Let's not *squander* the last days of summer vacation sitting around inside!

SQUEAMISH (SKWEE mish) *adj.* easily shocked or sickened

Stacy is too *squeamish* to sit through a horror movie that has a lot of blood in it.

Olivia might have made a good doctor except for the fact that she was *squeamish*, and fainted at the sight of blood.

STAGNANT (STAG nunt) *adj.* not moving or flowing; not changing

Because of the lack of rain, the river stopped flowing into the little pond, and the water became *stagnant*.

Life in Dullsville was stale and *stagnant*; everyone did exactly the same thing every day, and you always knew what people were about to say to you before they even opened their mouths.

STAMINA (STAM uh nuh) *n.* endurance; the ability to keep doing something without getting tired

To be a marathon runner, you have to build up enough strength and *stamina* to run twenty-six miles.

"I used to be able to drive all day and night without stopping," mumbled Dad. "But since I turned forty, I don't even have enough *stamina* to drive eight hours without resting."

STEALTH (STELTH) *n.* the ability to move or do something quietly and secretively, without being noticed

Cats use their *stealth* to sneak up and pounce on mice and birds.

"The burglar we are hunting is a man or woman of incredible *stealth*," said the inspector. "Those diamonds were stolen right out from under our noses!"

STIMULATE (STIM yuh layt) *v.* to stir up, excite, or boost the activity of something

Thomas found that going for a short jog *stimulated* his creativity.

"I've just had the most *stimulating* conversation with a man who just got back from a mountain climbing expedition," gushed Fenella.

My Aunt Kate drinks tea after dinner because she says it *stimulates* digestion.

STRENUOUS (STREN yoo us) *adj.* demanding great effort and energy

Ice hockey is a *strenuous* sport.

"I know I said we should get outside and do something," said Roger, "but I was thinking of something a little less *strenuous* than mountain biking up the Matterhorn."

After he had his appendix removed in an operation, Brian had to avoid *strenuous* exercise for a couple of weeks.

STUDIOUS (STOO dee us) *adj.* devoted to study

Larry is a very serious, *studious* boy, but for some reason he gets nothing but Cs in school.

After one semester in college, Carl realized he wasn't cut out for the *studious* lifestyle and decided to quit and go get a job.

SUBCONSCIOUS (sub KAHN shus) *adj.* below the level of awareness

George misplaces his catcher's mitt every week before baseball games, and his mother thinks it's because he has a *subconscious* desire to quit the team, but doesn't want to admit it.

Steven is always getting in trouble at school, but the principal doesn't think he's a bad kid, just someone with a *subconscious* need for attention.

SUBDUE (sub DOO) *v.* to conquer; to bring under control; to lessen in strength

The Aztec tribe was easily *subdued* and quickly destroyed by the Spanish forces led by the explorer Hernán Cortés.

The police *subdued* the crowd of angry people who were marching to city hall demanding the resignation of the mayor.

Note: The word *subdued* can also be used to mean quiet and understated, or low in intensity.

The flowers and *subdued* lighting created a very romantic atmosphere.

Dad likes *subdued*, conservative ties, not bright, floral ones.

SUBSEQUENT (SUB suh kwent) *adj.* happening or coming after, later, or next

I was completely confused by all the characters and events in the first chapter of *The Emu Enigma,* but *subsequent* chapters cleared things up for me.

Ansel's plans for Thanksgiving included a turkey feast, a *subsequent* nap, and an afternoon of football viewing.

SUBTLE (SUT ul) *adj.* slight; not obvious

Whenever Penelope leaves a room, she leaves the *subtle* scent of her perfume in the air.

"Even the most *subtle* change in the temperature of this room could ruin my experiment!" screamed the scientist.

Jane's makeup is very *subtle*.

SUCCUMB (suh KUM) *v.* to give in or give up; to be overpowered

Carlo and I begged for weeks before Dad finally *succumbed* and let us get a puppy.

Even though everyone else in the office was sick with the flu, Lee refused to let his body *succumb* to the illness.

SUITOR (SOO tur) *n.* a man who woos a woman or tries to win her affection

Penelope had so many *suitors* calling her all the time, her father finally got her her own phone line.

My Aunt Charlene has a very charming *suitor* who brings her flowers and plays his banjo for her.

SULTRY (SUL tree) *adj.* very hot and humid

Even sitting by an open refrigerator did little to cool us off on this *sultry* day.

SUPERFICIAL (soo pur FISH ul) *adj.* on the surface; concerned only with what's on the surface; shallow

Amazingly, Allan fell all the way down the rocky hill and only wound up with a few *superficial* cuts.

I told Amanda that judging people by how they dress or wear their hair is very *superficial*.

After a *superficial* examination the doctor told me I had no broken bones, but the X rays showed I had two cracked ribs.

SUPERNATURAL (soo pur NACH ur ul) *adj.* having to do with or being outside or beyond what can be explained by the laws of nature; beyond what is normal, natural or explainable

Even though countless people have reported seeing them, ghosts are considered *supernatural* beings.

Superman uses his *supernatural* powers, like flying and seeing through walls, to protect the innocent and fight the bad guys.

SUPERSTITION (soo pur STISH un) *n.* a belief that a certain act or event foretells or predicts another event, even though the two things have no logical relation

The belief that putting a hat on a bed will bring bad luck is a *superstition*.

There is a *superstition* that if the palm of your right hand itches, you'll be getting some money soon, but if the palm of your left hand itches, you'll be getting into a fight.

Note: A person who has superstitions is *superstitious* (soo pur STISH us).

Professional athletes are often *superstitious*; they believe using a certain bat, eating a certain dish for dinner, or listening to a certain song before a game will help them win.

SUSCEPTIBLE (suh SEP tuh bul) *adj.* easily affected; sensitive

Lonny is *susceptible* to colds; he gets sick if he so much as gets his feet wet in the rain.

Rudy found it hard to stay on a diet because he was *susceptible* to the temptation of dessert.

SUSPICION (suh SPISH un) *n.* the act of believing something with little proof

My lunch had disappeared, and I had a strong *suspicion* that the dog was the sandwich thief.

Note: Someone who is full of suspicion is *suspicious* (suh SPISH us).

My old Uncle Herman is *suspicious* of anyone from the big city.

SYMPATHY (SIM puh thee) *n.* the ability to understand another person's feelings; pity or sorrow for another person's unhappiness

Yolanda's friends called to express their *sympathy* when they heard about the accidental death of her goldfish.

When my parents told me we were moving to another state, I was sad to leave my friends. My teacher said she felt *sympathy* for me because she moved around a lot as a kid, and knew how hard it was.

Note: To show or feel sympathy is to *sympathize* (SIM puh thyze).

It was hard for us to *sympathize* with the rich boy who was complaining and crying because his parents wouldn't buy him another new pony.

SYNOPSIS (si NOP sis) *n.* a short outline of a story or topic

A good book report should be more than just a *synopsis* of the plot.

Tim missed the first few minutes of the movie because he was getting popcorn, so Nancy whispered a quick *synopsis* when he got back to his seat.

SYNTHETIC (sin THET ik) *adj.* not of natural origins; artificial; not natural

"I'm sorry to tell you this, but you paid $10,000 for a necklace made of *synthetic* rubies," said the jeweler.

Wool and cotton are natural fabrics, but nylon and polyester are *synthetic*.

TANTALIZE (TAN tuh lyze) *v.* to tempt someone with something, but keep it out of reach

I was *tantalized* by the beautiful pies locked in the rotating display case.

"It's cruel to *tantalize* the dog with that drumstick when you know you're not going to give him any of it," huffed Dinah.

TARNISH (TAR nish) *v.* to dull the shine of; to stain or disgrace

Exposure to the wind and rain had *tarnished* the brass lamppost.

Peter's record of straight As was *tarnished* by one D in chemistry.

TEDIOUS (TEE dee us) *adj.* long, slow, and boring

Making spaghetti sauce from fresh tomatoes is such a *tedious* task.

Dorian's explanation of why the sky is blue was so *tedious*, I lost track of what he was saying.

TEMPERATE (TEM pur it) *adj.* mild; moderate; restrained

The weather was *temperate* during the first week in March, but snowstorms hit us again in the middle of the month.

The harsh, fiery old headmaster of the academy finally retired, and the students were glad to see a younger, more *temperate* man take his place.

TENEMENT (TEN uh munt) *n.* a run-down, often overcrowded, apartment building

At the beginning of the 1900s, many Europeans came to the United States with very little money and were forced to live in *tenements* in big cities like New York and Chicago.

TENTATIVE (TEN tuh tiv) *adj.* not final or firm; unsure

We set a *tentative* appointment for Marcy to get braces on her teeth, but we will have to delay it if she gets a chance to play the flute on television.

The baby took three or four *tentative* steps before falling down on his padded behind.

THWART (THWART) *v.* to keep from happening; to block or prevent

Bad weather *thwarted* our plans for a wheelbarrow race to the Pam's Ice Cream Palace.

Thank goodness we have superheroes like the Tick around to *thwart* the evil plots of fiendish criminals!

TIMID (TIM id) *adj.* shy; easily scared

The little girl was too *timid* to come out from behind her mother's legs to say hello.

Dexter was so *timid* he was frightened by the sound of the doorbell ringing.

TOLERANCE (TAHL ur uns) *n.* the practice of respecting the beliefs of others; the ability to endure or put up with something

Tolerance of different religions is one of the most important tenets of the United States government.

Mimi has no *tolerance* for heat; she sweats and turns almost purple whenever the temperature goes over seventy degrees.

Note: Someone who has *tolerance* is *tolerant*. A *tolerant* parent *tolerates*, or puts up with, more than a strict parent would. Not many parents will *tolerate* bad behavior.

TORMENT (tor MENT) *v.* to cause great pain; to annoy

The mean little boy *tormented* grasshoppers by tearing their legs off.

After we had been driving for about thirty minutes, I began to be *tormented* by the thought that I had forgotten to turn off the oven before we left.

TOXIC (TOK sik) *adj.* poisonous

The dye used on these Christmas tree ornaments is *toxic,* so parents should be careful to keep small children from putting them in their mouths.

The river used to be full of fish, but they were all killed by the *toxic* chemicals dumped into the water by the plastics plant.

TRANSCRIBE (tran SKRYBE) *v.* to write or type a copy of

Dorothy liked the speech so much, she *transcribed* every word.

Note: Once you have *transcribed* something, you have a *transcript* (TRAN skript).

You can often buy *transcripts* of television shows by sending a request to the network.

TRANSPOSE (trans POHZ) *v.* to reverse or switch in placement or order

Melvin was a fast typist, but often *transposed* the letters of words, so that "fort" became "frot" and "bird" became "brid."

TRAUMA (TRAW muh) *n.* a serious shock with lasting effects

For little children, being left with a babysitter for the first time can be a *trauma.*

Note: An experience that causes trauma is *traumatic* (traw MAT ik).

For Maggie, missing an episode of her favorite soap opera "As Time Drags On" is a *traumatic* experience.

If you've had a trauma, you have been *traumatized* (TRAW muh tyzed).

Being shut in the clothes dryer overnight had *traumatized* the cat.

TRITE (TRYTE) *adj.* uninteresting because of overuse; stale

The phrase "pretty as a picture" is too *trite* to do justice to Allison's good looks.

Candy and roses are *trite* Valentine's Day gifts.

TURBULENT (TUR byuh lent) *adj.* stirred up or disturbed

The thunderstorm and *turbulent* winds made air travel impossible.

The civil rights movement, the women's rights movement, and the widespread objection to the Vietnam War made the 1960s a *turbulent* decade in American history.

TYCOON (tye KOON) *n.* a wealthy, powerful businessperson

Donald Trump—who owns casinos, hotels, apartment buildings, and other properties worth millions and millions of dollars—is a real estate *tycoon*.

Mr. Franklin, who owns the paper mill and several other businesses in our town, is a local *tycoon*.

TYRANT (TYE runt) *n.* a ruler with total, unrestricted control who is often harsh and cruel

Jane was okay as a coworker, but when she was promoted and took charge of our department she became a complete *tyrant*, firing people for no reason and forcing everyone to work seven days a week.

Note: A tyrant enforces and expresses *tyranny* (TIR uh nee), which is absolute or oppressive power exerted by a government or ruler.

Before she had the chance to fire me, I told Jane I refused to put up with her *tyranny* and I quit.

ULCER (UL sur) *n.* a sore in or on the body, usually in a moist area

Ignatius had a painful *ulcer* on the inside of his cheek that kept him from enjoying his Thanksgiving dinner.

Aubrey's stressful job gave him a stomach *ulcer* that hurt him whenever he ate.

ULTERIOR (ul TEER ee ur) *adj.* beyond what is seen or admitted

Ben said he was just trying to be useful when he helped Dad change the oil on the car, but he had an *ulterior* motive: he knew that the faster he could get the oil changed, the sooner his father would leave town for the weekend, and the sooner he could invite all of his friends over for a party.

In the story of Hansel and Gretel, the witch gives the hungry children some food, but her *ulterior* plan is to fatten them up so she can eat them.

UNANIMOUS (yoo NAN i mus) *adj.* having the same opinion; in complete agreement

After fifteen long rounds, the judges made the *unanimous* decision that Julio Cesar Chavez had won the boxing match.

The students were *unanimous* in their objection to their teacher's cruel and unusual decision to give them a test the day they got back from their winter break.

UNBEKNOWNST (un bi NOHNST) *adv.* without the knowledge of

"If someone fed Fido the leftover steak, it was *unbeknownst* to me," claimed Edgar.

UNBRIDLED (un BRYDE uld) *adj.* uncontrolled; wild

Nancy had an *unbridled* affection for Vince—there was nothing she wouldn't do for him, and she couldn't bear being apart from him.

UNCONSCIOUS (un KON shus) *adj.* not awake; not aware

After she fell off the jungle gym and hit her head, Isabella was *unconscious* for five minutes.

Neville, who thought he was the life of the party, was *unconscious* of the fact that everyone was bored to tears by his silly jokes.

UNCOUTH (un KOOTH) *adj.* crude; unrefined; unmannerly

After he ate the pudding with his fingers, wiped his mouth on the tablecloth, belched loudly, then spat into his water glass, Cedric's mother moaned, "How could I have possibly raised such an *uncouth* son?"

"Your manners were fine," Kyle's friend assured him, "but flicking your cigarette ashes in the antique vase and calling their modern art collection 'finger paintings' was a little *uncouth*."

UNDERMINE (UN dur myne) *v.* to weaken by wearing away or attacking the foundation

Greg's midnight ice cream feasts were *undermining* the effects of his diet and exercise program.

Sylvia's boss *undermined* her authority by contradicting instructions she gave and overriding rules she made for her department.

UNEASY (un EE zee) *adj.* nervous and unsure

Amanda's mother was *uneasy* about letting her stay by herself for the evening, even though she was eleven years old.

Caroline is *uneasy* driving by herself late at night.

"I have the *uneasy* feeling that someone is watching us," said Shaggy.

UNFOUNDED (un FOUN did) *adj.* having no factual support; not backed up by facts

"All those stories about me skinny-dipping in the hotel fountain are completely *unfounded*," said Monica. "No one can prove a thing."

Reports of aliens landing in the cornfields have proved to be *unfounded*—no trace of any such landings can be found.

UNKEMPT (un KEMPT) *adj.* messy; untidy

Evelyn, who had stayed up late studying and slept in her clothes, showed up for the exam looking sleepy and *unkempt*.

Marian keeps the top down on her convertible whenever she drives somewhere, so her hair tends to be *unkempt*.

The security guard was very embarrassed when he found out that the *unkempt* man in the shabby jacket he had just thrown out was, in fact, Albert Einstein, the famous scientist and guest speaker.

UNWIELDY (un WEEL dee) *adj.* hard to carry or manage because of shape or size

The box of posters wasn't heavy, it was just so large and *unwieldy* it was hard for one person to carry alone.

Brandon was used to driving a small sports car, so he found the bus kind of *unwieldy*.

UPHEAVAL (up HEE vul) *n.* a sudden, strong disturbance

The assassination of President John Kennedy caused a great *upheaval* across the country.

Our neighborhood was thrown into a state of *upheaval* when the fifth pet in one week was found with all its fur mysteriously shaved off.

UPHOLSTERY (up HOHL stur ee) *n.* the materials used to stuff and cover furniture

We had to have the cat declawed because she was destroying the *upholstery* on the couch and chairs.

"All true luxury cars have leather *upholstery*," declared Mario.

VACATE (VAY cayt) *v.* to empty; to leave or exit

The people *vacated* the burning building as quickly as possible.

Nothing can *vacate* an auditorium faster than my Aunt Myrtle playing her accordion and singing her polka version of "You Light Up My Life."

Tommy and his roommates were ordered to *vacate* their apartment after the landlord got several complaints about their loud band practices.

VACILLATE (VAS uh layt) *v.* to change your opinion or course of action back and forth

We all waited in the living room while, upstairs, Vicki *vacillated* between wearing flats or high heels.

"We don't have time to stand here *vacillating* between chocolate cake and coconut cake," said Tina. "The surprise party is supposed to start in ten minutes!"

VAGRANT (VAY grunt) *n.* a person who wanders from place to place with no permanent home or *adj.* wandering

When he was in his early twenties, my uncle lived as a *vagrant* musician, playing his tuba for money in cities across the country.

At night, *vagrants* come and sleep on the park benches.

VAGUE (VAYG) *adj.* unclear; not definite or precise

Patrick saw the *vague* shape of a person coming towards him through the fog, but by the time he realized it was Count Dracula, it was too late to run.

Paula was *vague* about her plans for the weekend, so we suspected she had some sort of secret meeting.

Stan's teacher told him some of the arguments in his report were too *vague*, and that he should use examples to back up his points.

VAIN (VAYN) *adj.* useless; having no effect

We were forced to call a tow truck after several *vain* attempts to push the car out of the deep mud.

Note: *Vain* also means conceited, or overly pleased with one's looks or abilities.

Jon was so *vain*, he thought every girl who smiled or said hello to him had a crush on him.

Everyone thought Eugenia was *vain* because she was always admiring herself in the mirror.

VANDAL (VAN dul) *n.* someone who destroys or harms another person's property on purpose

The statue of George Washington was spray-painted purple by a group of young *vandals*.

Note: To act like a vandal is to *vandalize* (VAN du lyze).

The teenagers were accused of *vandalizing* several statues around town.

VANQUISH (VANG kwish) *v.* to defeat or destroy totally

Tina *vanquished* her fear of water by taking swimming lessons at the YMCA.

Napoleon's army was finally *vanquished* in the disastrous battle at Waterloo.

VEER (VEER) *v.* to swerve

I had to *veer* to the left to avoid running into the fallen tree in the road.

The car *veered* dangerously close to the cliff.

VELOCITY (vuh LAHS i tee) *n.* speed

Nolan Ryan could throw a baseball at a *velocity* of over one hundred miles per hour.

Driving at high *velocities* is especially dangerous when the roads are wet.

VENERABLE (VEN ur uh bul) *adj.* worthy of respect, usually because of age or position

The Sacred Heart Academy is a *venerable* Catholic school for girls.

The *venerable* minister was loved by everyone in the church, even though he had started to give the same sermon several weeks in a row and often forgot what he was talking about in the middle of a sentence.

VERDICT (VUR dikt) *n.* the jury's decision at the end of a trial; a judgment

"What's your *verdict*?" asked Aunt Faye, after we sampled her latest pecan pie recipe.

The jury took two days to reach a *verdict* of "guilty" in the Hawlsey murder trial.

VERIFY (VER i fye) *v.* to prove or determine the truth or accuracy of something

Most employers will *verify* the information you put on your application before hiring you.

The FBI tried to *verify* reports of an invasion of space aliens in Omaha.

Before the radio station would give him the tickets he had won, Roy had to *verify* his identity by showing the DJ his school ID card.

VERSATILE (VUR suh tul) *adj.* useful for many purposes; capable of many things

Keenan is a *versatile* actor; he can be a villain, a hero, or a comedian.

This new white shirt is very *versatile*; it goes with all my other clothes, and I can wear it on casual and dressy occasions.

VERTICAL (VUR ti kul) *adj.* upright; standing up on end, rather than flat on a side

Most libraries stack their books in *vertical* rows.

The suit was black with thin *vertical* white stripes.

VICE VERSA (VYSE VUR suh) *adv.* the other way around; in reverse order

Kathy borrows Bobby's bike whenever she needs it, and *vice versa*.

"It's the man's job to ask a woman for a date, not *vice versa*," said my grandfather.

VIGOROUS (VIG ur us) *adj.* strong and full of energy; done with a lot of energy

After six months of good care at the stable, the horses were healthy and *vigorous*.

The pitcher's trainer gave his arm a *vigorous* rubdown after he pitched nine tough innings.

VIRULENT (VIR uh lunt) *adj.* very harmful; infectious; mean

Doctors are urging everyone to get a flu shot this season because an especially *virulent* strain of the disease has been going around.

Susie started screaming the most *virulent* insults she could think of when she saw her best friend holding hands with her boyfriend outside the movie theater.

VIVACIOUS (vye VAY shus) *adj.* lively and full of spirit

Belle is usually a giggling, *vivacious* girl, but for some reason she is feeling sad today.

Vivian decided to play something light and *vivacious* at her piano recital.

VOLITION (vuh LISH un) *n.* a conscious act or choice; the power of independent choice

Her parents were stunned when Michelle, of her own *volition*, offered to share the last piece of cake with her sister.

Farley had about as much *volition* as a jellyfish; he simply did what he was told.

VOLUNTARY (VOL un ter ee) *adj.* done by free choice

Participation in the school blood drive is completely *voluntary*; no one will force anyone to give blood.

Brad made the *voluntary* decision to give up playing on the football team in order to pay more attention to his schoolwork.

VULNERABLE (VUL nur uh bul) *adj.* open to harm, injury, or attack

Homes without locks on the windows are *vulnerable* to burglary.

Achilles, the great Greek hero, had only one spot on his body that was *vulnerable* to knives, swords, or arrows: the back of his heel.

WALLOW (WAHL oh) *v.* to roll around, as in water or mud; to give in to a state of mind or way of life

The hippopotamus *wallowed* happily in the muddy bank of the river.

"I wish you'd quit *wallowing* in self-pity," said Nell to Bea. "I assure you your bangs will grow out eventually."

WARRANT (WOR unt) *n.* official permission; official written permission

The police needed a *warrant* from the judge before they could search the warehouse owned by the suspected cheese thieves.

The teachers have the *warrant* of the school board to use strict discipline in the classrooms.

Note: *Warrant* can also be a verb meaning to deserve or to call for.

Does coming home fifteen minutes late really *warrant* such strong punishment?

WARY (WAYR ee) *adj.* on guard; cautious

Evelyn made a slow, *wary* search of the dark, abandoned house.

Be *wary* of people who come up and offer to carry your bags in the airport; they might try to rob you.

WEARY (WEER ee) *adj.* tired; worn down

The long walk from his broken-down car to the gas station had made Fred *weary*.

After years of wars and battles, the soldier grew *weary* of fighting and longed for peace.

"I'm *weary* of all this arguing," snapped Mom. "Either shut up or speak nicely to each other."

WINCE (WINS) *v.* to flinch or start from shock, pain, or embarrassment

Zach *winced* as his mother tried to pull the piece of glass out of his foot.

Hearing the tape of myself singing in the shower made me *wince*.

WITNESS (WIT nis) *n.* a person who saw or heard an event and can tell others about it or *v.* to see or hear an event

There were seven *witnesses* to the car accident.

Jack was sitting on a bench across the street, and *witnessed* the whole accident.

WOO (WOO) *v.* to try to get the affection or favor of

Percy *wooed* Gwendolyn with poetry, flowers, and soft music.

The grocery store tried to *woo* shoppers with sales and giveaways.

YIELD (YEELD) *v.* to surrender or give over; to provide or give forth

A yellow traffic light means you should slow down and *yield* the right of way to traffic from another direction.

The Texan rebels at the Alamo refused to *yield* to the much stronger forces of the Mexican Army.

This year, my garden *yielded* several baskets full of tomatoes.

ZEAL (ZEEL) *n.* enthusiasm for a cause or goal

"I've never seen someone file papers with such *zeal*," Ms. Roth told her assistant.

Bruno poisoned the rats with great *zeal*.

Answers

✍ **QUIZ #1** ✍
1. S 2. S 3. O 4. S 5. O 6. O 7. S 8. O 9. S 10. S 11. O

✍ **QUIZ #2** ✍
1. S 2. O 3. S 4. O 5. O 6. S 7. O 8. S 9. S 10. O 11. O

✍ **QUIZ #3** ✍
1. c 2. a 3. d 4. a 5. b 6. c 7. d

✍ **QUIZ #4** ✍
1. c 2. j 3. f 4. m 5. b 6. e 7. n 8. l 9. a 10. k 11. i
12. d 13. h 14. g

✍ **QUIZ #5** ✍
1. f 2. d 3. i 4. k 5. b 6. a 7. g 8. h 9. l 10. m 11. c
12. j 13. e

✍ **QUIZ #6** ✍
1. S 2. S 3. O 4. O 5. S 6. S 7. S 8. O 9. O 10. S
11. O 12. O

✍ **QUIZ #7** ✍
1. O 2. O 3. O 4. O 5. S 6. O 7. O 8. O 9. S 10. O 11. S

✍ QUIZ #8 ✑
1. c 2. a 3. a 4. c 5. b 6. a 7. d 8. c 9. d 10. b
11. d 12. b

✍ QUIZ #9 ✑
1. f 2. h 3. b 4. k 5. m 6. g 7. c 8. l 9. j 10. a 11. e
12. n 13. i 14. d

✍ QUIZ #10 ✑
1. e 2. g 3. a 4. d 5. j 6. k 7. b 8. h 9. m 10. l 11. c
12. f 13. i

✍ QUIZ #11 ✑
1. S 2. S 3. S 4. O 5. O 6. O 7. O 8. O 9. O 10. O 11. O
12. O 13. S 14. S 15. S

✍ QUIZ #12 ✑
1. O 2. S 3. S 4. O 5. S 6. O 7. S 8. O 9. O 10. S 11. S
12. S 13. O 14. S 15. O

✍ QUIZ #13 ✑
1. c 2. c 3. a 4. d 5. d 6. b 7. b 8. c 9. a 10. d 11. a

✍ QUIZ #14 ✑
1. b 2. a 3. e 4. g 5. i 6. c 7. m 8. l 9. d 10. k
11. h 12. j 13. f

✏️ QUIZ #15 ✏️
1. e 2. i 3. d 4. j 5. a 6. l 7. c 8. b 9. g 10. k
11. h 12. f

✏️ QUIZ #16 ✏️
1. S 2. S 3. O 4. S 5. S 6. O 7. S 8. O 9. S 10. O 11. O
12. O 13. O

✏️ QUIZ #17 ✏️
1. O 2. O 3. O 4. O 5. O 6. S 7. S 8. O 9. S 10. O
11. O 12. S

✏️ QUIZ #18 ✏️
1. b 2. c 3. d 4. a 5. c 6. a 7. d

✏️ QUIZ #19 ✏️
1. h 2. l 3. a 4. m 5. f 6. n 7. c 8. k 9. i 10. b 11. g
12. d 13. j 14. e 15. o

✏️ QUIZ #20 ✏️
1. h 2. a 3. d 4. l 5. b 6. j 7. f 8. m 9. e 10. i
11. n 12. c 13. k 14. g

✏️ QUIZ #21 ✏️
1. O 2. S 3. S 4. O 5. O 6. S 7. S 8. O 9. S 10. O 11. O
12. O 13. O

✍ QUIZ #22 ✍

1. S 2. O 3. O 4. S 5. S 6. O 7. S 8. S 9. O 10. S
11. O 12. O

✍ QUIZ #23 ✍

1. c 2. a 3. d 4. a 5. c 6. b 7. d 8. a 9. d 10. d

✍ QUIZ #24 ✍

1. b 2. d 3. i 4. e 5. a 6. f 7. j 8. c 9. h 10. g

✍ QUIZ #25 ✍

1. d 2. a 3. f 4. i 5. c 6. g 7. j 8. e 9. k 10. h 11. b

✍ QUIZ #26 ✍

1. O 2. O 3. S 4. O 5. O 6. O 7. S 8. O 9. O 10. O 11. S

✍ QUIZ #27 ✍

1. d 2. c 3. c 4. a 5. a 6. d

✍ QUIZ #28 ✍

1. g 2. a 3. c 4. d 5. h 6. j 7. b 8. e 9. i 10. f

✍ QUIZ #29 ✍

1. b 2. h 3. i 4. e 5. j 6. c 7. g 8. k 9. f 10. d 11. a

✍ **QUIZ #30** ✍

1. S 2. S 3. O 4. S 5. S 6. S 7. O 8. S 9. O 10. S 11. S
12. S 13. O 14. O 15. S

✍ **QUIZ #31** ✍

1. b 2. a 3. b 4. a 5. d 6. c 7. d

✍ **QUIZ #32** ✍

1. d 2. g 3. i 4. e 5. j 6. c 7. b 8. l 9. n 10. m 11. f
12. h 13. k 14. a

✍ **QUIZ #33** ✍

1. c 2. i 3. j 4. g 5. k 6. a 7. m 8. n 9. l 10. e 11. h
12. f 13. d 14. b

✍ **QUIZ #34** ✍

1. S 2. O 3. O 4. S 5. S 6. S 7. O 8. S 9. O 10. O

✍ **QUIZ #35** ✍

1. a 2. c 3. e 4. h 5. d 6. g 7. i 8. f 9. b 10. o 11. j
12. m 13. n 14. l 15. k

ABOUT THE AUTHOR

C.L. Brantley has worked for The Princeton Review since 1991 as an editor and author. Prior to teaming up with them, she worked in the software, telecommunications, and entertainment industries as a copywriter and speech writer. Her other books include *Word Smart Junior*, *Writing Smart Junior*, and *Kids Go! Austin*, a travel guide for children visiting the Austin, Texas area.

Brantley holds a B.A. in English, an M.S. in mass communication, and is working toward a Ph.D. in Computers and English Studies. She currently lives in Texas, where she studies, teaches, and writes. Her favorite color is red, and her favorite saying is, "Hey, at least I'm not dead." She sincerely hopes that you enjoy this book.

We Know Tests!

Use our 20 years of experience to raise students' standardized test scores.

State Assessment Solutions for Educators and Parents

- **Homeroom.com:** Assess, analyze, remediate
- **Professional Development:** Educating educators
- **Diagnostic Test Booklets:** Benchmarking student performance
- **Test-Specific Prep Books:** Providing proven strategies

For more information

call 1-800-REVIEW-2
or email K12sales@review.com

Go to *www.homeroom.com* for a *free 30-day test drive* and product demo!

Award-Winning

The **Princeton** *Review*

Smart Junior Guides

for Kids in Grades 6–8

GRAMMAR SMART JR., 2ND EDITION
0-375-76259-0 • $12.00

MATH SMART JR., 2ND EDITION
0-375-76260-4 • $12.00

SCIENCE SMART JR.
0-375-76262-0 • $12.00

WORD SMART JR., 2ND EDITION
0-375-76257-4 • $12.00

WORD SMART JR. II, 2ND EDITION
0-375-76258-2 • $12.00

WRITING SMART JR., 2ND EDITION
0-375-76261-2 • $12.00

*Winners of the
Parents' Choice Award!*

AVAILABLE WHEREVER BOOKS ARE SOLD